THE ANALYTIC FIELD

The EFPP Book Series

Series Editors: *Dimitris Anastasopoulos and Monica Lanyado*

OTHER TITLES IN THE SERIES

- *Counter-transference in Psychoanalytic Psychotherapy with Children and Adolescents*
- *Supervision and its Vicissitudes*
- *Psychoanalytic Psychotherapy in Institutional Settings*
- *Psychoanalytic Psychotherapy of the Severely Disturbed Adolescent*
- *Work with Parents: Psychoanalytic Psychotherapy with Children and Adolescents*
- *Psychoanalysis and Psychotherapy: The Controversies and the Future*
- *Research in Psychoanalytic Psychotherapy with Adults*
- *The Therapist at Work: Personal Factors Affecting the Analytic Process*
- *Invisible Boundaries. Psychosis and Autism in Children and Adolescents.*
- *The Development of Consciousness: Psychoanalysis, neuroscience and child development.*

THE ANALYTIC FIELD
A Clinical Concept

Edited by

Antonino Ferro
and Roberto Basile

published by

KARNAC

for

The European Federation
for Psychoanalytic Psychotherapy
in the Public Health Services

First published in 2009 by
Karnac Books Ltd
118 Finchley Road
London NW3 5HT

British Library Cataloguing in Publication Data

A C.I.P. for this book is available from the British Library

ISBN-13: 978-1-85575-781-3

Typeset by Vikatan Publishing Solutions (P) Ltd., Chennai, India

Printed in Great Britain

www.karnacbooks.com

CONTENTS

BIOGRAPHIES OF THE CONTRIBUTORS

LAURA AMBROSIANO Psychologist, is a Training and Supervising Analyst of the Italian Psychoanalytical Society. Among her most recent publications: *Ululare con i lupi: conformismo e reverie (Howling with the wolves: conformism and Reverie)*; The analyst: His professional novel, IJPA 2005; *La spinta a esistere. Note cliniche sulla sessualità oggi.* (The Drive to Exist. Clinical notes on sexuality today).

ROBERTO BASILE, MD, is an analyst of the Italian Psychoanalytical Society. Among his most recent articles: *Countertransference and the characters of the psychoanalytic session,* (together with A. Ferro in Scand. Psychoanal. Rev. 2008) and Flaming Red: A Session with Agnese (IJPA 2006).

CLÁUDIO LAKS EIZIRIK, MD, is a Training and Supervising Analyst of the Porto Alegre Psychoanalytic Society and an Adjunct Professor of the Department of Psychiatry, Federal University of Rio Grande do Sul, Brazil. He is currently the President of the International Psychoanalytical Association. Among his most recent works: *Psychoanalysis in a Changing World (IJPA 2008);* On the Therapeutic Action of Psychoanalysis. (Psychoanal. Q. *2007); Psychoanalysis as a Work in Progress. (IJPA 2006); Becoming (and Remaining) an Analyst in Latin America. (Psychoanal. Inq. 2005).*

ANTONINO FERRO, MD, is a Training and Supervising Analyst of the Italian Psychoanalytical Society. He has written eight books, most recently: *'Psychoanalysis as Therapy and Story Telling'; 'Seeds of Illness Seeds of Recovery'; 'Mind Works. Technique and Creativity in Psychoanalysis'.*

EUGENIO GABURRI, MD, is a Training and Supervising Analyst of the Italian Psychoanalytical Society (SPI). He has published several articles and books on psychoanalysis, among which:

Emozione e interpretazione: psicoanalisi del campo emotivo (Emotion and interpretation: psychoanalysis of the emotional field). *Ululare con i lupi: Conformismo e reverie* (Howling with the wolves: conformism and Reverie), *La spinta a esistere. Note cliniche sulla sessualità oggi.* (The Drive to Exist. Clinical notes on sexuality today).

JAMES S. GROTSTEIN, MD, is Clinical Professor of Psychiatry at the David Geffen School of Medicine, UCLA, Training and Supervising Analyst at the Psychoanalytic Center of California and the New Center for Psychoanalysis, Los Angeles. He has recently published *A Beam of Intense Darkness: Wilfred Bion's Legacy to Psychoanalysis* and has another book which is soon to be published: *"...But at the Same Time and on Another Level": Psychoanalytic Technique in the Kleinian/ Bioninan Mode: A Beginning.*

LUIS KANCYPER, MD, is a Training and Supervising Analyst at the Argentinian Psychoanalytical Association. He is author of six books and among his most recent ones: Jorge Luis Borges o la pasión de la amistad (Jorge Luis Borges or the passion for friendship), El complejo fraterno (The fraternal complex), Adolescencia: El fin de la ingenuidad (Adolescence, the end of ingenuity).

CLAUDIO NERI, MD, is Professor at the Faculty of Psychology 1', University 'La Sapienza' of Rome, visiting professor at the University 'Lumière Lyon 2' and 'Descartes Paris 5'. He is a Training and Supervising Analyst for the Italian Psychoanalytical Society. He is author and editor of numerous books, amongst which: *Group, Dreams in Group Psychotherapy* and *Lire Bion* (Reading Bion).

THOMAS H. OGDEN, MD, is the Director of the Center for the Advanced Study of the Psychoses, a Supervising and Personal Analyst at the Psychoanalytic Institute of Northern California and a member of the Faculty of the San Francisco Psychoanalytic Institute. He has written eight books, most recently, *Rediscovering Psychoanalysis: Thinking and Dreaming, Learning and Forgetting; This Art of Psychoanalysis: Dreaming Undreamt Dreams and Interrupted Cries; Conversations at the*

Frontier of Dreaming; and *Reverie and Interpretation: Sensing Something Human.*

CARLOS SOPENA, MD, is Training and Supervising Analyst at the Madrid Psychoanalytical Association. Among his articles: *Fragment of the Analysis of an Hysterical Patient* (IJPA 1991). He is the Editor of *Hamlet. Ensayos psicoanalíticos* (Hamlet: Psychoanalytic essays).

RUDI VERMOTE, MD, is Member of the Belgian Society of Psychoanalysis. He is Head of the Hospitalisation Based Treatment of Personality Disorders and the Outpatient Psychoanalytic Psychotherapy Services at the University Psychiatric Hospital of the University of Leuven (Louvain), Campus Kortenberg and Head of the Postgraduate Training in Psychoanalytical Psychotherapy, University of Leuven. He is author of the book *Reading Bion.*

INTRODUCTION

The concept of the analytic field originated in the 1960s from an insight by two Franco-Argentinian analysts, Madeleine and Willy Baranger. Exploring the relational vertex in psychoanalysis, these two authors realized that the "analytic dyad" creates a dynamic field—that is, a situation between two persons "who remain unavoidably connected and complementary" as long as they share the analytic situation and are "involved in a single dynamic process. In this situation, neither member of the couple can be understood without the other", for in the analytic field all the current and emerging structures depend on the interaction between the two participants.

For a long time, the idea of the analytic field remained confined to the geographical area of Latin America. One reason for this may have been the linguistic difficulty of exporting a type of thought whose origins did not lie in the English-speaking world, while another was perhaps the problem presented by the introduction of a notion that was "foreign" in so far as it was capable of bringing about a Copernican revolution in the observational vertex of psychoanalysis. Yet the concept did filter through to other countries, albeit slowly, and came to play a vital role in, for example, Italian psychoanalysis, while influencing the International Psychoanalytical Association to publish a book in which the subject plays a prominent part (*Truth, Reality, and the Psychoanalyst: Latin American Contributions to Psychoanalysis*, edited by Sergio Lewkowicz and Silvia Flechner). In addition, in 2008 the *International Journal of Psychoanalysis* assembled a number of contributions on the subject in a single volume and published the original paper by Willy and Madeleine Baranger in English.

According to our view, the field concept permeates the thought of many very different analysts, resulting in a wide range of contact points extending for instance from Bion to Ogden, from Grotstein to Ferro, or from Corrao to Eizirik, and of course ultimately also including authors unrepresented in this book.

Until now, however, no book has ever attempted to compare and contrast contributions on field theory and at the same time to explore its clinical and technical implications. The present volume is intended for the first time to link together many of these writings and to provide an initial wide-ranging survey of the subject—for it is our contention that a theory of the field in its various loci can also be inhabited by different theories.

Field theory readily lends itself to a multi-pronged approach of this kind because it opens the way to a dimension in which free rein is given to the elements of dreaming, narration, and deconstruction. This aim is accomplished in terms not only of the purely theoretical aspect, but also of its powerful implications for the theory of technique: while taking up a position close to all relational theories, field theory has a strong technical specificity of its own, in that it breaks for the first time with the idea of making the here-and-now explicit in the session and of consequent transference interpretation. As a result, the relational aspect in effect becomes a stream flowing through the field; this river then widens out into a vast lake in which there is time for characters to emerge, to sink into the depths, to return to the background or to take the stage again. Reality in the field is more virtual in nature, involving characters who are progressively subjected to a process of casting in order to express the types of functioning active in the field. All the field's characters are born of the mental mating of the two members of the couple, namely the two minds; there is so to speak a continuous summoning up of characters and players, or an ongoing assignment of roles directed towards making the deepest levels of the field more and more susceptible to explicit expression. The story proceeds by the mechanisms of the compulsion to repeat and of projective identification, which are used for constant rereading of the current relationship and for constantly rendering it explicit. Considered in these terms, listening in the analytic field is reminiscent of the kind of listening described by Betty Joseph in her contributions on the transference as a total situation, or alternatively of certain aspects of relational theories. However, field theory differs from the latter in some major respects. Firstly, in field theory the two minds in the session form a novel structure that is not only the sum of the two mental lives, but also something completely new. Again, the analyst's unsaturated interventions permit continuous expansion, by way of narrative transformations and transformation in dreaming. At the same time, while sharing in the events of the field with the patient, the analyst maintains an area of asymmetry which is his film about the film. Meanwhile the patient likewise makes his own film about the film.

In line with field theory itself, we considered it best for us not to tie together the thread linking the various contributions in this book and their sequence, but instead to allow the reader to conceive his own dreams and thoughts about the articles presented. One can discern in each paper the connections and references to Latin American and post-Bionian psychoanalysis, in the sense of a psychoanalysis interested more in extending thinkability than in recovering past events. In other words, field theory changes the paradigm of analytic work from the unveiling of a hidden meaning to facilitating the possibility of thinking for oneself of possible new meanings. The psychoanalytic laboratory then becomes dedicated not to what has been but to what may be in the future.

A particular aim of this book is to present not only theoretical discussions of field theory, but also contributions on clinical work and technique. For this reason we have given preference to articles with a substantial clinical component which exemplifies their specific underlying technical theory. In the Babel of psychoanalytic languages, clinical practice is in our view the most effective way of comparing psychoanalytic models.

In conclusion, we would like to express our particular thanks to Dimitris Anastasopoulos for his patience and perseverance in keeping track of the successive phases in the production of this book, from suggesting the idea to rereading all of its parts and also to his contacts with the publishers, Karnac Books; without his enthusiasm, this book would never have seen the light of day.

CHAPTER ONE

The universe of the field and its inhabitants

Antonino Ferro and Roberto Basile

The inhabitants of the field

The analytic field is inhabited by innumerable real and virtual presences in the process of aggregation, and a valid comparison might be with the universe as it is understood today. For the analytic field coincides with the unrepeatable "universe" that is born at the beginning of each session, only to be temporarily suspended when each session comes to an end. The field is inhabited by certain principal characters, who could be called the protagonists, as well as by supporting actors and, finally, by extras; moreover, all these presences can constantly change their roles. However, human characters (or even non-anthropomorphic ones) represent the most mature part of the field. They could be likened to the constellations discernible in a starry sky. The field is the locus of an infinite number of other phenomena, most of them unknown. An axiom of the field might be that the "Big Bang" occurs at the beginning of each session—and the "Big Crunch" at the end.

Characters constitute the outcome of operations carried out further upstream. Their status is always complex and they do not correspond to the persons to whom they bear a superficial resemblance. The characters of the session are the fruit of mental operations performed by analyst and patient and reflect the mental functioning of both, as well as their proto-emotions, emotions and unknown aspects. In other words, they are holograms of the mental functioning of the analytic couple; but they also include kinds of functioning that would, in other languages, be said to be split off, or not yet accessible to thinkability. Characters enter and leave the session tangentially; others, having entered tangentially, become protagonists; while others still immediately take essential parts. From this point of view, whatever the patient talks about, he or she is describing a form of functioning of the field.

Let us look at an actual session. It is taken from the fourth year of analysis of a patient called Salvatore. Because I am going to be away for a congress, followed by some public holidays, we are about to have two weeks with only two sessions each instead of the usual four.

Patient: I feel very excited today: I have finally bought the motorbike. I had terrible trouble yesterday: a Turkish patient in jail had some pseudo-epileptic seizures in which he was banging his head, scratching himself in despair and rolling about on the floor. The guards then called a priest because they thought the devil might have got into him—that the demon himself was there—so the priest came along with his cross. Then he had another fit, so they thought an exorcist was needed.

Analyst: (*thinking that the motorbike is telling us about having to go on two wheels instead of four and that the Turk represents an as yet indecipherable reaction of his in the form of rage and despair at the cancellation of the two plus two sessions, he confines himself however to the following comment*). Well, analysts have always taken courses in exorcism, and maybe on the one hand you're pleased at having to stand on two wheels [the motorbike] for the two weeks when we'll be having only two sessions, but on the other, we have the crosses, like the crossing out of the two sessions, and perhaps these crossings out on your Turkish "orbital" part cause seizures.

Patient: (*laughing*). You know, when I was small I used to go and watch films with a friend of mine who lived in Corso Cavour [where my consulting room is located!] and once I saw *The Exorcist*: it really terrified me.

Analyst: (*thinking that the patient was frightened by my getting too close to his potential "Turkish" side, I say only the following*). What a coincidence about the address!

Patient: (*laughing out loud*). My mum and dad aren't on speaking terms: mum would like him to take his work more seriously, and to do things more exactly and correctly; dad does what he can, but can't manage to get everything working to perfection—sometimes there are "gaps" in the organization.

Analyst: (*thinking that he is describing two different modes of functioning of mine, of the field and of his own*). So, your mum is a Hapsburg and your dad's a Bourbon—and then there's me causing all these gaps!

Patient: I don't think I'm seriously annoyed about the four sessions we'll be missing. At home there's rust on the gate, and it needs to be treated with Ferox [a product that removes rust from *iron*, iron being the meaning of my surname, Ferro, in Italian], and then the rust would go away.

Analyst: (*thinking that he is angry with me, the man with the "iron" surname*). In Latin it would be *Ferox/ferocis*—in other words, getting ferociously angry instead of secretly building up rust!

Patient: But I *am* angry; I can get angry now—maybe not with you, but where I work there were two members of staff who didn't show up and I really am able to express the anger aroused in me.

Analyst: ... and there's someone else who isn't going to show up soon, if I'm not mistaken!

Just as the universe is full of stars approaching the end of their lives and others just coming into being, these processes being underlain by a whole series of subatomic, electrical, magnetic and other phenomena, so the field has a generational matrix of its own, which draws on proto-emotional, archaic, fragmented states and works them up into "characters". These wizards of the formation of "psychoanalytic matter" are the functions that inhabit the field and, by inhabiting it, constitute it.

This is what Grotstein (2007) calls the "dreaming ensemble"—i.e., all the functions that transform the proto-sensory and the proto-emotional into pictograms (Elias Mallet de Rocha Barros, 2000), oneiric (dream) thought and holograms. One could use terms such as the α-function of the field, the oneiric thought of the field or the contact barrier of the field, but I am less concerned with naming these functions than with describing the mental operations that are performed. These mental operations can proceed in two possible directions in seeking to create new constructions of sense. The first involves the transformation of ß-elements from obscure places in the field (ß-elements are Bion's equivalent to proto-sensations) into α-elements (which are Bion's equivalent to material for dream thoughts) (Bion, 1962), while the second concerns the achievement of possible new compositions, but only after a process of deconstruction—as in a town-planning situation where there is to be a change in function: the obsolete structures must be "deconstructed" first. All these "constructive" operations could be described as effecting the alphabetization of ß-elements.

However, there are not only constructive forces, for in the universe of the field, two different "dragons" confront each other—namely, the contrasting phenomena of "transformation into dreams" and "transformation in hallucinosis". While the former seeks to produce images—provisional, dynamic meanings—the latter reverses oneiric functioning and gives rise to certainties and blockages of the field.

Another bipolarity that strongly characterizes the life of the field is the oscillation between unsaturated and saturated interpretation. Before an interpretation becomes a classical transference interpretation, it must often undertake a long journey, which we shall now attempt to follow through its various stages from unsaturation to saturation.

.......\.........

+ ***** ....:::::::::

ooooo****_______

At the beginning of many patients' analyses, fragments of proto-emotions are present:

These could be called *proto-sememes*.

The proto-sememes must be gathered in, organized and transformed to a higher level, thus eventually generating *micro-sememes*:

G / –
A C – I I
Y- L – I
N – A – I
I – [F]
▯ E Γ L
- I Z S

The micro-sememes must in turn be organized in such a way as to create *basic sememes*—for example, JEALOUSY.

This, either by itself or in combination with other basic sememes, must next be *contextualized to fit the apparent situation*:

> "King Kong gets jealous of X when …"

A further stage in the work of the field is *apparent contextualization together with an explicit personification*:

> "At school you are jealous of X when …"

In this way we arrive at *contextualization and reversed explicit personification*:

> "You're afraid I'm jealous when you …"

Finally, at journey's end, we have *contextualization with direct explicit personification*:

> "It seems to me that *you* are jealous when I …"

"School" or "King Kong" will of course be thought of as locations in the present field; in other words, an interpretation in effect travels from an unsaturated interpretation *in* the field to an unsaturated interpretation *of* the field, then to an unsaturated interpretation in the transference, and lastly to a saturated interpretation in the transference.

This suggests that patients are also always talking about the oneiric level of the functioning of the analytic couple, and, further, that what a patient says after an interpretation is also a dream about that interpretation: hence the characters who appear signify the way in which the patient heard the interpretation.

In this connection, let us see what happens, and how it is signalled by the field, when the analyst "goes offside".

A competent analyst brings a clinical case to supervision, saying that she has failed to respect the setting: she has replied to an urgent text message from a patient and agreed to meet the surgeon who was to operate on her inner ear.

In the session the patient had mentioned the operation *for hearing* that she was shortly to undergo. After the surgery she had described how *hearing* had become something terrible for her, saying that sounds were devastating. The surgical team had included an engineer who modulated the receptivity of the complex implant she had had fitted in a difficult neurosurgical operation.

The patient had commenced her four-session-a-week analysis on a face-to-face basis because she was deaf and had to lip-read. She had a devastating history behind her. The emotional situation in which she had grown up was very low-grade: her mother was a high-class prostitute and the patient herself had been repeatedly abused from early adolescence by both family members and her mother's clients. The father was a violent man who had spent many years in prison. The patient described herself as "lesbian", attracted only to women. She had the appearance of an ugly, burly boy with a simian element—a "gorilla-like woman" according to her analyst. Yet below the surface a hidden, obscured kind of beauty could be glimpsed.

The patient's emotional situation could be illustrated by the following diagram:

♀♂♂♂♂
♂♂♂♂
♂♂♂♂
♀
♂♂♂♂
♂♂♂♂

That is to say, her mind is subject to continuous abuse by protomental contents—represented by the symbol ♂—which re-emerge in uncontainable, unmetabolizable form because the containing parts of the mind (♀) lack the necessary capacity.

The analyst goes "offside" not by "venial" instances of acting-out but when she shifts her listening vertex onto an external reality which, owing to its brutish and degraded nature, imposes itself on her listening. This impedes the specificity of analytic listening in the session which should always come first, like a kind of magic philter applied to the patient's material: "I had a dream." By failing to use the analytic magic philter, the analyst loses the specificity of analytic communication: she overlooks the patient's message that, through the work of analysis, through the *im-pianto* [*impianto*, the Italian for implant, contains the word *pianto*, which means crying], and through the painful introjection of a new function, she is becoming *capable of hearing and feeling* [the same word, *sentire*, means both in Italian] the emotions she had previously had to leave unheeded because they were too excruciating. The analysis is precisely the set of operations, surgical or otherwise, that enable her to be no longer deaf to her pain and to the intense emotions she has kept at bay in order to survive. Now there is a "new world of sound" with a surgeon-analyst and a "sound"-engineer-analyst that permits an increasingly modulated form of listening to emotional states.

This is not to say that the result of analytic listening should then be communicated to the patient explicitly and directly; instead, mediation might be necessary through the characters of the "surgeon", the "engineer", the "implant", the "operation" and the "surgery". However, what cannot be avoided is a dreaming kind of listening, the kind that we activate by preceding the patient's narration with the "I had a dream" mentioned above, because that and that alone is specific to us. The aim of analysis is to develop the patient's ability to "dream"—and hence to transform, metabolize and therefore forget—the excesses of sensoriality and proto-emotions which, unless digested and "dreamed", lead to suffering and symptoms.

Our attention must be directed not towards homosexuality as real genital behaviour, but towards its metaphorical significance. For example, in this case I am thinking of the patient's quest for a relationship with a receiving and available mind that is required to provide a model of receptivity. The "simian" side must find a place and be listened to; this will constitute a ♂♀ relationship, which is metaphorically heterosexual and can then be introjected by the patient.

The more "real", "dramatic" or "objective" the situation narrated by the patient, the more the analyst is at risk of losing the magic philter.

The field, then, is permeated by turbulence, by whirlwinds and sometimes by tsunamis of ß-elements, which find, in the process of transformation into dreams, the transformational container that leads from disorganized potentialities to possible forms of representation.

The concept of the field is rendered even more complex by all the virtualities at work in it—as it were, parallel worlds or universes that subsequently coalesce into narrations which come to life in accordance with the receptive capacity of the dreaming ensemble. Breaking down the latter, we encounter "night dreams", which become dreams of the field at the moment in which they are narrated. In field theory, dreams are not material that tell solely of the patient's mental state in the night when they were dreamed, but also partake of the here-and-now of the analytic situation through the choice of the moment when they are brought and the form in which they are brought, as well as, of course, through their content.

Another aspect worth exploring is the contribution of the analyst's mental state to the creation of the field. If the analyst's mind has turbulences of its own (or at least predominantly of its own) or is involved in the turbulences of the field, that is not necessarily a disadvantage—provided that the analyst is aware that what happens in the field is co-determined by the contributions of patient and analyst alike. This will now be illustrated by a clinical example.

One Monday I thought I had had a good session with Lucilla. In the next session she brings a dream: she is in a desolate place, a kind of dump full of rubbish; walking in this litter-filled space, she sees three ugly, dirty, witch-like women sadistically ill-treating a kitten. As she goes on through the darkness of the dump, more and more witches appear, arousing more and more anxiety. She is very afraid, but then a car full of *"virgili urbani"* [a slip of the tongue for *vigili urbani*: in Italian *vigili* are police, but the word is similar in sound to *Virgilio*, the Italian for the Latin poet and mentor figure Virgil] arrives and picks her up. The car is driven by a "fat policewoman" who seems not to take her story seriously; but although the patient is afraid of being "dumped" from the car, she is kept inside. In a second dream, an established couple is, to her surprise, plunged into crisis; she takes their little girl in her arms, but the child slips out of her grasp and falls to the ground—though she seems not to have sustained a lethal injury.

I ponder over these dreams. I think of the time when I told her the dates of my holiday, even though that was several sessions ago, and realize only then that in the previous session I was preoccupied with a "personal" concern that had caused me to miss a few sentences pronounced by the patient, although I had, I thought, soon got back on her wavelength. I now ask her if anything had struck her about the last session. She immediately answers: "At one point I felt that you weren't listening to me."

This enables me to show her what happens when she experiences me as being less present in the session: she feels "dumped", thinks she is worthless, no more than garbage to be got rid of in my eyes. Next she is progressively assailed by feelings of rage, pain and despair, which she fears are looming over her (the witches). But then she feels that I am close to her again, although unsure of my reliability; she is afraid of being dumped again, and when all this happens, a good couple—the two of us—is plunged into crisis, and trust (the little girl) falls to the ground, although no permanent damage has been done.

"You couldn't have summed up my feelings any more accurately than that," she says, adding: "Absolutely perfect; not a crease or blemish to be seen." "Yes," I reply, "it's not for nothing that my name means 'iron'"[1] (in our analytic language, my name stands for an iron to get rid of creases).

We are now able to start working on the roots of the "fear, and experience, of not being listened to", this time on another stage—that of her infancy and history.

But how are we to see this stage? As we venture ever further into the depths and margins of the field, we come upon areas of incipient oneiric functions and sensory turbulence.

The field we are considering is one that is multispatial, multidimensional, holographic and oneiric; it is a field that comes to life in the analytic encounter. Each individual is the bearer of a "psychic field" of his or her own, inhabited by turbulence and intrapsychic possibilities of all kinds. In the analytic field, the "subjective fields" of each participant flow together, giving rise to a new entity that is much more than the mere sum of its predecessors. The field takes on characteristics (Ferro, 2005 and 2009) that can be described as follows:

- The field becomes a place and moment where the emotional turbulences activated by the analytic encounter are manifested.
- The field becomes the place-and-time of the promotion of stories and narrations that are the outcome of the process of alphabetization of the proto-emotions present in the couple.

- The field is the matrix which, by way of the capacity for reverie and availability for being in unison, promotes the development of the ability to contain and of the α-function (Ferro, 2006).

Transformations of the field are mediated by an ongoing process of co-narration between analyst and patient, who become "two authors in search of characters" (Ferro, 1992, 2002), alphabetizing the proto-emotions and facilitating their constant evolution.

In the field, the semantic halo of the concept of interpretation is expanded so as to include all other unsaturated, seemingly conversational input from the analyst. Central to the field is the analyst's reverie—i.e., his ability to make contact with his waking dream thought (and its constituent subunits) and to narrate it in words, thereby bringing about transformations of the field itself. The narrative derivatives of the patient's waking dream thought and of the α-elements of which it is composed are equally important. The patient's narration can be seen, from a certain vertex, as an ongoing renarration of how he or she "presents in the form of frames of a film" the field's elements, events and lines of force. In this sense, there is no material brought by the patient that is not relevant to the field.

It is essential for the complexity of the present field, which is horizontal in nature and lives in the here and now, to be supplemented by an equivalent vertical complexity, which also includes the multigenerational aspect: so time enters the analyst's consulting room.

We thus find ourselves in a geometry not only of the "internal world" and of the "relationship", but also of "histories" and their transmission. It is no longer the analyst and the patient who are active and present with their two-dimensional "photographs" of parents, uncles and aunts and grandparents to be interpreted and stripped of their disguises by transference interpretation. Instead, we are in the presence of three-dimensional characters belonging to different temporalities who ask, or need, to be able to take the stage in their own right: at this point, any interpretation "in the field" is a transference interpretation. In this dimension, the analyst must in my view submit to being permeated by these transgenerational lyophilized elements (Faimberg, 2005) which await only the fluid medium of reception of the field in order to take on "substance" and history.

We are thus confronted with a complexity for which we are not always equipped. Some other points too are worth considering here—for instance, how the narrating function of the field may extend to pockets of unthinkability in the analyst as well as the patient. The transgenerational aspects of the analyst enter the room in the form both of the personal element and of the transmission of the analytic function from one generation of analysts to the next, including the analyst's blind spots (to which the field, if only we listen to it, may fortunately draw attention!). The need here is to retrace the history, including our own history as analysts—not as a rite, but as a way of discovering transgenerational legacies.

There is much food for thought here on the concepts of projective identification and emotional turbulence; in cinema terms, the situation can be likened to the beginning of *Jurassic Park*, in which residual traces of DNA in the soil overcome animal extinctions and ferocious, mysterious dinosaurs are brought back to life: in the same way, the mind cannot develop unless certain split-off elements are restored to the present.

While the "double multipersonality" (Baranger M. and W., 1961–62) of analyst and patient previously opened the way to myriads of possible universes along the axis of space, now it inevitably reveals to us a plethora of ramifications in time. As Borges puts it, we find ourselves in a "web of time—the strands of which approach one another, bifurcate, intersect or ignore each other": the world of uchronias, or utopias in history. The world of uchronias is one whose history has diverged from history as we know it, historical events being replaced by hypothetically possible ones. This opens the way to possibilities which are mere exercises in terms of the history of civilization (what if General Custer had won the battle of Little Big Horn …?); in the case of a personal history, however, by virtue of the process of *Nachträglichkeit* and its assignment of new meaning, these can become new thought, new realities of the future and—why not?—also of the past. Indeed, it seems to me that the possible rewriting of a history that never was can open up vast new prospects and is the most precious gift that analysis can confer.

A place for Cochise

An important and somehow arbitrary operation is the "fact" we choose as being the organizer of the discourse of the patient (it is arbitrary only to some extent, if it originates from an inspiration that the analyst is able to detect/accept). Of course, this operation is based on the "negative capabilities" of the analyst and on his/her capacity for reverie.

An experienced colleague asks me for a consultancy due to a dramatic situation he is going through. I get the first bits of information over the phone—as he lives in a nation in the far North. In the last few weeks, both he and his family have been protected by body guards because of the threats made by one of his patients.

This patient, I am told by my colleague during a session, has threatened him because analysis caused him to lose the joy of living, made him get married, become a father, find a job in a bank, but all this prevented him from finding "true life". He lost all the women he could have had, had to give up the custom-built cars he used to own when he was young, the travels he could have made. In short, the price was too high, and now he wants to get back at his analyst by killing himself after slaughtering the analyst's family. The analyst incidentally tells me that the patient continues to get some special creams from Switzerland to treat a worrying rash.

What speaks to me as *chosen fact* is the rash, the red skin, a tangential element, i.e., the "redskin". A redskin who terrifies all the pale faces (white men). But I wonder why. A redskin cannot be so scary.

I enquire about the age of both the patient and the analyst.

The patient will turn 40 and, around the same time, the analyst will turn 50.

Here is the key: the "redskin" of the patient, with his flaming arrows, sets fire to the "redskin" of the analyst. The very same redskin with which the analyst had lost contact and which caught fire upon the crisis of his fiftieth birthday (and the fortieth of the patient).

A life spent working in a bank, a life spent in the consulting room, is quite unacceptable to the redskin (the redskins!), who claims revenge and makes threats. A painful mourning process, for the many existential potentials given up, has to be carried out. A mourning process of accepting reality is preceded by telluric shocks of anger.

Having tactfully helped my colleague to re-establish contact with his own "redskin" has enabled him to contain the patient's redskin without fearing his own so much, so that each of them was able to find a way to give some relief and space to his own redskin.

I should say the three of us, since I, myself, was about to turn 60, and as a child one of my favourite heroes was Cochise, who makes the most of circumstances so that his own space and right to exist are acknowledged, both of which had been ignored for a long time.

The dreaming of the field

Loredana's medals

Loredana was a woman of about 35 who presented with a narcissistic type of pathology; she claimed "not to need analysis as a patient" but wanted it only "for professional reasons", as a "psychiatrist working with difficult patients". "Well, I do have some emotional difficulties as well." I noticed her need to deny her own suffering but did not mention it explicitly, and was struck by the interest in the Arab world which she then expressed to me: she had nearly studied oriental languages instead of medicine, and was fascinated by the Arab world—by the enormous wealth and great poverty of those countries.

From the beginning this analysis was greatly at risk of being broken off, and was marked by acting-out and hints of a negative therapeutic reaction—until I realized that, as a dream suggested, Loredana "could not afford treatment that was too expensive" (on the emotional level).

I recall that after some of my interpretations a "child brought into the resuscitation ward after swallowing nails" took the stage; and that, after any interpretation I felt I could give directly, immediately "a little girl who was almost blinded by receiving too much oxygen in the incubator" would appear. On the other hand, if I was aware of the overdose of interpretation I was administering and toned down my comments, this would be received and signalled by the arrival in the session of "an oculist who helped the little girl by non-intrusive treatments, so that she had good prospects of recovering her sight". Again, if I had been experienced as over-efficient, she would immediately mention the "Chief Physician who had been on a management course and functioned in electronic-brain mode all the time". In a particularly significant session, after I had given a direct interpretation connecting the intense rage she was able to experience following a rage-ridden dream with something that had caused her a great deal of suffering—a deep wound that had always been denied—Loredana interrupted me in terror, exclaiming: "What's happening, what's happening? I can see the mask in the picture opposite lifting up ..." It is hardly necessary for me to say that, in the picture on the opposite wall, there was no mask in motion, and indeed no depiction of a mask at all.

I realized that my interpretations were bursting the bounds of the "container" (♀) and giving rise to extreme persecution. If I then interpreted this persecution or the feelings generated by my interpretations (envy, jealousy or intolerance of dependence), she would skip sessions, bring accounts of furious rows, or talk about the terrible relationship she had with her brother, who rejected anything that came from her—rejection and contempt. It became clear to me that there was no point in interpreting all this in the transference and that I must modify my usual technique. There then appeared "Luigi", her new boyfriend, who "lets himself be driven by me, is caring, affectionate and not at all stupid, but is less experienced than I am". I used carefully dosed interpretations in following her account of this love story, which set other possible suitors aside: "Ulisse", who wanted sex more than anything else (he appeared whenever I "touched her" with transference interpretations), and "Carlo", who was capable of platonic friendship only (he took the stage when I was too reserved and distant). Luigi seemed to be the right middle ground, and they were soon married. A baby was promptly on the way, and seemed to have two connotations: a defensive one relating to the "cost" of her analysis, and a "creative" one.

The pregnancy enriched Loredana's emotional life, which began to be experienced and narrated through the emotions activated, which she "discovered" in the "little girl". For a long time her own separation anxiety was brought in the form of "little Marta's anxiety" (the child cried in despair whenever her mother went away); her own jealousy was called "Marta's jealousy when she is told that a new little brother is on the way"; and her own needs were "Tommy's unstillable hunger, bordering on greed".

So, for a long time, we had to stick with the story as narrated (albeit with my absolute conviction that we were exclusively talking about and working on the emotional and mental facts of the consulting room), until it eventually became possible to find a more explicit way of allowing Loredana to approach emotions recognizable as her own.

The "lots of medals" of a dream from the early stages of her analysis gave way to "lots of holes (needs)" from a later dream that had been concealed by the medals-as-prostheses.

Now began a period in which Loredana set about re-owning split-off geographical areas of her mind. Her dreams became populated with gypsies, immigrant pedlars, Arabs who were sometimes as furious as "Marta" (when she was angry Marta was so incomprehensible that she might as well have been speaking Arabic) and sometimes seeking asylum ... Then came "Lassie", the faithful creature able to find his own way home.

The very sick children she was now beginning to treat by psychotherapy now took the stage; each represented the particular problem that was currently concerning us—and here again, a long, indirect interpretative route had to be followed.

Next to appear was "Claudia", who had a school phobia due to her fear of an over-demanding teacher (whenever I increased my interpretative dosage), or who had a phobia of fruit because it meant; indicated the end of dinner-time, when daddy would leave; "Marina", who was so in love with her boyfriend, who didn't take care of her as she would have liked; and many other characters, each with his or her own "theme".

I shall now present two sessions illustrating this style of working.

Session

I announce an increase in my fees from New Year (it is October). The patient skips the next two sessions. What does it mean when an analyst increases his fees from "New Year"? In the words of the Italian saying, *anno nuovo, vita nuova* [new year, new life]: perhaps the analyst had in the back of his mind the idea of embarking on a renewed analytic life in a higher gear (and at higher emotional cost).

Monday

Patient: The last few days have been terrible: an unbelievable workload at the clinic that I couldn't cope with; then Marta went down with otitis, and on top of everything the car wouldn't start ... Marta can't stand Tommy: she's been ill-treating him, hitting him because she's so angry with him. Then she had an episode of night terror ... and if her father went anywhere near her, she screamed her head off ... it must be the Oedipus complex!

Analyst: (*this slips out; I at once feel that it is excessive, not well cooked*). It must be the increase! (*I then add the following, without at the time realizing that I might perhaps have inwardly taken the rage at the "Arabs" upon myself.*) I wonder if we can connect the skipped sessions—everything that has happened in the last few days—with my asking for an increase: maybe it aroused emotions in you that you couldn't cope with ... Your ear hurts when you hear certain requests ... You weren't able to get yourself going to come along here ... you're so angry with me and afraid of me ... (*and, who knows, perhaps the "incredible workload" mentioned by the patient is the higher gear the analyst wishes to engage for the analytic work*).

Patient: (*after a few minutes' silence, during which I feel a kind of discomfort and await her reply to what I said*). Something terrible happened to Marcella (I told you about her some time ago): she was raped in a garage by a former boyfriend who has become a drug addict: as revenge for her having left him, he raped her.

Analyst: (*note how the patient responds to the transference interpretation, partly by introducing to the field a new character, Marcella's ex-boyfriend, a drug addict and a rapist ... I refrain from transference interpretation, which has proven too violent for the patient in this connection, and give preference to an "unsaturated" interpretation—that is, one that does not overtly reveal the transference but instead remains on the level of the characters of the session. A "saturated", transference interpretation would explicitly and directly describe how the patient experienced my words as a rape, in my rage at her having abandoned me for two sessions because I think they would have been intolerable. Instead, I comment as follows*). It must have been a terrible experience for "Marcella" to be violently assaulted, and by someone she had been close to as well, whom she may well have trusted.

Patient: Yes, but at the same time she always has her new boyfriend close by, whom she can talk to; he is affectionate and understands her well.

Analyst: That may help her to digest the assault somehow. (*Here again, I opt not to "defrost" the transference, but of course I consider that the patient's communication is a reference to* *my last interpretation, and that I was then experienced rather like an affectionate boyfriend whom she can at last speak to and whom she can freely trust.*)

Patient: (*after a few minutes' silence*). While playing with Marta I thought how much difference there is between a "real mouse" and Mickey Mouse, the cartoon character book, and then I thought of a film I saw on TV about ants that had grown to enormous size after being exposed to radiation: they attacked two people who were fond of each other ... Animals like mice really can make you afraid.

Analyst: (*what aspect of the patient is Marta, whom she has brought in at this point in the analysis? I imagine she may be a reference to the creative, generative elements of the session. I refrain from an interpretation that would decode the "mice" as living, frightening emotions and "Mickey Mouse" as the feeling contained in the narrative interpretation; and I do not interpret the "radiation" as my dangerous words that unleash terrible furies*). So mice are dangerous: they also carry rage! .... (in Italian the term "rabbia" (rage) means both "anger" and "rabies")

Patient: And the plague too ... I remember a comic strip where enormous ants invade the earth under the guidance of extraterrestrials ... and people did not know how to defend themselves ... And I recall a frequent dream of mine, of enormous ants coming out of a wound in my body.

Analyst: (*I refrain from interpreting the invasion of feelings infesting her mind, from which she does not know how to defend herself, me and the analysis*) But there are remedies for both rage and the plague—and then, rage and ants do not come from nowhere: in the dream they emerge from a wound, so "someone" must have hurt you ...

Patient: Ummm, yes, the increase ... You know, in the consulting rooms where I work, my friend, who is also a colleague of mine, wants to put up the rent, and that's causing me a lot of problems, as she is asking too much.

Analyst: (*I do not address the obvious split between the increased rent and my increase in fees, and reflect on the cost—including the emotional cost—of the analysis for this patient*). But is your friend so inflexible that you couldn't perhaps talk about it again and reach an agreement?

Patient: (*after a few minutes' silence*). I read in the paper that Superman had died ...

Analyst: (*I desist from interpreting the retraction of her projection of omnipotence on to me*). And maybe the days of Superwoman are over, now that you can be wounded and have "economic" difficulties (*I am thinking of the emotional cost of the analysis*).

Patient: Well, now I'm confident that my friend will grant me a short deferment; I'll certainly talk to her about it next week, when we've arranged to meet here in Pavia.

A few months later

Patient: I felt awful on Tuesday: leaving the kids all by themselves—I just couldn't do it, so I didn't come ...

Analyst: And then on Wednesday there was my phone call (*cancelling her session, and leaving her feeling all by herself like her children*).

Patient: Yes, I was afraid you had done it to get even with me ... Then I told myself that couldn't be ... Then I had a dream. I must say first that I had seen a TV documentary about Pygmies who were very resentful about the devastation white people were inflicting on the forest; in the documentary they said they filed their teeth to make them very sharp; this was very useful for meat instead of using knives, but it was terribly painful because they also cut into the dentine and pulp underneath the hard parts ... Well, in the dream, my brother came home crying and screaming with pain: he had had something done to his teeth; maybe they had been cleaned. He was suffering terribly, and I tried to give him something—aspirin or the like—but it had no effect. I stood it for a while, I tried to help him, and then I left.

Analyst: What does all this suggest to you? (*It is also important to help the patient to expand his or her own thought. On the one hand, this may help the analytic couple to allow new aspects to take the stage—perhaps ones the analyst has not yet thought of—while, on the other, it generates a narrativopoietic capability in the patient.*)

Patient: Well, that's not difficult: it makes me think that I'm feeling pain and suffering ... the sessions when we won't see each other ... in the past I'd never have been able to admit it ... if I'm suffering like this, how on earth will I ever be able to do without you? Well, basically, I must say that one reason why I didn't come on Tuesday was that I didn't want to hear you tell me your summer holiday dates ...

Analyst: And then the thought that "the kids would be left all by themselves" made you feel awful.

Patient: I know what you mean ... it's true.

Analyst: What is also true is that now this pain at being left all by yourself can be owned; you can take care of it and look for remedies, even if the pain then gets intolerable ... and then you leave, just like in the dream. Another thought I had was that skipped sessions, or holidays, are like damage done to the Pygmies' forest ... and the Pygmies in fact put me in mind of "Calimero"[2] children, little black creatures, because they're neglected. Right then, let me tell you the dates of the summer holidays: from ... to ...

Patient: (*after a few minutes' silence*). On the ward there's someone called Michele, who is very angry. He can't stand the Chief Physician, who is the one who makes decisions ... he says he will leave within a year ... that he doesn't want to come any more ... he was furious because a little girl couldn't have the analysis she needed—he was fuming with rage ...

Analyst: Michele threatens to leave when he feels that something is unfair, a "high-handed act", and basically also because he is coming to the defence of a little girl who needs analysis ... he is sort of getting his own back, as you were afraid I was doing by cancelling Wednesday's session after you skipped Tuesday's. (*In this interpretation, I am cautiously bringing in the transference more explicitly, even if the main emphasis is still on interpretation of the character Michele, whom I see as a reference to myself.*)

Patient: Yes, Michele is too angry; he really would leave, but on the other hand he would then start over again, and then leave again ... every time he feels put upon ...

Analyst: Ummm: Michele's rage, the Pygmies' sharp teeth for tearing into meat like knives—I think they're also telling us about your rage after I mentioned the holidays to you; but let's not forget that the filing of teeth is very painful, as it is in the dream for your brother … and that your tender, affectionate parts are suffering through all this, and Michele is restrained—but perhaps also understood in his rage, and above all in his suffering. It's like your brother in the dream when you want to give him a remedy, the aspirin. What might the aspirin be?

Patient: Well, I decided to go away for a month this summer … I'm going to Sicily, to get far away from my mother; I'll feel calmer there …

Analyst: So maybe you'll be killing two birds with one stone: "Michele" will be pleased to be going away for a month … away from the mother or whoever causes him pain … but the "pulp and dentine" will also be happy to be in Sicily, where you imagine I too will be … (*the analyst is Sicilian*).

Patient: (*after five minutes' silence*). At last I can see what it says under that picture: "hand-coloured". A picture that's hand-coloured by the artist is worth more and is finer …

Analyst: Oh, the picture … that picture has been important for us both.

Patient: Yes … the balconies opposite my house (*the reference is to a psychotic little girl whom she "saw" and on whom we worked for a long time*).

Analyst: The other one too … (*referring to the "hallucinations/frames from a waking dream film when she saw the mask move"*).

Patient: When I was trying to make Valentina say something today, she drew me a dog with spectacles on, a scarf and a pipe—a nice little sniffer dog; she put a hand in front of its mouth as if to say: that's enough for today!

Analyst: A word is enough to the wise … (*the transference is omnipresent, although only hinted at, in the last few exchanges of this session too. This style has enabled us to "sniff out" the patient's situation without too many persecutory experiences, and at the end of the encounter a new character makes its appearance: the nice little sniffer dog …*).

Although I feel that this approach helped with the working up, metabolization and transformation of very primitive emotions, the next session, here reproduced in indirect form, showed me that it was insufficient.

I have had to postpone Loredana's session by one hour.[3] At the beginning of the session, as Loredana begins to speak, I am distracted by feelings of intense rage at the poor postal service, as a result of which letters are not being delivered on time and are also likely to get lost. I then manage to listen to the patient again: she is meanwhile telling me that she has seen one film in colour and another in black and white. In the first, an unwanted little girl in a house commits suicide and her brother takes his revenge by killing everyone responsible for her death. The other is a sad story set in Pavia, about a doctor's wife who dies in childbirth, but her baby girl survives.

It is not difficult for me to think up for myself an exhaustive interpretation of content (the furious feelings initially triggered in PS by my postponement—despair, fury and revenge—and the same feelings revisited in the depressive mode, with acceptance of the loss of the session and of the birth of the new session). On other occasions the patient has shown that she does "not yet have a place" to accommodate interpretations that stem from me, so I give an unsaturated interpretation, merely drawing attention to the differing affective tones of the two films.

After a short silence, the patient says: "I've just remembered a dream: I was washing some sweaters of mine with the extra-delicate program, which is very good for fine woollens, but because the spin cycle with this program is also extra-delicate, the sweaters were still soaking wet and I was afraid they would be too heavy for the washing line."

I see the washing machine as the transformational, elaborative function of the mind, which takes in dirty material and returns it washed and dried so that it can be worn. However, the ideal transformation from ß-elements (the dirty washing) into α-elements (clean, dry washing) here fails at least in part, and the result is only partially satisfactory: the washing is clean but cannot yet be worn. I ask her if she thinks a normal wash might ruin the sweaters, to explore whether a more explicit transference interpretation might ruin our work. She answers "no", because they have now been washed several times with the extra-delicate cycle, so they are no longer likely to get spoilt. She adds that she was thinking of her sister Carmen, who once had a rug washed and hung out on the line, but couldn't use it until it was dry, and this had made her cry a lot.

In the past it was vital to subject the material brought to her sessions to a delicate wash—in other words, I had to stay on the level of "unsaturated" interpretations for a long time. At this point, though, I feel that I can program a normal wash (which is now expected and wished for), and I relate, in the transference, the feelings of the first dream to the second: the experiences of the "sister" who cannot wait and the new capacity to tolerate her emotions. The path to a transference interpretation can often be very time-consuming, especially in the early years of an analysis, even with less seriously ill patients, or indeed when the work is at an advanced stage where particularly difficult new departures are imminent.

The patient comments: "Now I understand all the rage I was feeling yesterday, quarrelling with everyone ..." (and I in turn understand the rage I felt at the postmen who failed to deliver the mail on time).

A year later the situation looks very different. It has become necessary for us to "speak to each other clearly", and I have tried to make sense of a lot of things that happened in the last few months which I had not understood. I was also able to confront the "no" problem: Loredana could not pronounce the word "no" or accept it when someone said it to her—this was one of the roots of her "being well behaved at all costs". I was able to say "no" to her and discover with relief that the "Arabs" were now no longer so dangerous.

Let us consider the events in order.

Loredana unexpectedly asks me if we can change from the usual four sessions a week to three, as the town where she lives is "quite a way from Pavia" and the children need her. I am unsure how to take this request, and am even more disconcerted when she asks me if I think it will be much longer before she can terminate her analysis.

I am unprepared. She then starts telling me about a conflict that has broken out on the ward between her and Dr Sirti, an efficient, energetic neurologist who, however, does not want to bother with psychological problems. Who will the Chief Physician choose as his Assistant?

I find it hard to get my bearings. I play for time because the situation is unclear to me.

One Monday

She arrives coughing, with a heavy cold. She tells me she is angry with the Chief Physician because she does not know if he will grant her the status of Assistant, which would allow her to manage her own cases; she certainly has the seniority and experience, but is afraid he will penalize her for the time off she took for her two pregnancies.

She has also had a dream: she was in a food shop and had a big blanket in her trolley; feeling that maybe she did not need it, she was not sure whether to give it to a woman standing nearby or to keep it. There was also a second fragment: she was with the trolley outside the shop with lots of useful things that she had bought, but the route of the road had not yet been marked out; the reality was difficult, there was no connection to anywhere else, and she did not know what to do.

In Italian the Assistant Chief Physician is called *Aiuto*, a word that also means "help". I tell her that it seems to me that there are two parties in her, still warring with each other: one would like to give up the fourth session and after that the blanket of the analysis because she thinks she no longer needs it, but perhaps that is not all there is to it, as she also has a cough and a cold—so can she already contemplate doing without the blanket? All the same, she has done a lot of work and learnt a lot, and she has a trolley—a place to contain her things—and she could not tolerate it if I, her Chief Physician, failed to acknowledge her acquisitions.

Yet I am not satisfied. What is it that is still worrying me? Is it reasonable to reduce the number of sessions? To terminate? Has the time come? Or is something not right?

Perhaps I can accept her plan … it is sensible … I talk to her about it in terms of "it's something we can think about"—but I am not at all convinced.

She comes to the next session upset and in tears, twenty minutes late: the Chief Physician has no confidence in her and will surely choose her neurologist colleague as his Assistant; he does not set any store by the investigation of mental problems. She still has some hope of successfully putting her case to the old and respected Chief Physician in Pavia.

Then she brings a dream: it is about Daniela, a psychologist doing a psychotherapy course, who, however, does not want to have analysis, and three or four English people reading a newspaper … and then she is looking for her spectacles.

I now feel able to put things together: the distance she was complaining about; the children's need to have their mother near them; the question "Who shall I choose to help [*aiuto*] me?"; Loredana and her interest in delving into the psychological depths versus the "efficient-neurologist-cum-Daniela who does not want to go down into the depths".

I tell her that the dream opens up some pathways for us: "Daniela" is telling us that she does not want to delve into the depths in her analysis, so she comes along late; that she wants to cut down on her sessions; that she is angry because she is afraid I have not immediately taken her side; that she reacted phlegmatically and with a stiff upper lip like an "Englishman"; and that I now feel that, using my rediscovered old Chief Physician's spectacles, I can choose her as Assistant [i.e., as *aiuto*—for help]. I therefore tell her that I disagree with Daniela about the three sessions, and about terminating.

She leaves in silence. Next time she tells me that this was the first "no" of her entire life, that it didn't kill her, and that the Chief Physician has chosen her as his Assistant.

The analyst's "no" in effect acts as a limit set to the expansion of the process of containment. In this case, it is not a limit imposed by harshness as such, but by the strength of the analyst's mental capacity to think a new thought in that situation. The analyst could alternatively have said something like "You ought to stay in analysis at four sessions a week because that is what the rule of psychoanalysis dictates." Such a response would have constituted a flight into orthodoxy, which would have been incomprehensible to the patient. Instead, the analyst generates a "no" of his own after having been able to dwell for a long period in uncertainty, based on his own capacity to dream about the patient's dream.

This process is received by the patient's mind, and in addition it seems that his/her history too is being rewritten: the Chief Physician chooses her as his Assistant [for "help"] and not Daniela. So, once again, the patient is the analyst's best assistant/helper and colleague.

Notes

1. [Translator's note: The Italian idiom in the patient's comment means literally "You don't make a crease", and the analyst's name (Ferro) means iron, so the allusion is to an iron that could iron out the creases.]
2. [Translator's note: "Calimero" is a dumpy, childlike cartoon figure from Italian commercials.]
3. Usually I would simply tell the patient that I am not able to have a session at the usual time and would then wait for the patient to ask for it to be postponed, and I would accept or do my best to fit the reality of my schedule; in this case, however, because I knew that she would want to reschedule the session when possible, I myself suggested the postponement.

References

Baranger M. e W. (1961–62). La situacion analitica como campo dinamico. In: *Problemas del campo analitico*. Kargieman, Buenos Aires, 1969, 128–164.

Barros, E.D. (2000). Affect and Pictographic Image: The Constitution of Meaning in Mental Life. *International Journal of Psychoanalysis 81*: 1087–1099.

Bion, W.R. (1962). *Learning from Experience*. London: Heinemann.

Faimberg, H. (2005). *The Telescoping Of Generations: Listening To The Narcissistic Links Between Generations*. London and New York, Routledge.

Ferro, A. (1992). *The Bipersonal Field: Experiences in Child Analysis*. Routledge, London, 1999.

Ferro, A. (2002). Some Implications of Bion's Thought: The Waking Dream and Narrative Derivatives; *International Journal of Psychoanalysis, 83*: 597–607.

Ferro, A. (2005). 'Commentary' on Field Theory by Madaleine Baranger and on The confrontation between generations as a dynamic field by Luis Kancyper. In *Truth Reality and the Psychoanalyst* (Eds.), S. Lewkowicz and S. Flechner IPL London.

Ferro, A. (2006). Clinical implication of Bion's thought. *International Journal of Psychoanalysis. 87*: 989–1003.

Ferro, A. (2009, in press). Transformations into dreams and characters of the psychoanalytic field, Opening lecture at the IPA Conference in Chicago, 2009.

Grotstein, J.S. (2007). A Beam of Intense Darkness. Karnac Books, London.

CHAPTER TWO

On the therapeutic action of psychoanalysis

Cláudio Laks Eizirik

When Freud (1912) recommended the adoption of a state of "evenly suspended attention", he meant that the analyst should be open to whatever arises, without prejudices of any kind, and without systematically seeking confirmation of any previous hypothesis. Adopting this position could help him in the delicate and what is even now the somehow mysterious process of the therapeutic action of psychoanalysis.

In his seminal paper of 1934, Strachey stated that the final result of a psychoanalytic treatment is to enable the patient's whole mental organization, which was held in check at an infantile stage of development, to continue its progress towards a normal adult stage. The principal effective alteration consists, according to him, in a profound qualitative modification of the patient's superego, from which the other alterations would follow for the most part automatically. This modification of the patient's superego is brought about in a series of innumerable small steps through mutative interpretations, which are effected by the analyst by virtue of his position as the object of the patient's id-impulses and as an auxiliary superego. However, according to Strachey, the fact that the mutative interpretation was the ultimate operative factor in the therapeutic action of psychoanalysis does not imply the exclusion of many other procedures (such as suggestion, reassurance, abreaction, etc.) as elements in the treatment of any particular patient. (Strachey, 1934).

From then on, several authors, following along these and many other lines, suggested ways in which the analyst could come closer to what the patient is trying to communicate and thus operate more effectively in order to produce psychic change. All these contributions—coming from different analytic schools—help us today, in our daily work, to attempt an analytic technique that aims at a therapeutic action.

In this chapter, I will briefly review some contributions from Klein and post-Kleinian authors, and then outline with some detail the ideas put forward by the Barangers and other Latin American authors, and finally present some clinical material in order to illustrate the ways I think psychoanalysis acts therapeutically.

Melanie Klein presented a short contribution on the criteria for the termination of an analysis to the British Society, in 1949, in which her views on the therapeutic action are indirectly stated: "Have persecutory and depressive anxieties been sufficiently reduced in the course of the analysis, and has the patient's relation to the external world been sufficiently strengthened to enable him to deal satisfactorily with the situations of mourning arising at this point? By analyzing as fully as possible both the negative and the positive transference, persecutory and depressive anxieties are diminished and the patient becomes increasingly able to synthesize the contrasting aspects of the primitive objects, and the feelings towards them, thus establishing a more realistic and secure attitude to the internal and the external world. If these processes have been sufficiently experienced in the transference situation both the idealization of the analyst and the feelings of being persecuted by him are diminished; the patient can cope more successfully with the feeling of loss caused by the termination of the analysis and with that part of the work of mourning which he has to carry out by himself after the end of the analysis" (Klein, 1949, p. 204).

As can be seen, the therapeutic action of psychoanalysis, according to Klein, would happen through the rigorous maintenance of the analytic setting, so as to keep transference as pure and uncontaminated as possible; emphasis on transference as the central focus of analyst-patient interactions; a belief that the transference situation is active from the beginning of the analysis; an attitude of active receptivity rather then passivity and silence; interpretation of anxiety and defense together; and mainly *emphasis on the transference interpretation as the agent of therapeutic change.* (Segal, 1967).

More recently, post-Kleinian analysts, without radically changing these basic points, developed new ways of understanding psychic life, and as a consequence, of explaining the therapeutic action of psychoanalysis. For instance, many authors have discussed the importance of what the patient does in contrast to the content of what he says. Among them, Betty Joseph has particularly emphasized this contrast as a starting point for her understanding of the way patients very early on in their lives and in the analytic situation adapt to their objects and attempt to control them through projective identification, a mechanism first described by Klein (1946), but whose full usefulness was only developed by Bion's container/contained formulation (1959).

Joseph's aim is to discover where the alive, immediate emotional contact between patient and analyst is, this being a prerequisite of true understanding. She stresses that much of what the patient communicates in a session is not expressed in terms of words but though the use of words to carry out actions, that is, to do something to the analyst, or to put subtle pressure on the analyst to do something to the patient. The analytic task is to accept the pressure to do or to feel some particular thing, reflect on the fact that one is being subjected to it, and then make a limited and precise interpretation only about the immediate action. She avoids interpretations with two or more contrasting statements and premature links with bodily expressions and conceptualizations of unconscious fantasy and with known facts of the patient's history, which she calls "the plausible interpretation." She does so because in her view then both patient and analyst lose the immediate emotional reality, and have what is in effect a safe theoretical discussion about a third person, the patient. Her method particularly stresses the repetition of infantile defenses, the attempt to draw the analyst into behavior that will evade painful emotional confrontations by attempting to maintain or restore an age-old system of psychic defense. (Joseph, 1975, 1985; Spillius, 1988). The continuous analytic work along these lines shows how to accept therapeutic limitations, from learning to contain and to use constructively feelings of therapeutic discouragement. This will bring a slow and consistent psychic change; this constitutes her way of formulating the therapeutic action of psychoanalysis.

Willy and Madeleine Baranger, analysts of French origin, both trained in Argentina, where they became prominent authors, presented their ideas about two main concepts that can shed light on the therapeutic action of psychoanalysis in several contributions, mainly in their paper "The analytic situation as a dynamic field" (1961–2). Their concepts of the dynamic field and unconscious fantasy represented the convergence of various contemporary currents of thought, such as the ideas of Kurt Lewin, the Gestalt theory, and the developments of notions due to Melanie Klein, Susan Isaacs and Wilfred Bion.

They describe different aspects of the analytic field: its spatial aspect, resulting from the particular features of the physical environment of the consulting room and variations in distance or proximity between analyst and patient; its temporal dimension, as indicated by the rhythm and length of sessions and the separations or interruptions occurring within the analytic process; and its functional configuration, due to characteristics of the setting—i.e., the different roles assumed by patient and analyst.

The main focus of their interest, however, was the study of the unconscious dynamic of the analytic field. Their central hypothesis is that the regressive situation of the analysis gives rise to a new Gestalt, a bipersonal or basic unconscious fantasy of the couple, different from the fantasies of the patient or the analyst considered individually. This fantasy underlies the dynamics of the analytic field—whether it be in motion or in stasis. This notion was inspired by the description of the mechanism of projective identification (Klein, 1946) and the structure of unconscious fantasy (Isaacs, 1948), as an expression of the totality of mental life, comprising both instinctual (libidinal and destructive) impulses and mechanisms of defense against these impulses. The Barangers see the analytic field as the stage for the *mise-en-scène* of the patient's primitive fantasies. The assumption that unconscious fantasies are brought into the present in the analytic field lies at the root of one of the main characteristics of the field, its radical ambiguity, in the sense that everything and every event in the field can be understood at the same time as being or meaning something else. Their approach differs to some extent from that of Klein and Isaacs in its emphasis on the idea that the analyst needs to understand not only the projection of the patient's fantasies, but also the processes arising between patient and analyst. This shared unconscious fantasy is conceived as a new structure that "can in no way be regarded as determined by the patient's (or, of course, the analyst's) instinctual impulses, although the impulses of both are involved in its structuring. Nor can it be seen as the *sum* of the two internal situations. It is something created *between* the two, within the unity they constitute during the session—something radically different from what each of them is individually". (Baranger and Baranger, 1961–2, p. 20, apud De León, 2002).

As a consequence, the words of the interpretation not only disclose unconscious contents of the patient's psychic reality, but are also a form of "doing with the patient". The interpretation must fundamentally be directed towards the here and now of the relationship with the analyst. The analyst's attention must be focused on the present of the analytic situation, and not on the discovery or reconstruction of facts from the past, or on the regressive reproduction of the fixation points and libidinal stages of infantile development.

The importance assigned to the analyst's participation led the Barangers to examine the role of countertransference as an instrument of technique. The analyst, to the extent that he is the depositary of different aspects and objects of the patient's self, assumes a multiplicity of varying functions. Thus he must continuously observe his countertransference if he is to understand the successive unfolding of the patient's fantasies. In later formulations, the Barangers (1979, 1983) stressed the importance of maintaining analytic asymmetry. Taking into account Racker's idea of counter-resistance, they showed that the link between the patient's resistance and the analyst's counter-resistance can become chronic. This gives rise to the formation of a bulwark in the analytic field, maintained by both of them alike. They defined this bulwark as "a neo-formation set up around a shared fantasy assembly which implicates important areas of personal history of both participants and attributes a stereotyped imaginary role to each" (Baranger et al, 1983).

M. Baranger suggested (1993) that the attitude of analytic listening—an important part of the way psychoanalysis acts therapeutically—is diametrically opposed to the mental position of the observer or experimenter in the physical and natural sciences. The latter plans his/her observations and experiments on the basis of his expectations, which depend both on his general knowledge of his discipline and on the idea or discovery that he considers may cause science to progress. He works with prior concepts that organize the same observation, in order to verify or falsify them. On the other hand, the psychoanalyst must beware of mentally obstructing access to the unforeseen, to surprise, which is precisely what he hopes for as a characteristic of the emergence of the unconscious.

But, as M. Baranger stresses, this is not a passive or naive form of listening. It is in fact guided by the analyst's full listening resources, among them the analytic theory that provides him an implicit framework to accommodate his discoveries. Each analyst develops a scheme of reference, according to M. Baranger, which is constituted by his theoretical allegiances, his knowledge of analytic literature, his clinical experience—especially his failures—what he was able to learn about himself in his analysis, and his identifications with his analyst and supervisors—as well as the theoretical fashions which periodically sweep through the psychoanalytic movement. My own approach to analytic neutrality (Eizirik, 1993) also attempts to include an emphasis on the difficult and yet unavoidable need to keep a certain critical distance towards analytic theories that might impair our listening.

What does the analyst listen to? Madeleine Baranger proposes that what defines analytic listening and distinguishes it from any other kind of psychotherapy is that it attempts to listen to the unconscious. In other words, the analyst listens to something other than what he is being told. But to imagine that he seeks a latent content that exists behind the manifest content would be to reify something dynamic. The unconscious is not behind but is elsewhere. Instead of adopting the well-known spatial metaphor of the structure of the mind, Baranger suggests the idea of the need to find the unconscious meaning somewhere in disguise, as a sort of a riddle that the analyst is challenged to face. The listening of the analyst consists, thus, in decentering the patient's discourse, stripping it down in order to find a new centre, which in this moment is the unconscious.

It is possible to consider that there are three factors involved: 1. The patient's explicit discourse; 2. The unconscious configuration of the field (unconscious fantasy of the field), which includes the transference/countertransference; 3. What corresponds at this point to something unconscious in the analysand, which must be interpreted. It is by virtue of the mediation of the unconscious configuration of the field that the patient's unconscious can express itself and the analyst can find an interpretation. These are the main elements that take part in the therapeutic action of psychoanalysis, as formulated by W. and M. Baranger.

I would like to turn now to another contribution, the one proposed by Haydée Faimberg (1996), at present a well known French analyst, but who began to formulate these ideas when still working in Argentina. She links the function of analytic listening to Freud's concept of *Nachträglichkeit,* which she defines as the retroactive assignment of meaning, rather than mere deferred action, and derives the notion of listening to listening from their combination. She proposes a dialectical conception of time, with interpretation involving three logical phases, which are respectively incumbent on the analyst, on the patient and on both. So the patient speaks and listens from a position dictated by his unconscious identification, which also causes him to reinterpret the analyst's interpretations and his silences. By listening to the patient's reassignments of meaning to his interpretation, the analyst can discover the patient's unconscious identifications and, together with the patient, thereby facilitate the process of psychic change. By the function of listening to listening, Faimberg proposes that it is possible to overcome the dilemma of whether the analyst with his interpretation or the patient with his own reinterpretation of it is right.

And finally I will mention some of my own contributions to the issue of analytic neutrality, since I think this might help us understand why the analytic therapeutic action is so difficult. I have been considering the problem of analytic neutrality since 1993, in successive papers, and in spite of recent criticisms to this concept, I still see it as an important tool, once we accept the need of including in it several elements, and also its unavoidable ambiguity. In my view, analytic neutrality is the position, not only behavioural but also emotional, from which the analyst, in his/her relationship with the patient, without putting aside the necessary empathy, observes the following features, while still keeping a certain possible distance in relation to each of them:

1. The patient's material and his/her transference;
2. The countertransference and his/her own personality;
3. His/her own values;

4. The expectations and pressures from the external environment;
5. Psychoanalytic theory (theories).

It must be stressed that only continuous psychic work about these 5 points can grant the analyst the possibility of having analytic neutrality as a tool and an aim at the same time.

Such a position does not imply an absence of spontaneity or naturalness. Instead, the awareness of the importance of maintaining a certain possible distance in relation to those five aspects is the element which permits us an increasing and deeper contact and communication with the patient's inner world, which aims at reaching the therapeutic objectives of both analyst and patient. "A certain possible distance" is a deliberately ambiguous expression. It admits the need of a distance, but acknowledges it is relative; at the same time, with the word "possible" the attempt is to emphasize that we are dealing with a position constantly threatened, by inner and outer influences which we try to keep under control, as far as possible.

The patient's material and his transference constitute, par excellence, the field of the analytic process. The free floating attention is the instrument which permits us to follow the patient's associations and his movements along the session and process. When listening, using all technical and personal instruments developed in the course of analytic training, and rooted in successive life and professional experiences, we are also acting as the scientist who observes. I think it is a mistake to suppose that the scientific attitude has been substituted by a different one; the observer's subjective dimension added to it, just like what happens in other fields of knowledge. But, in its essence, the search for a possible objectivity is still on.

Countertransference, considered as a set of emotional reactions provoked in the analyst by the patient, is one of the most important additions to the analytic field as an instrument of observation and information about the patient. However, there must be a distinction between the analyst's countertransference and his own personality, both in its healthy and pathological aspects.

The risk of not thinking about this aspect arouses in us the temptation to consider countertransference as a sufficient proof of what is happening with the patient, in agreement with Steiner's warning (1992). The possibility of an adequate utilization of countertransference depends on the extension and depth the personal analysis can reach, as well as on the self-analysis which should be later performed. The analyst's personal issues (or his personal equation, already mentioned by Freud in 1926) are aspects deserving constant attention. In particular, the narcissistic elements stressed by Rosenfeld (1987), have shown to be potentially the most harmful to the maintenance of true analytic neutrality. In my view, countertransference is also influenced by questions related to gender and the different stages of the life cycle (Eizirik, 1995).

These are the main elements which I take into account to consider the ways psychoanalysis can act therapeutically.

Let us now see how these ideas can help us with a sample of clinical material.

The patient, a woman in her early fifties, has been in analysis for many years now, with important psychic changes. She is considering the idea of ending her analysis, an idea that is present in the analytic field.

This is a Monday session, one week before the summer break. The patient begins the session telling me about a weekend in which she had a long conversation with her husband, who was complaining about his therapist and thinking about ending his treatment. In spite of knowing consciously that he has a lot of emotional problems, she agreed with him, encouraged him to end his treatment and felt glad imagining that he could be able to live without therapy.

At this point, I thought to myself: how can she be so blind to his real condition? But I kept silent.

She goes on to say that afterwards she was observing the way her husband related to friends and how much he used to speak and behave like a helpless child, which produced irritation in her. She then criticized him fiercely. One day later, at lunch, when their only son, in his twenties, told them he was planning to spend some months travelling abroad, the husband reacted with hostility, saying he would not help him. The patient, in her words, got mad at the husband, who was not able to appreciate the progress of the son, in his struggle for independence. She again criticized him fiercely, exactly at the moment in which he was trying to speak more calmly with the son.

I told her that she was mad at herself, for not noticing that the husband needed to stay in treatment, and that possibly she was seeing herself in the husband, because she also wanted to end her analysis, but perhaps was not convinced that this was the best moment for it.

She reacted to this interpretation with an intensity that is peculiar to her, similar to the one she showed at the lunch discussion. I could not avoid engaging in a sort of argument with her, trying to show her the way she was behaving towards me, and her attempt to deny how difficult it was for her to feel the pain of a prospective end of analysis.

Repeating something she had done in recent sessions, when she was responding to this interpretation she called me by the name of the husband. When I pointed out to her this slip and asked her what it could mean, she began to laugh and said maybe she was in love with me, adding that this kind of joke was unthinkable some time ago. "What else could it mean?", I asked her. She said maybe she wished her husband could listen to her and talk with her the way I did, maybe she wanted to feel at ease with him as she felt in her analytic sessions.

This allowed us to analyze her feelings of deep commitment to me and to her analysis, something she used to feel with her mother when she was a child, and her fear of losing me and of losing all she had achieved in these years. After all, by projective identification, the husband was said to behave as a child, and she prefers to see herself as a strong person, able to leave home, as the son wanted to do, and to take care of herself. Furthermore, I also pointed out the fact that we were near the summer break, something that could contribute to the feeling of being left abandoned. At the same time, she was more able to joke, and to enjoy her life, and when she said she could be in love with me she was expressing, in a disguised way, how much we were able to work together in her analysis.

She was silent, after this, seeming somehow distant. The former lively contact, in which we apparently enacted the scene of a couple arguing, was lost at this moment.

Listening to listening, as proposed by Faimberg, led me to think that I was focusing my interpretations on the possibility and the wish of the patient to end her analysis. This was something which I was, in principle, in agreement with, but at the same time I had my own reservations. In this second outlook, I had the impression that I might have been dealing with what Betty Joseph describes as the plausible interpretation, meaning the risk that both patient and analyst can lose the immediate emotional reality and have what is in effect a safe theoretical discussion about a third person, the patient.

What came to my mind was the fact that something was missing here. The unconscious, as Baranger would say, possibly was elsewhere, and not where I had imagined I saw it. Yes, the end of analysis was a possibility to take into account, but there was something else. And this was, most possibly, the relation of the patient with her own internal frail and lonely child—something she saw in her husband.

What led me to this new hypothesis? The slip in which she called me by the name of her husband, immediately after presenting him as a helpless child. Now I suppose she was telling me: you might imagine that I am in love with you, or that I wish my husband could relate to me the way you do. This might be a part of it. But you are blind, however, to what really makes me sick, anxious, desperate: when I feel like a motherless child, and cannot tolerate it. It is not because the analysis will end someday, or because there will be a summer break, it is because this is something I have always felt and I do not know whether someday I will be able to live with it, without using so many defenses. This is what really makes me so anxious, desperate and full of doubts and uncertainty about myself, my way of feeling and of relating to others.

I tried to say something of this to her, and this apparently brought us closer again.

How could we know that this might be a better understanding of her feelings, mental state and communications? Only by means of paying careful attention to the subsequent material, which I did in the following sessions. I was then able to find some evidence that supported this latter understanding. Moreover, the proposed plausible interpretation also had a countertransferential origin, because I had a double feeling towards this patient, which I could only identify after that session: I was concerned that she could be willing to end her analysis before having achieved a more solid psychic change, and I was also feeling I would lose a patient with whom I was passing so many good analytic hours. These feelings were making the best possible position of neutrality difficult for me to maintain at this moment.

Only when we allow ourselves to perform the function of listening to listening to what is happening in the analytic field can we be able to have a better way of identifying with the patient and his/her internal reality.

Sometimes we must listen to contributions from other fields, as they can also help us in our daily profession. When I was writing this paper, I was at the same time reading Philip Roth's latest novel "The Human Stain", and I was struck when I found the following lines.

After proposing one of the clues for the dramatic situation he pictures, and describing the empathic way the narrator relates to the main characters, Roth writes: "How do I know she knew? I don't. I couldn't know that either. I can't know. Now that they are dead, nobody can know. For better or worse, I can only do what everyone does who thinks that they know. I imagine. I am forced to imagine. It happens to be what I do for a living. It is my job. It's now all I do". (2000, p. 213).

In our own job, if we allow ourselves not only to observe, but also to identify and to imagine, through successive projective and introjective identifications, we might be able to build with each patient a specific analytic field, in which we can aim to do our best to analytically listen to what happens in his/her psychic reality.

In order to summarize what I am suggesting in this chapter, my view is that the therapeutic action of psychoanalysis rests in the unique experience of being listened to and understood by another in a new way, in what was described as the analytic field, which leads to the patient acquiring a new understanding of him/herself, thus reducing his psychic pain and becoming more free to enjoy his/her own capacities. This is the way to obtain insight as a result of the experience of being understood in a new, fuller way than any previous experiences provided.

This is one way of formulating the therapeutic action of psychoanalysis, one among many, but the one that makes me often feel the continuous fascination of our impossible profession.

References

Baranger, M., Baranger, W. (1961–62). The Analytic Situation as a Dynamic Field. *Int. J. Psycho-Anal.*, 2008, *89*: 795–826.

Baranger W. (1979). 'Proceso en espiral' y 'campo dinamico'. *Rev. Urug. Psicoanal.*, *59*: 17–32.

Baranger, M., Baranger, W., Mom, J. (1983). Process and Non-Process in Analytic Work. *Int. J. Psycho-Anal.*, *64*: 1–15.

Baranger, M. (1993). The Mind of the Analyst: From Listening to Interpretation. *Int. J. Psycho-Anal.*, *74*: 15–24.

Bion, W.R. (1959). Attacks on Linking. *Int. J. Psycho-Anal.*, *40*: 308–315.

De Leon, B. (2002). Libro Anual de Psicoànalisis XVI 217–238 San Paulo Escuta LTDA.

Eizirik, C.L. (1995). Contexto scio-economico e formao psicanalitica. *Rev. Psicanl. Porto Alegre*, 2: 277–288.

Eizirik, C.L. (1993). Entre a escutaeainterpretação: Um estudo evolutivo da neutralidade psicanalítica [From listening to interpretation: An evaluative study of psychoanalytic neutrality]. *Revista de Psicanálise da Sociedade Psicanalítica de Porto Alegre*, 1: 19–42.

Faimberg, H. (1996). 'Listening To Listening'. *Int. J. Psycho-Anal.*, 77: 667–677.

Freud, S. (1912). Recommendations to physicians practicing psycho-analysis. The Standard Edition of the Complete Psychological Works of Sigmund Freud, Volume XII (1911–1913): 109–120.

Freud, S. (1926). Inhibitions, Symptoms and Anxiety The Standard Edition of the Complete Psychological Works of Sigmund Freud, Volume XX (1925–1926): 87–178.

Isaacs, S. (1948). The Nature and Function of Phantasy. *Int. J. Psycho-Anal.*, *29*: 73–97.

Joseph, B. (1975). The Patient Difficult to Reach In: Psychic Equilibrium and Psychic Change: Selected Papers of Betty Joseph: Edited by Elizabeth Bott Spillius and Michael Feldman. New York: Tavistock/ Routledge, 1989.

Joseph, B. (1985). Transference: The Total Situation. *Int. J. Psycho-Anal.*, *66*: 447–454.

Klein, M. (1946). Notes on Some Schizoid Mechanisms. *Int. J. Psycho-Anal.*, *27*: 99–110.

Klein, M. (1950). On the Criteria for the Termination of an Analysis. *Int. J. Psycho-Anal.*, *31*: 204–204.

Rosenfeld, H. (1987). Impasse and Interpretation, *New Lib. of Psycho-Anal.*, *1*: 1–318. London: Tavistock.

Roth, P. (2000) The human stain, Vintage Books, New York.

Segal, H. (1967). Melanie Klein's technique In The Work of Hanna Segal New York: Jason Aronson, 1981 pp. 3–24 First published in Psycho-analytic Techniques ed. B. B. Wolman. New York: Basic Books.

Spillius, E. (1988). Melanie Klein Today, Vol. 1, *Mainly Theory*, London: Routledge.

Steiner, J. (1992). The Equilibrium Between the Paranoid-Schizoid and the Depressive Positions. *New Library of Psychoanalysis*, *14*: 46–58.

Strachey, J. (1934). The Nature of the Therapeutic Action of Psycho-Analysis. *Int. J. Psycho-Anal.*, *15*: 127–159.

CHAPTER THREE

The enlarged notion of field in psychoanalysis

Claudio Neri

Key words: Field; Transformations; Alfa Function; Narration; The Analytic Third

This paper has been divided into two sections. The first part focuses on a comparison between field and other notions that, although somewhat similar to field, don't exactly coincide with the term. The second section begins with the paragraph on alfa-function and develops the idea of "enlarged field".

The origins of the concept

M. and W. Baranger, F. Corrao

The first works in a (dual) psychoanalytic context which introduce the bi-personal field concept are by Madeleine and Willy Baranger and propose a broadening of the Kleinian school psychoanalysis through concepts that come from Gestalt psychology and Merleau Ponty's "in situation" psychology of man (1964). «The structural characteristics of the analytic situation require a necessary description with the help of the field concept. The analytic situation has its own spatial and temporal structure, and is oriented along determinate dynamic lines of force; it has its own laws of development, general and momentary objectives. This field is our immediate and specific object of observation». (Baranger and Baranger, 1961). Considering that both patient and analyst take part in the same dynamic process, the Barangers (1978) recognize the individuals that are involved in the field, the field that they themselves produce and in which they are immersed. The field isn't the sum of inner situations that belong to members of the couple, nor can it be amenable to one or the other, instead, it takes the form of a third element with independent qualities and dynamics. The analytic field, defined as such, is made up of three levels. The first level corresponds to the formal aspects and the basic contract (setting), the second level corresponds to the dynamic aspects of the manifest content and verbal interaction, and the third corresponds to the functional aspect of integration and insight as regards unconscious bi-personal fantasy. The unconscious bi-personal fantasy represents the most original aspect of the Barangers' proposal and it combines Kleinian concepts with those of field: it is in fact made up of the overlap of projective identifications belonging to the two members of the analytic pair. The unconscious bi-personal fantasy is the specific object of analysis, the scope is to mobilize the field and allow the projection and introjection processes to reactivate themselves, as their paralysis causes sufferance.

As the paper develops it will appear clearer how this reference, which is tightly bound to Kleinian theory is also the Baranger's most dated contribution as it defines the mechanisms, formation and development processes of the field in a very specific and binding manner. The current perspective tends to add value to the possibility of grasping through the notion of field, the even more evasive elements and those that are difficult to determine; as Carla De Toffoli (2005) observes. She said that when «something happens that goes beyond the usual space-time parameters, that surpasses individual boundaries, that isn't containable in known categories [...] so it can be useful to resort to the Field model, so that the experience can be reflected and somehow be thinkable, in order for it not to be lost».

F. Corrao (1986) sees psychoanalysis as a specialized practise through the transformation of sensorial and emotional experiences into thoughts and meanings. He develops a notion of field that is coherent with this perspective. «The field [...] can be described on the basis of its transformations [...], it doesn't appear to be confined by any perceptive factual observational viewpoint, but [...] it refers to eventual phenomenological movements, [...] invisible and anyhow deductible [...]» (Corrao, 1986, p. 120). His theory on the curing process focuses on the transformations and evolutions of the psychoanalytic field (including the analyst, the patient and the theories). The consequence of giving value to the notions of transformation and field is that of abolishing a stable distinction between subject and object that are considered to be functionally reversible.

The Italian school

Before proceeding with the part of the paper dedicated to differentiating the field notion from similar concepts, I would like to clarify one aspect of the discourse that I shall be developing. Over the years, through contributions made by many psychotherapists and analysts, there have been numerous definitions made of 'field'; sometimes these definitions have been contradictory and incompatible. Hence, I won't add an original definition of my own as I prefer to give a reinterpretation and a link to what I consider to be the most significant contributions. Furthermore, I don't intend to outline a complete and exhaustive picture of the phenomenon of field, but, instead, I shall be focusing only on aspects that seem of greater use in clinical practice. I also want to clarify that this article is mainly based on the work of Italian group psychoanalysts and psychotherapists who have sparked off a lively debate on this topic: Riolo (1986; 1997), Correale (1991), Di Chiara (1997), Gaburri (1997), Chianese (1997), Ferro (2003).

Due to an old tradition which goes back to Federn and Weiss and that was further continued by Perrotti, Musatti and Servadio, Italian psychoanalysts have been trained to monitor each and every moment of what occurs in the session; particularly the modification of sensations, atmospheres and bodily experiences. They search with constancy for an emotional contact with the patient, they accurately follow each tiny exchange—made up of silences, gestures, changes in space and modifications in posture—between the patient and themselves that sustains, modifies and determines the therapeutic relationship. I will briefly underline how this focus of attention has been resumed in recent studies and in particular by psychoanalysts who are part of the Boston Change Process Study Group (2005, p. 694).

The perceptions are noted in the analyst's mind as useful observations for the development of the session; they may however not be noted as observations, but transformed into images, fantasies and narrations that at the appropriate time can be shared (or not) with the patient. The annotation, transformation and eventual communication doesn't overlap or substitute interpretation, it lies, instead, side by side with interpretation, redefining the position and the importance. A change in classical technique results from this: the analyst's receptivity, attention given to the context, the transformations that take place on non-verbal elements (extra-verbal, ultra-verbal), tolerance for doubt become an important therapeutic key alongside capacity of interpretation and above all interpretative modulation (Ferro, 2005).

In parallel to what I have described and summarized, in Italy the interest for the field notion has grown, it has brought about an original elaboration of the concept that in my opinion hasn't been sufficiently acknowledged within the international circle. In 1994, the national congress of the Italian Psychoanalytic Society that was held in Rimini was on "the analyst's answer and transformations of the analytic field". An important outcome of such reflections was an increased awareness of two particular points. First of all, the field concept is only useful if we stop considering it to be a comprehensive psychoanalytic theory, and, moreover, if we consider it alongside other theories and models, like, for example, the theory based on transference and counter-transference. If the concept of field is used in this manner it allows us to better explain some dimensions of the analytic situation and to have a more complete perspective. The second point is that the field notion needs to be enlarged and included alongside other concepts that make it complete and usable in practice. I'm referring particularly to Alfa function, narrative function, transformation and evolution in O, which I will subsequently discuss.

Atmosphere

Before presenting the main topic—proposals for the use of the field notion in clinical practice—I will differentiate the field notion from other similar concepts with the use of some examples.

Sometimes the terms field and atmosphere are used as synonyms. Nevertheless, atmosphere and field don't coincide. The term field suggests greater complexity when compared to atmosphere. Field isn't only an atmosphere: a whole series of interacting functions depend on field. More precisely, field is the ensemble of conditions that allows these functions (empathy, attention, attunement, reception, interpretation, etc., ...) to interact positively or else be blocked, inhibited or subverted. To further explain this point, I shall use an example taken from a hospital environment.

> When a doctor or a nurse starts their shift, they usually enquire in an apparently generic manner: "What is it like today?" They are in fact asking not what the atmosphere is but what the overall general situation of the ward is. When this information has been received, other more specific questions on emergencies or on any particular cases will be made. The order in which the doctor who starts the shift asks questions corresponds to something that has been taught through experience: an emergency or a complicated clinical problem are dealt with in a different way in accordance with how the ward "is," if there is tension, chaos, alarm. When resolving clinical problems one needs to take account of the variables that don't solely regard the patients but correspond to functions that are carried out by different members of staff, the relationship between themselves, the relationship between staff and patients. All of this is summed up in the concise question that the doctor asks when starting the shift: "What is it like today?"

Field differs from atmosphere because it sustains the ensemble of functions which are necessary for the ward and the analytic situation to work.

I'd like to point out a further difference between field and atmosphere; field corresponds to mental states that can be lived—contemporaneously—or alternatively—inside the mind or in the environment, on the other hand, atmosphere is a condition that is usually attributed to the environment only.

Bond

The concept of bond was introduced by Pichon-Rivière and then developed above all by René Kaës and Janine Puget.

The term bond (vinculo), according to the original definition (Pichon-Rivière, 1979), contemporaneously refers to "object relations" and "interpersonal relations". The bond represents a complex structure that includes the subject, the object and the relationship between them, at both an internal and external level. For example, we can talk about a "brotherly bond" because there are fantasies to do with brothers and sisters, but also because of the real interpersonal relationship that exists between a brother and sister: that is; there are always two sides, one is internal and the other is external.

Contributions made by R. Kaës (1993; 1994) and J. Puget (Puget, Berenstein, 1997) describe the bond as a particular unconscious psychic reality, that is separate and different for each of the subjects that are connected by the bond. According to Evelyn Granjon (2005), the concept of field is wider and more structured than that of bond. The effects of the bond manifest themselves within the field; however, the field doesn't merge or produce them.

We can see a greater parallelism between field and bond in Anna Maria Nicolò's definition (2002, p. 186): «[...] the bond constitutes the relational background into which our clinical work inserts itself, and in which all the characters from the inner world belonging to the patient and analyst move. It forms the relational scenario of the analytic stage. Such a scenario in certain situations [...] can be mobile and variable, and not particularly influence the emotional development of the story. On the contrary, in other situations it may represent the dominant element that overcasts the story itself and the dialogues between characters».

Setting

As I mentioned before, M. and W. Baranger, consider the setting to be one of the constitutive levels of field. I don't agree with their point of view, and I consider it more useful to keep the two concepts separate. In other words, I don't agree with underlining the formal aspects (space, time, agreement), for which field would constitute «a true and proper structure that creates itself between analyst and patient and that allows the analysis to develop» (Ferro, 1990, p. XV).

Field, as I intend it, does not coincide with setting, and diversely to setting, isn't relatively invariant. The configuration is made up of some elements that are stable in time, and others that can change from one moment to the next. These changes can influence the patient, the analyst and the quality of their relationship. The relative mobility and elasticity of the setting are linked to properties of the field. I think my manner of considering the field concept could usefully be placed alongside that of J. Bleger's. According to Bleger (1966; 1970) the analytic situation can be studied by pointing out the aspects that constitute a process (dynamic setting), the phenomenon that we interpret (1967, p. 237), and aspects that represent a frame, a "non-process" (institution setting). The institution setting includes the more stable dimensions of the relationship (the place, the time, the payment for the session, etc., ...) and it works as a deposit for the psychotic aspects of personality.

As long as it is constant and unaltered, the institution setting is "mute," it acts as a background to the analytic process and guarantees a symbiotic form bond. Furthermore, Bleger presents an interesting observation: in the institution setting, the 'not changing' part of identity is generally deposited and doesn't correspond to the psychotic part, but also includes some elements on which a more mature identity are based.

Bleger's formulations add a certain depth to the idea of field as a trans-personal pool of ideas, feelings and emotions that are present in a couple or in a group. Individuals contribute by depositing internal emotions, feelings and even split parts of their self (Perrotti, 1983), up until an amalgam is composed of differing elements that no longer corresponds to the single participants, nor to their relationship, but that conditions both.

Analytic relationship

Loewald (1960; 1960a) considered a relationship to be a highly developed form of psychic dialogue and interaction in which two or more people interact. A relationship takes place contemporaneously at various levels; the essential nucleus of meaning of the term refers to interaction amongst individuals, as in centres of psychic activity, which are highly organised and relatively autonomous. Even if those involved in the relationship are relatively autonomous, at the same time they are dependent for their own development and preservation in remaining in the affective, social and cultural field that belongs to that relationship. In other words, the field has a nutritive and supporting action on individuals and on the relationships that take place. On the contrary, in other circumstances the field may have an emptying and paralyzing action.

S. Mitchell (1988)—in a similar manner to Loewald—feels that the study of psychic life can't be centred on the individual, who is considered as a separate entity, and the vicissitudes of his drive desires, but it should focus on the field interaction in which the individual is born and fights to establish contacts and express himself. The analytic inquiry implicates participation, observation and the discovery and the transformation of these relationships and of their inner representations.

I consider that "relationship" and "field" form a system in which the functions of each vary when the general conditions change.

More precisely, I'd like to affirm that individuals (analyst and analysand) are the source of activity and of the organization and intentionality that are present in analysis. The relationship is the context in which such activity comes to life and the field is a basic dimension of the relationship. Incidentally, I remember a similar thought that was expressed by Alice and Michael Balint in their article on the analyst's emotional response published in 1939. The analytic situation isn't a "sterile" field, but it is "doubly individual", permeated by a highly specific climate which is connected to both participants and to their particular relationship.

At other times a particular type of field manifests itself. It doesn't manifest itself as a basic dimension of the relationship but as something that is present, taking the place of a relationship that no longer exists or before establishing a relationship. I shall make use of an extract taken from a clinical case to highlight a situation in which field activation substitutes a relationship.

> Over the last two years, Roberto, a forty year old man has shut himself in at home. He tells the doctor and nurses who go to see him that he's subject to the electromagnetic field waves caused by Radio Maria. Roberto has called the carabinieri on numerous occasions to have his house disinfested from the "Radio Maria field", unsuccessfully. The healthcare staff at the Mental Health Centre combined psychotherapy with medication and they hypothesised that the magnetic field represented a particular

> type of unity between the patient and his mother who had died a few years previously. The mother and the residual relationship show themselves as "Radio Maria field".

The image of the "electromagnetic field caused by Radio Maria" represents both a mental state and a physical condition of imprisonment.[1]

Common and shared space

The idea of common and shared space is a recent and interesting line of thought. R. Kaës (2003) presents this idea as a consequence to a general change in psychoanalytic models and the introduction of new tools (group analysis, couple therapy, etc., ...) that "open" psychic space (of dream, of psychoanalysis) putting it into a relationship with inter-subjective space. In my opinion, Kaës' most interesting notion is on common and shared oneiric space, considered as «a porous, strange and sometimes disquieting space» (Kaës, 2002). In order for this space to be created it is necessary for the participating individuals to have undergone a process of common regression. However, Kaës rightly warns us that «the notion of regression that is common to two or more subjects needs to be managed with certain shading», as in this case, it's about light and reversible types of regression and depersonalisation. Regression and depersonalisation aren't in themselves enough for this space to be created: «The notion of common regression [...] indicates the participation in something that belongs to more than one person. Having this thing in common doesn't mean that it is automatically shared [...]» (Kaës, 2002). Sharing is made possible by the activation of an "inter-individual and above-individual apparatus" that puts individuals, their psychic apparatus and oneiric spaces into relation.

The common group space, similarly to "analytic space" (Viderman, 1970), is a sort of place—both imaginary and real at the same time—in which life takes place and exchanges are developed (Rouchy, 1998). Kaës' model is essentially based on alliances and unconscious contracts; its main reference is based on Freudian metapsychology.

"Common and shared space" doesn't coincide with the notion of field, that in my view, as we will see shortly—is tightly bound to Bion's concept of evolution in "O".

Field and transference

It isn't easy to say where to place field in respect to transference. In Caesura (1977, p. 57) Bion hypothesizes that the distance between field and transference isn't as big as it initially seems: «there is much more continuity between autonomically appropriate quanta and the waves of conscious thought and feeling than the impressive caesura of transference and counter-transference would have us believe».

Bion's proposal is suggestive, but not completely convincing. It can be said that field and transference overlap to a great extent and that it's difficult to differentiate one from the other. We can, however, say that certain phenomena that belong to the field are highly distinguishable from transference, and, as a matter of fact, interfere with its functioning. I prefer to keep the two notions separate; as I pointed out when concluding the paragraph on "The Italian School" (also see Neri, 1988).

I shall return to this matter further on in the paper, in the paragraph entitled "The dream of the dance".

The third

I shall now try to point out certain specific characteristics of the field. The field is a product of the relative-like connection and mestizo of the analyst and analysand (or of the psychotherapist and group members). The words have carefully been chosen. "Product" refers to the fact that the field has different characteristics to those of the individuals that contribute to its make-up, that also differ from the sum of their characteristics. "Relative-like" points out how the field is generated by fondness and empathy that converge, creating something that is relatively stable and also creating temporary events that show up in a certain session or at a certain point of the session. "Mestizo" not only points to affinities between the analyst and analysand, but also character traits and disparate affective and cultural elements that contribute to the creation of the field. I would like to underline that I use the term "mestizo" in a positive sense, as an expression of tolerance, openness and summarizing capabilities.

A couple or a group produce a field and at the same time are influenced by it. This definition highlights the proximity between "field", "thirdness" and "analytic third". Andrè Green (2005) writes: «The necessary and satisfactory conditions to establish a relationship are that there be two terms. This simple ascertainment [...] places the couple as a more fertile theoretic referent amongst all the theories that have unity as a base. [We can go one step further and add that there isn't] any interest in being trapped in the dual relation»; T. Ogden, working on these ideas, created the concept of analytic third. This concept is used by Ogden to understand the phenomena that take place during the session.

T.H. Ogden (1997; 1999) defines the intersubjective analytic third as the result of the exchange of the analyst's and the analysand's states of reverie, in which the analytic process «involves the partial giving over of one's separate individuality to a third subject, a subject that is neither analyst nor analysand, but a third subjectivity that is unconsciously generated by the analytic pair» (Ogden, 1997). If on the one hand the "third" is the product of an unconscious exchange of the two members, on the other hand it's what defines the patient and analyst as such; in other words, an analyst, an analysand and an analytic process don't exist outside of this. The "third" is in dialectical tension with the individual subjectivities of the participants; this corresponds to an experience that is continuously in evolution. This may be different for each member of the couple, and may therefore reflect the asymmetry within the analytic relationship.

Madeleine and Willy Baranger ably described the collusive and pathological side to the phenomenon with the names "bulwark" or "bastion". The "bulwark" is an «immobile structure that slows down or paralyzes the analytic process that appears in the field, as a result of the unconscious link between the analyst and patient» (Baranger, Baranger, Mom, translator's translation).

Another way of seeing the question can be expressed through the words of Mitchell (1997, p. 128) who writes: «the analyst participates and inevitably always exactly co-creates that which he is trying to comprehend together with his patient». It's useful to consider the concept functional aggregates as introduced by Bezoari and Ferro, and defined as «an analytic production of the pair [...] a first level of shared symbolization» (Bezoari, Ferro, 1992, p. 401). The functional aggregate is the outcome of transformation processes that the analytic pair carries out to gather and represent what happens at the deepest levels of emotional exchange, the «elaboration of "functional aggregates" coincides with a switch from plain figures, with a single vertex, to holograms, i.e., three dimensional images that take shape in the multi-subjective space and can be simultaneously seen from different perspectives, as they are produced by at least two sources of light» (Bezoari, Ferro, 1997, p. 142).

Changes in the field

Field characteristics can change through spontaneous evolution; they can also be modified (involuntarily, unknowingly or intentionally) by people that share the same space or relational situation.

Saul Bellow (1997) in the paragraph that I will quote—uses terms such as "spreading", "scattering", "sprinkling". These words suggest that the variation of the psychological field that exists between two or more people can be used not so much to invest directly in the other person, but by modifying the shared medium.

> «Madge crossed her arms and walked back and forth. She was extremely restless. She went between the glass doors, passing into the long living room as if she were inspecting the sofas, the settees, and the Persian carpets, putting something of herself into them again. Something sexual? Something criminal? She asserted her significance. She wasn't about to let you forget it. She spread, she scattered, she sprinkled it. She hadn't done time for nothing. When I met her, she made me think of a course in field theory, and I mean psychological field theory, for which I registered in my student days, having to do with the mental properties of a mental region under mental influences that resembled gravitational forces.»

In order to explain this type of phenomenon, M. and W. Baranger (as I hinted at before), refer to projective identification. Instead, I prefer to focus on the synchronization of basic, somatic and mental functions (for example: breathing, muscle tone, anxiety, relaxation, attention), and of the breaking up and alteration of such synchronizations.

The characteristics of the analytic field also change when taking the mental states that take place in the patient's mind into account. The variation of field characteristics, along with the patient's verbal and non verbal communications, associations and dreams give the analyst a representation of the route that the patient is taking during a session and during the whole analysis in the exploration of his world that is made up of relationships, fantasies and memories. The following paragraph is from a book on reporting by Ryszard Kapuściński—it immediately points out how field characteristics can change, thus having an influence on people's lived experiences that are in its range. In The Shadow of the Sun (1998, p. 108) Kapuściński describes a taxi journey on the island and city of Lagos:

> «The apartment [where I live] is located in the centre of town, on the island of Lagos. The island was once a staging area for slave traders, and these shameful, dark origins of the city have left traces of something restless and violent in its atmosphere. You are made constantly aware of it. For instance, I may be riding in a taxi and talking with the driver, when suddenly he falls silent and nervously surveys the street. "What's wrong?" I ask, curious. "Very bad place!" he answers, lowering his voice. We drive on, he relaxes and once again converses calmly. Some time later, we pass a group of men walking along the edge of the road (there are no sidewalks in the city), and at the sight of them the driver once again falls silent, looks about, accelerates. "What's going on?" I ask. "Very bad people!" he responds. It's another kilometre before he is calm enough to resume our conversation.
>
> Imprinted in such a driver's head must be a map of the city resembling those that hang on the walls of police stations. Little multicoloured warning lights are constantly lighting up on it, flashing, pulsating, signaling places of danger, sites of attacks and other crimes. These warning lights are especially numerous on the map of the downtown, where I live».

It's as if terrible memories (that are now in the background) were tied to a territory (Lagos, the slave driver island) and tangible field negativity: «something restless and violent that stirs in the air». This "field negativity" is made up of an ensemble of mental states (that correspond to different points of the field-place-deposit); each of them able to pervade both the driver's and Kapuściński's perceptions and lived experiences: you go to a certain neighbourhood of the city and you transform, you're in danger and therefore you become a somewhat shady character.

A railway metaphor

Kapuściński's book brings to mind the famous analogy with which Freud (1913–14) compares the patient to a passenger, seated in a train compartment, and the analyst to a railway expert. The patient-passenger, freely associating, describes his emotional states as if they were the different scenes of the changing landscape that he sees from his window. However, he doesn't know the meaning of what he is describing and, even less, the meaning of the journey as a whole. The analyst-expert of railways, instead, is not only able to follow the whole associative pathway but also give it meaning.

Besides the similarity of the chosen images, there are some substantial differences between what Freud says and Kapuściński's work. The first difference regards the fact that the device that Freud singled out, assumes that the analyst doesn't have direct access to the fantasies-landscapes; he is instead informed of them only indirectly through what the patient tells him. Instead, for Kapuściński, what is said by the driver is not the only source of information: Kapuściński "himself" also perceives the change of atmospheres and sensations as they cross the different city neighbourhoods. The second difference is that throughout the example of the two people in the compartment—Freud is essentially aiming at describing the particular "tandem work" that patient and analyst do, in order to transform the unconscious fantasies into conscious and meaningful communications. Kapuściński, on the other hand, wants to underline how travelling through different city neighbourhoods causes a change of thoughts, fantasies and of the mood and communication between the two people.

Alfa function

How can the psychotherapist modify the negative, binding or even perverted characteristics which may have taken place within the analytic field?

To at least answer this question partially, it is necessary to place the field notion alongside the "alfa function" notion and to "dissolve the emotions into narrations". Throughout the close connection with these notions, the notion of field itself changes, becoming what I would like to define as the enlarged notion of field.

The alfa function corresponds to the ability of operating transformations in sensorial experiences, in tension and in emotions. More generally, in all the external and internal elements which urge and press the mind and personality of an individual. The structuring of a child's alfa function doesn't occur due to an autonomous development, but instead, it depends on that of the mother and of the other people who take care of the child. Firstly, the mother "digests" through her own alfa function, the sensorial feelings that the child, who is still immature, is not able to metabolize. Later, the child—relying on the mother's function—will structure and activate his own alfa function.

Some of the manners in which the therapist's alfa function operates during the session may be clarified by referring to rêverie. Rêverie—as denoted by the common use of this word in French—is a relaxed and dreamy state, a light form of aimless daydreaming. When referred to the analytical situation, rêverie corresponds to the «analyst's capability to acknowledge the patient's pre-verbal or verbal communications, capability of reception which is accompanied by a concomitant elaboration activity» (Di Chiara, 1992).

Emotions ⇔ narrations

The expression "dissolving emotions into narrations" indicates a theoretical and technical approach, which gives great importance to the possibility that a certain sentiment or lived experience may be expressed. For this approach—the importance of expressing—is equal to that of understanding and giving a meaning (Baruzzi, 1981). Working along the lines of this approach, the idea of transformation becomes central and, for the most part, absorbs that of interpretation.

It must be underlined that the concept of narration here is used in a much different manner from the way it has been used by American psychoanalysts, for example by Roy Schafer, who mostly underlined the aspect related to constructivism and relativism of the narrative function. Schafer thinks (1983; 1992) that it's possible to consider "tales of life", which are slowly produced during the course of analysis, the analyst's theories of reference, interpretation and the analytical relation itself as structures or narrative performances, that have a fictional, mutable and transformable character.

Instead, in this perspective which I present, the reference to narration is connected to the possibility of grasping, giving shape and therefore making something, which is present only in an implicit way or only at an emotional level, representable or thinkable. "Dissolving emotions into narrations" means operating a transformation through which emotions and lived experiences that are too condensed are expressed through words, scenes and narrations. The putting into words that I refer to does not coincide with classical interpretation, but, rather, it represents a precursor or a substitute. It is characterized by some aspects (spontaneity, immediateness, proximity to the pre-conscious dimension), that are somewhat similar to free association; it is also characterized by narrative form and images.

The notion on "dissolving emotions into narrations" may also be referred to as "emotion ⇔ narration". This annotation (emotion ⇔ narration) not only highlights the transformation which has the expression of emotions as an outcome, but also a reciprocal operation. It highlights how narration has the capacity of allowing emotions to surface, emotions which up until that moment had been dispersed or simply perceived as tensions (Corrao, 1992; Neri 2004 and 2007).

Emotions and feelings aren't usually considered to be on the same level as thoughts; as factors of organization and orientation. However, I think that the surfacing and expression of new kinds of feelings is fundamental in the process of knowledge, change and in the total reorganization that is undertaken in analysis. As the authors of the Boston Change Process Study Group (2005) also observed: «we can say that [emotions and feelings] are the most important and complex products that emerge from human interactions».

The dream of the dance

Along the lines of this theoretical and technical approach, dreams aren't considered to be an undeciphered text, but rather a first form of expression and containment of emotions and lived experiences; which will undergo subsequent transformations, throughout the dream-telling in the session and the dialogue between patient and analyst (Friedman, 2002). Here is a clinical example.

Nino: "I dreamt that I was in a room with some other people, colleagues from the mental health centre where I work. I started dancing with Annarita, the psychologist at the centre; just to make the situation cheerful. The dance became faster and more and more intense. Annarita started to laugh. After a while I laughed with her. The laughter carried on. We fell on the floor."

Nino adds some associations.

Nino: "For many years Annarita and I have had a very positive relationship. We've conducted a group of "severe patients" together which had very positive results. Afterwards, I started up a second group at the centre: the "culture-group". During the same period Annarita started a music-therapy group. Annarita's group didn't really work out very well due to some technical problems. She slowly transformed it to the point of having it become a twin group with the one I was conducting, with the same formula".

Whilst listening to the patient, I understand that his relationship with Annarita, rather than sexual coupling, is more of a going along together, synchronized and supporting one another.

Nino: (continues) "At present, the relationship between Annarita and me has changed. There is still strong respect, but a sort of suspicion has sparked off between us. It's still an intense relationship, but moving towards light conflict, rather than friendship. I've decided to not continue with my "culture-group" this year. The group that came to an end last year was very rich and productive. This year, though, we are missing the central idea around which the group could work".

I think that if Nino doesn't continue to conduct a group that had worked so well, there must have been and still is something that represents a big obstacle.

Nino: (keeps talking, then, once this part of the discourse is finished, remains in silence). "The situation at the Centre is in general very conflictual. There is a litigious, violent and disruptive contraposition between the head physician and the person responsible for the outpatients' clinic. The conflict has spread, it's gone beyond the Centre itself: it has involved the mayor, the local politician and other key figures in the city".

Two possible types of intervention come to mind. The first is to put the dream and the associations in relation to the transference. The dream, read in this perspective, would signal an erotic sense of the relationship between the patient-Nino and me-Annarita. The over-warming of the analytical relationship would have a destabilizing effect on the structure of the patient's Self and could lead to a break-down of the analysis («the laughter continued even more, we fell to the ground»). On a different level, the erotic transference would find a connection with the persecutory transference that would then progressively spread through in the positive relationship between the patient and the analyst-Annarita. This second aspect of the transference, up until now, has been kept relatively distant, as it is split and projected onto a secondary scene which is represented by the relationship between the head physician-analyst and the patient-responsible for the outpatients' clinic.

I'm not fully convinced of these thoughts on the dream and on the associations. It contrasts with the perception I have of the relationship between Nino and Annarita as being something that proceeds as unison rather than as coupling. Further more, I didn't perceive any erotic sense and/or persecution in the atmosphere of the session, but rather a sense of suffering, anxiety and preoccupation. The dance appeared to me a way of contrasting and modifying such feelings of suffering, anxiety and preoccupation, introducing cheerfulness (as Nino said) or possibly excitement (as it seemed to me).

The second intervention—coherent with the idea that the dream is a first form of containment and expression of emotions which are searching for a more complete and detailed expression—is possibly guided by the idea that Nino wishes to actually share what he is living with me. This thought doesn't see me-analyst as one of the characters of the dream but rather as the addressee of the dream and of the narration. Therefore, I choose this second way of reading the dream and cautiously intervene by signalling excitement rather than emphasizing the erotic sense.

Dr. Neri: "It seems to me that there is growing excitement".

Nino: "Why do you say excitement? What I'm feeling at the Centre is—rather—boredom, impossibility of participating".

Dr. Neri: "The dream shows increasing excitement. The laughter brings Annarita and yourself to the ground".

Nino remains silent. He seems rigid and uncomfortable. He's probably waiting for me to give the dream a collocation by pointing out a context. The identification of a context is in general essential for a cognitive and emotional transformation to take place.

I think that it's very painful for Nino to see the risk of the conflict between the head physician and the person responsible for the outpatients' clinic spreading to the entire Centre. Some years back, the Centre in which he was working burnt down, forcing him to change job and live elsewhere, in a nearby town.

I decide to intervene as much as possible in regards to what the patient has said in his associations to the dream.

Dr. Neri: "I thought that the dream could represent the present situation at the Centre where you work, and shows how you're living this situation".

Nino: (starting to cry softly). "There is mounting laughter in the dream, but I think it stands for the opposite: increasing crying".

I'm strongly touched by Nino's pain, which suddenly showed up. The eventuality that what he invested in may crumble, makes him suffer a lot. I think that having a better understanding of what his role is in the event could help him.

Dr. Neri: "The dream also shows the functions which you and your colleagues carry out at the Centre".

Nino: "Actually, Annarita and I are key figures at the Centre. If our relationship, which has already become more conflictual, should eventually break, the Centre wouldn't be the same anymore".

The session is drawing to an end. I think it appropriate to intervene once again, not belittling the seriousness of the situation or distancing the pain Nino is feeling, but putting effective regulation into practice which will allow the patient to leave the session feeling less oppressed. A film and a dance scene come to mind: the dance occurs in the ballroom of a ship that is close to a catastrophe. Furthermore, the image of a beautiful, shapely actress dancing with the protagonist of the film comes to mind.

Dr. Neri: "It's somewhat similar to the dance party on the Titanic".

Nino: (seems to be relieved by my implicit reference to the images of the movie and he starts to talk in a clear voice once more). "Some things are going well ... perhaps I could position myself in the Centre in this way ..."

From blocking-up to "non direction" to resuming communication.

This last intervention—about the dance in the ballroom of the Titanic—offers an example of the insertion of a narrative element which has the function of regulating the field's affective quality during the session. I'd like to ponder over this aspect of therapeutic work. This could be carried out not only by "associative-narrative intervention" but also by other forms of intervention.

I would like to give two more brief clinical examples; both of them represent a situation in which the session is dominated by coldness, uneasiness and difficulty in communicating. In these cases interpreting the "non communication" is not enough; rather, it's necessary to transform it before an interpretation is possible and useful. The first clinical case considers the situation as seen from the point of view of the psychoanalyst's lived experience.

> During some sessions, there is the activation of a sort of magnetic shield in me or between me and a certain patient who keeps my possibility of relating with him and what he is expressing distant. The activation of this shield provokes a reaction in the patient, who feels lost; he either becomes logorrheic or, on the contrary, closes up. I also get tired through the unconscious effort of maintaining the active shield.
>
> However, if I succeed in renouncing understanding what is happening and let go of my thought and fantasies completely, I get closer, I feel better. I become more interested. I gladly accept sharing any discourse or any mental state. I'm able to resume the work together with the patient.[2]

This way of proceeding could be considered as a regulation process of the analyst's mental state, following Bion's proposals (without memory, without desire, without comprehension). Furthermore, it could also be considered as a temporary possibility of the analyst of relying on a third subject (the field) and its own capability of readdressing the communication between himself and the patient.

A freely fluctuating dialogue

The second clinical example highlights a similar situation to the one I have previously described, but in this case it is considered from the patient's point of view. The contact is resumed and achieved through a short, freely fluctuating dialogue, a sort of chat (Strozier, 2001, translator's translation).

> At a certain point of the session the patient is in such a state of anguish that he's not able to say anything else. He remains in silence, and his distress visibly increases.
>
> I understand that the patient is pointlessly struggling. I therefore fill the space/time with silence and difficulty—which has been created in the session—with some kind of talk of not much importance. On certain occasions, I pose a question on a topic that is familiar and not of conflict to the patient (for example, plans for the evening or for the weekend).
>
> On other occasions, I'll comment or summarize what has occurred over the last weeks. Other times still, I'll propose a short story to reconstruct the whole picture. However, I always narrative elements, a voice.
>
> These interventions aren't similar; they're actually the opposite to interpretation of resistances that I myself would have made at the beginning of my work as a psychoanalyst.
>
> When a situation of stalemate and impossibility to talk has been reached, waiting evenmore isn't going to help; as a matter of fact it can lead to a tug of war. Interpreting is often counterproductive. It's useful to reintroduce a "conversation" that allows the patient to take up the discourse once again. I have noticed, in many circumstances, that my words and the calm acceptance that they express manage to dissolve excess embarrassment or fear. The atmosphere of the session soon becomes warm once again. Progressively, the analyst and patient create islands of contact and shared direction. Analytic work can resume.

Language and structuring of the field

In which way can a psychotherapist facilitate the establishing and lasting maintenance of field characteristics which are favourable to analytical work?

Kohut (1984) and Anzieu (1975) have underlined the importance of affective investment on the fragmented and rising aspects of the patient's personality (also see Neri, 1998 and 2005). They have also pointed out that the analyst must be sufficiently autonomous in reference to the individual and institutional Superego.

Italian psychoanalysts have particularly focused their attention on "tolerance of the limits of understanding". A particular form of such tolerance is the unsaturated interpretation. Tolerance—actively and tenaciously exercised, session after session—promotes a specific configuration of the analytical field, which allows the "shadows of being" to pause, thus maintaining their own obscurity. This then allows the surfacing of unheard thoughts and the development of a new search for meaning (Gaburri, 1998). The tolerance I'm talking about must not be mistaken for fatalism, renunciation or detachment; it is, indeed, an active exercise, which tends to contrast the tendency to adhere to explicit or implicit requests, originating from the internal or the external, to give meaning to what happens. The drive to give meaning and definition gains strength from the connection with powerful needs. That is, the institutional Superego and "automatic conformism", more generally from the "valency" which is characteristic of every man for being part of the herd and which then leads him to bind with others according to a "basic assumption". If the therapist adheres to requests of this type, which can become pressing and imperious, he produces apparently solid knowledge and constructs scenarios of superficially reassuring predictability, but leads the analysand and himself to a dead end.

The language of the analyst

I'd like to add something with regards to the language with which the psychoanalyst intervenes in the session. I've learned a lot in this regard by contact with therapists who work with small children. Many prefer to intervene directly in the game rather than give a verbal interpretation of the play and the development of the playing scene by moving an element of the game, adding a character, proposing a change in the game. For example, they don't tell the child: "the game you're playing with the elephant, the lion and the little monkey always reaches the same outcome. The Dad-lion and the Mum-monkey destroy everything; therefore the little monkey is left alone with a broken house". Instead they add a character or propose a possible different step of the play scene: "the little lion friend of the little monkey arrives, (I'll place him here) let's see if the little lion can help" (Lugones, 2005).

Even the analyst who works with adult patients can use the language that the analysand uses in the session. Hence, he can present his observations and interpretations, not as a meta-discourse that comments what the patient is saying but by directly entering his discourse. Antonino Ferro (2005) refers to "co-narrative transformation" and "dialogical cooperation".

The first necessary condition for these types of intervention to be successful is that the psychotherapist must have invested interest and participation into the patient's language and the world of people, things, facts, ideas and feelings of which he is object. Secondly, the analyst must not translate the analysand's discourse into psychoanalytic language and then retranslate this into the language of the analysand; he must simply talk with him. Psychoanalytic language remains momentarily in the shadow of the therapist's mind, although it is in some way present through his words.

Spirally proceeding dialogue

Before proceeding with a clinical explanation, I want to underline how this use of language also implies that the analyst adopt a particular perspective, which regards dialogue and listening. Luciana Nissim Momigliano writes (1992, pp. 28–29): "the psychoanalytic thought of the meaning of a bi-personal field (assertion renewed in an important work by M. and W. Baranger), in which the two who form the analytical pair are considered to be involved in the same dynamic process, so much so that neither of the two can be understood inside the situation without the other—but in which the roles are asymmetrical, [...] it's coherent with the idea that in the session there is the development of dialogue". Langs (Langs, Stone, 1980), proposes a «thought of analytic dialogue as something having a spiral-form progression, as it is made up of sequences of events, that can be described as follows: a communication takes place (usually coming from the patient, more rarely from the analyst), a formulation/intervention (generally made by the analyst and more rarely by the patient), a new communication follows, that is an answer. Now we are used to listening out for this answer, in its conscious and unconscious aspects of confirming/acceptance, or refusal of what we have proposed through our interpretation, but we're not as well trained in taking into consideration this aspect of the sequence, in which each communication is so tightly linked to the previous one. Placing oneself in this perspective, means that one can notice how many of the patient's so called "free" associations don't only communicate the characteristic elements of his inner world, that we traditionally call transference to the analyst, and mobilize the counter-transference, but they also establish a message for the analyst in the actuality of the relationship, and an answer, that is not usually direct, but expressed through derivatives, both from his interventions and silences».

A fragment of Renato's analysis

Twice a week, Renato takes a train or car and has a two hour journey to come to analysis. He often spends the whole session explaining things that he knows about on various subjects and matters. Sometimes his explanations are very rich in detail, but they are never boring.

Throughout the years, this way of his has caused many different thoughts in me. I thought that our relationship could have been a re-edition of the one he had with his father, to whom Renato was closely attached and who died some years before. I thought that in some aspects of the Self, he was suffering great solitude. Renato, therefore, was coming to see me simply so that someone would spend time with him and would listen to the things he knew about and wanted to share.

Renato's life had gradually improved. Psychotherapy, in my opinion, has contributed to this improvement, although I can't say how much he has improved his awareness of the nature and root of his problems. Most psychoanalytical theories explain the changes that occur in the lives of patients as the result of a shared verbal comprehension between the analysand and the analyst (communicated in the form of interpretation) in particularly significant moments of the transference relationship. I don't want to attribute such exclusive importance to the comprehension and neither to the expression through words. The change—in my opinion—doesn't necessarily require the comprehension of something that has been expressed through words, in the meaning of an unconscious that becomes conscious. The change can be gradually achieved, through the minute exchange that takes place between patient and analyst. In some circumstances these changes don't even need to be expressed, but by means of contiguity, move into the life of the patient. The change may also be achieved due to the analyst's availability and to the favourable conditions of the field that have permitted the transmuting interiorizing to take place. That is, a process which permits one to absorb and transform those functions which are originally performed by the self-objects into an internal structure (Kohut, 1971; 1984).

Renato is now certainly able to carry on alone, with good affective regulation in his relationships and improved contact with his feelings and fantasies.

Nonetheless, Renato keeps coming to the sessions and continues to explain things to me, sometimes very special explanations, and other times less so.

Today he's talking about something that has to do with his daily life: washing dishes. He explains that using very hot, sometimes boiling water for washing dishes is useless, sometimes even counterproductive.

Out of curiosity I ask him for further explanation.

Renato clarifies that the soap enzymes are already active at forty degrees and that a higher temperature is not necessary.

I tell him that I didn't know about it and that I think it's a noteworthy piece of information.

The patient continues: "if you put the plates under boiling water, it creates a film that is very hard to remove".

I thank him, "I'll keep it in mind the next time that I'm washing dishes".

That same evening, once I get back home, I think back to this conversation. I also understand that the patient has asked me to be very cautious in his regard. My words could burn him and cause, instead of relief and will to cooperate, a defensive reaction. I had already given him a first spontaneous answer of consent during the session, when I told him: "I'll keep it in mind the next time that I'm washing dishes". Now, it's a matter of not so much explaining to the patient what happened during the session, but rather properly adjusting my way of intervening.

Over the years I've learned to understand Renato's language—an eloquent language even when he's talking of very simple things, a substantial and serious language and rich in affective requests. Renato has also discovered the great expressive potential of his own language. Our own way of communicating has also been created, (a psychotherapist-patient tandem language) which means a lot of listening on my behalf and a lot of explanations from Renato.

This work has transformed the analytic field, equipping it with new qualities which are similar to those of everyday life, however, still preserving other special and precious ones that belong to the analytic situation (Malamoud, 1994).

Renato felt accepted in analysis. In some ways he has also been accepted as a participant (a son) in my domestic life. Sometimes, when I'm having at dinner with my family, I might say, "did you know that when washing dishes ..., or to preserve food ..., etc., ..."

Renato has also had a prolonged and lasting experience of being in the analytic field, a field with very different characteristics to those of his family of origin.

Throughout this experience, he didn't make many judgements on his childhood and his family experience, but rather, put it all into perspective and was able to look at it with more sympathy and compassion.

Collective fantasies and myths

I will now momentarily put psychoanalysis aside and say something about group psychotherapy. The fundamental differences of field in relationship to group psychotherapy, compared to psychoanalysis, consist in the fact that, in group psychotherapy, the field is co-created by the analyst and by a multitude of people and certain phenomena which belong to that particular group. They are as a totality (primitive mentality, basic assumptions and work group) which manifest themselves. In the group's field, feelings, fantasies and thoughts acquire different resonance when comparing them to those of a traditional setting (dual). Messianic and apocalyptic collective fantasies and myths (Eden, Tower of Babel, Ur, etc., ...) strongly influence it. This doesn't mean that they are not active in a dual setting, but that they show up in a more evident manner within the group setting. I think it would be useful to recall Bion's observation (1961, p. 87): «The total of what is taking place remains the same, but a change of perspective can bring out quite different phenomena».

I shall be adding a short clinical case example that underlines an initial situation of blocked communication that is similar to those described in the first part of this work. I shall limit the presentation to interventions of the group analyst and those made by group members that help clarify the field characteristics that are present in the session.

> During the initial part of the session two dreams were told: the first was Carlotta's dream, in which there was a mixture of sexual and persecutory scenes, feelings of tenderness, excitement and solitude. The second was Bartolo's dream, long and contorted; he described a state of tension which then led to feelings of dejection and renunciation.

Valeria: «While Bartolo was telling his dream I leaned forward to pay more attention. Nonetheless, I wasn't able to follow what he was saying. It's as if I'd lost contact with what was happening in the group: nothing provoked anything».

Marinella: (who up until that moment had remained cuddled up in silence). «Today, I came to the session because the group is making me feel really good. But I come here from outside Rome. I'm exhausted. I really made an effort to get here».

Bartolo: «Today, I made an effort too. I came to the session using all my will power, because I knew it was important».

Valeria: «It was very hard for me as well».

Carlotta: «Quite the reverse, I've been counting the minutes to be here since this morning».

Dr. Neri: «Valeria tried to pay attention to Bartolo's dream, but she wasn't able to. Perhaps she was hindered by something. In the end, she gave up trying to understand and detached herself from what was happening in the group. Marinella, Bartolo and even Valeria say that they feel the importance of coming to sessions, but they also say that it's a big effort. Carlotta, on the contrary, has felt a drive to come to the session. It's as if two different series of feelings were being confronted: interest and fear. What arouses interest is now perceived as closer than how it was felt during sessions of the past months or weeks. It may be possible that new feelings and thoughts emerge and become perceivable».

Marisa: «I've been on the night shifts in the delivery room at San Camillo Hospital for a number of years now. There, I've often seen the hours before dawn. The delivery room at San Camillo has big windows that overlook the Colli Albani and you can see that gloomy and purplish hour that precedes sunrise. Sunrise is pink and beautiful. Dawn, on the other hand is Anxiety-provoking. Nevertheless, there is something beautiful about dawn too. A life made up of only sunrise would be boring and false, for life to be complete there must also be room for dawn».

The representation of the group's field that Marisa proposes highlights being born (the delivery-room). Giving birth to ourselves is one of the main objectives of therapy. The representation also explains why we must tolerate anguish and pain ("there must also be room for dawn"); it also underlines an evolutionary axis (the succeeding of dawn and sunrise; the birth).

The group members consider her intervention as a useful fine tuning of the context. During the last part of the session, and in the following sessions, they regain contact with what is drawing closer to the group's field, they actively concentrate on giving a name to things and to the feelings that they're living.

Evolution in O

In the above clinical sequence, I formulated two interventions in which I refer to the presence of something which attracts and at the same time scares. I would now like to explain the hypothesis and ideas on which those interventions are based.

It is sometimes possible to sense the presence of something which is not directly observable through the effects that it causes. For example, Einstein proved the existence of celestial bodies based on their power of curving light (Rushdie, 2005). In the same way, it is possible to prove the existence of an active nucleus (attracting and repelling) in the analytic field, which cannot be directly observed, but that has an influence—which is recordable—on what group members say, feel and act during the session.

Numerous group psychotherapists have highlighted the presence of a thematic nucleus, common fantasies which group members refer to, and are active at a preconscious level. I think that it's possible to recognise two nuclei, at two different levels: the first one corresponds to the theme and to the preconscious fantasies of the session (what is being said) and may be elaborated through a process of knowledge (what Bion calls "transformation in K"). The second one is, instead, made up of intense but shapeless fantasies. This second level nucleus cannot be directly known, it can however evolve through what Bion (1970) has defined "evolution in O", which is evolution of that which is unknown.

In my opinion it's very important for group members to be able to get into contact with this shapeless nucleus and participate in its evolution, because it's just as rich an experience with transformative and therapeutic potentials as comprehension promoted through interpretation.

The possibility of group members to "get into unison with O" is favoured by a series of factors.

During the session, it's necessary for the therapist to be in unison with the focal point and promote its taking shape inside the group.

The individuation of the focus is facilitated by a point of view by which group members and their interventions are considered as the expression of an overall meaning, which becomes accessible if we renounce a modality of thought which separates and classifies and if we assume a synchronic vertex. In past works (1995 [2007(3)]; 2004) I called it "searching the star shaped disposition" which allows the analyst to perceive and make non-homogeneous and poorly organized material significant, by individuating the presence of a "central nucleus" or of a "focal point" with which all elements are in relationship (Benjamin, 1933). When the analyst proceeds in searching for the "star disposition", he tends to value space more than time, more precisely, he tends to grasp the elements of the session in their synchronicity. With such a term, in agreement with the definition given by Jung (1948), I mean a perspective that is the opposite of causality, which considers essential « the coincidence of events [...] as meaning something more than mere chance» (Jung, 1948).

Conclusions

With the preceding paragraph, dedicated to the elicitation of the theoretical references that underline the clinical practice with groups, I draw up an overview on the concept of field. I use the term "view" to emphasize how this work is not an attempt to define a new notion, or even a new model of field. Indeed, my efforts with patients in the clinical practice have been to recognise, gather and enunciate a series of elements that are re-conductible to this notion of field.[3]

Summary

This article has attempted to re-propose the terms of a renewed comparison on an important subject: the clinical use of the notion of field. In the first part of the paper, I distinguished the concept of field with other closely bound but not overlapping concepts: atmosphere, bond, relationship and transference. In the second part, I presented the enlarged notion of field, which comes from the confluence of the idea of field with the concepts of Rêverie and the capability to dissolve emotions into narrations.

Notes

1. I wish to thank Giorgio Campoli and colleagues at USL "Roma A" in Via Boemondo for having told me about this patient and for the authorization to use it in my paper.
2. I've already published this and the following example in Neri 2003.
3. As a side note, I'd like to add some words for those who might be interested in having more historical information. The notion of field was introduced into psychology starting from the mid 50's on the basis of research and experiences on groups. Later on the idea of field gathered ground in psychoanalytic thought. The main authors are Kurt Lewin, Enrique Pichon-Rivière, Sigmund H. Foulkes and Wilfred R. Bion. Kurt Lewin (1951) defines field, in the social and psychological spheres, as a dynamic totality, capable of producing a sense of cohesion and belonging within a group, which manifests itself with the emerging of the "us" feeling, of common motivations and goals and implies a sort of group identity with which the individual becomes one. The idea of field expressed by Kurt Lewin (1948, p. 125) is particularly interesting for the linked definition of interdependent connection: «the field elements are not necessarily

similar amongst themselves, but once a bond of interdependence has been established, this will be stronger than a bond that is based on similarities». This means that the change of one of the elements of the field necessarily influences the state of all the others. More or less in the same years, these authors conduct research on groups that, although not explicitly including the notion of field, are based on a substantially analogous vision. Foulkes develops a model of group psychotherapy based on the psychoanalytic theory and at the same time centred on elements that are absolutely specific to groups, which is seen as a «a true psychological entity» (Foulkes, 1964, p. 77), «a living organism [... that] has moods and reactions, a spirit, an atmosphere» (Foulkes, 1948, p. 131). The central point of Foulkes' approach is the key concept of *network*, in the relational and social sense, of which the individual represents a knot; any type of communication or event inside a group's network gains significance thanks to a common substrate, which Foulkes defined as *matrix*. The matrix constitutes the picture of reference, «a basis of unconscious comprehension, in which complex reactions and communications are produced» (Foulkes, 1964). Wilfred R. Bion (1961) uses the term field, but his hypothesis on the group mentality, on the work group and on the basic assumptions describe an ensemble of collective forces, affects, representations and behaviours in which the productions and the lived experiences of the single individuals distance themselves from the individual source which has individuated them, converging in a sort of common *medium*, which is autonomous from the single individuals. Besides the contributions contained in *Experiences in Groups* (1961), the idea of "beta space" proposed in *Cogitations* (1992) is also useful and—as López-Corvo (2006) says—completes Bion's theoretical elaboration. The beta space is a "space" of "non thought" and "unthinkable" thoughts, in relation with a sphere that includes "constellations of alpha elements" (Bion, 1992, p. 314). The contribution of Enrique Pichon-Rivière (1955–1972) mainly consists in the concepts of "psychological field" and of "operative group". The *psychological field* represents a complex totality, which includes five classes of elements: the interpersonal context (the *entourage* or frame of situations and factors, human and physical, that continuously interact); the observable behaviour, spontaneous or provoked, which includes various forms of communication; the lived experience, that can be communicated through external behaviour or through verbal communications; the objective somatic changes and the productions of the subject's activities. Pichon-Rivière underlines how these dimensions have traditionally been taken into account one at a time, stating arbitrary and poorly realistic divisions, as if these elements «would not form a whole in a certain moment, in the "here and now" of any situation» (Pichon-Rivière, 1979). The main object of the psychological—and psychoanalytical—research is indeed the «"here and now" of a certain situation, of what is taking place». The *operative group* is defined as «an ensemble of people brought together by spatio-temporal constants, that integrate amongst themselves with an inner shared representation, they implicitly or explicitly propose a task, that constitutes the quality of the group» (Pichon-Rivière, 1955–1972). The task, both at a manifest and deep level, is the element which transforms an ensemble of people into a group and has, from Pichon-Rivière's point of view, an evolutionary potentiality (from the past to the future, from regression to progression).

References

Anzieu, D. (1975). *La psicoanalisi ancora.* In *Psicoanalizzare*, Borla, Roma. 2002.

Balint, A. & Balint, M. (1939). On transference and countertransference. *Int. J. Psycho-Anal., 20*: 223–30.

Baranger, W. & Baranger, M. (1978). Patologia de la transferencia y controtransferencia en el psicoanàlisis actual: el campo perverso. *Revista de Psicoanálisis, 35*: 1101.

Baranger, W., Baranger, M. & Mom, J.M. (1983). Process and Non Process in Analytic Work. *Int. J. Psychoanalysis., 64*: 1–15.

Baranger, W., Baranger, M. & Mom, J.M. (1988). *The Infantile Psychic Trauma from Us to Freud: Pure Trauma*, Retroactivity and Reconstruction.

Baruzzi, A. (1981). *Bion sull'esprimersi. Riv. Psicoanal., 27*(3–4): 136–147.

Bellow, S. (1997). *The Actual.* New York: Viking Press. p. 53.

Benjamin, W. (1933). On the Mimetic Faculty. In: W. Benjamin (Ed.), *Reflections.* New York, NY: Schocken.

Bezoari, M. & Ferro, A. (1992). L'oscillazione significati-affetti nella coppia analitica al lavoro [The Oscillation of Meanings-Affects in the Analytic Couple at Work], *Riv. Psicoanal., 38*: 381–403.

Bezoari, M. & Ferro, A. (1997). The dream within a field theory: Functional aggregates and narrations. In *Journal of Melanie Klein and Objects Relations, 17*(2): 333–348, 1999.

Bion, W.R. (1961). *Experiences in Groups.* London: Tavistock Publications.

Bion, W.R. (1970). *Attention and Interpretation*. London: Tavistock Publications. (Reprinted London: Karnac Books 1984). Reprinted in Seven Servants (1977e).

Bion, W.R. (1977b). *Two Papers: The Grid and Caesura*. Rio de Janeiro: Imago Editora. [Reprinted London: Karnac Books 1989].

Bion, W.R. (1992). *Cogitations* (Edited by F. Bion) London: Karnac Books.

Bleger, J. (1966). Psychoanalysis of the Psychoanalytic Frame. *International Journal of Psychoanalysis, 48*: 511–519.

Bleger, J. (1967). *Simbiosis y ambiguedad. Estudio Psicoanalitico*. Buenos Aires: Paidòs, 1978.

Bleger, J. (1970). El grupo como institucion y et grupo en las instituciones. In *Temas de Psicologia*. Buenos Aires: Nueva Vision, 1971.

Boston Change Process Study Group (2005). The "something more" than interpretation revisited: sloppiness and co-creativity in the psychoanalytic encounter. *JAPA, 53*(3): 693–731.

Chianese, D. (1997). *Constructions and the Analytic Field. History, Scenes and Destiny*. Routledge, 2007.

Corrao, F. (1986). *Il concetto di campo come modello teorico*. In Orme, vol. II, Milano: Raffaello Cortina, 1998.

Corrao, F. (1992). *Modelli psicoanalitici: mito, passione, memoria*. Roma-Bari: Laterza.

Correale, A. (1991). *Il campo istituzionale*. Roma: Borla.

De Toffoli, C. (2005). *Lo Psicoanalista ed il Campo Psichico*.

Di Chiara, G. (1992). *Tre fattori fondamentali della esperienza psicoanalitica: l'incontro, il racconto e il commiato*. In: Robutti A. e Nissim L. (a cura di), Antologia, Milano: Cortina.

Di Chiara, G. (1997). *La formazione e le evoluzioni del campo psicoanalitico*. In: Gaburri E. (a cura di), Emozione e Interpretazione, Torino, Bollati: Boringhieri.

Ferro, A. (2003). *Seeds of Illness, Seeds of Recovery. The Genesis of Suffering and the Role of Psychoanalysis*. London: Routledge, 2004.

Ferro, A. (2005). Réflexions à propos de I'interprétation. *Bulletin de la FEP, 59*: 44–46.

Foulkes, S.H. (1948). *Introduction to Group Analytic Psychotherapy*. London: Maresfield.

Foulkes, S.H. (1964). *Therapeutic Group Analysis*. London: Allen and Unwin, reprinted London: Karnac, 1984.

Freud, S. (1913–14). *On beginning the treatment*. SE. London: Hogarth Press.

Friedman, R. (2002). Dream-telling as a Request for Containment in Group Therapy—The Royal Road through the Others. In: Neri C., Friedman R., Pines M. (Eds.), *Dreams in Group Psychotherapy: Theory and Technique*. London: Jessica Kingsley.

Gaburri, E. (1997). *Emozione e interpretazione*. Torino: Boringhieri.

Gaburri, E. (1998). *Il Campo gruppale e la "non cosa"*. In: Rugi G., Gaburri E. (Eds.), Campo gruppale, Roma: Borla.

Granjon Evelyn (2005). *La notion élargie de champs. Son emploi en psychothérapie de groupe.* Discussion on the paper of Claudio Neri, presented at the EFPP congress, Metz 2–4 December 2005.

Green, A. (2005). *Key Ideas for Contemporary Psychoanalysis: Misrecognition and Recognition of the Unconscious.* Hove & New York: Brunner-Routledge,

Jung, C.G. (1950). *Foreword.* In: Wilhelm, R. & Baynes, C., 1967. *The I Ching or Book of Changes.* 3rd. ed., Bollingen Series XIX. Princeton NJ: Princeton University Press (1st ed. 1950).

Kaës, R. (1993). *Le groupe et le sujet du groupe: Éléments pour une théorie psychanalytique du groupe.* Paris: Dunod.

Kaës, R. (1994). *La parole et le lien: Processus associatifs et travail psychique dans les groupes.* Paris: Dunod.

Kaës, R. (2002). *La polyphonie du rêve: L'expérience onirique commune et partagée.* Paris: Dunod.

Kaës, R. (2003). *La polyphonie du rêve dans l' espace onirique commun e partagé.* Unpublished text.

Kapuściński, R. (1998). *The Shadow of the Sun.* London: Penguin Books. 2001.

Kohut, H. (1971). *The Analysis of the Self.* New York: International Universities Press.

Kohut, H. (1984). *How Does Analysis Cure?* In: A. Goldberg and P. Stepansky (Eds.), Chicago: University of Chicago Press.

Langs, R. & Stone, L. (1980). *The Therapeutic Experience and its Setting. A Clinical Dialogue.* New York: Aronson. Modifications in tecnique. The Psychotherapeutic Project, 2/3, 1981, 215–253 (quoted according to Nissim Momigliano L. (1992).

Lewin, K. (1948). *Resolving Social Conflicts.* New York: Harper and Bros.

Lewin, K. (1951). *Field Theory in Social Science; Selected papers.* D. Cartwright (Ed.), New York: Harper and Row.

Loewald, H. (1960). On the therapeutic action of psycho-analysis. *Int. J. Psycho-Anal.*, *41*: 16–33.

López-Corvo, R.E. (2005). *The Dictionary of the Work of W.R. Bion*. Karnac Books Uno spazio per il futuro.

Lugones, M. (2005). In: Lugones, M., Algini, M.L. (a cura di), Paura del futuro. *Quaderni di psicoterapia infantile*, 50.

Malamoud, M. (1994). *La Danse des pierres. Études sur la scène sacrificielle dans l' Inde ancienne*. Paris: Le Seuil, 2005.

Merlau-Ponty, M. (1964). *The Visible and the Invisible*. Evaston, Ill.: Northwestern University press, 1968.

Mitchell, S. (1988). *Relational concepts in psychoanalysis*. Cambridge, MA: Harvard University Press.

Mitchell, S. (1997). *Influence and Autonomy in Psychoanalysis*. Hillsdale NJ: The Analytic Press.

Neri, C. (1987). *L'impatto del pensiero sull'individuo e sul gruppo*. In: Neri, C. et al. (a cura di), Letture Bioniane, Roma, Borla.

Neri, C. (1988). *Champ de l'expérience groupale: un homologue ou un analogue du transfert dans le situation de la cure?* Revue de psychoterapie Psychanalytique de Groupe, n. 12–13.

Neri, C. (1995 [2004⁷]). *Gruppo*. Roma: Borla.

Neri, C. (1998). *Eustokhìa e Sincronicità*. In: Rugi G., Gaburri E. (Eds.), Il campo gruppale. L'istituzione, la mente del terapeuta e gli scenari del gruppo. Borla, Roma.

Neri, C. (2003). Presentazione. In: Gaburri, E., Ambrosiano, L. (Eds.), *Ululare con i Lupi*. Torino: Boringhieri.

Neri, C. (2003a). Free Associations, Free Flowing Discussions and Group Thought. *Group Analysis*, *36*(3): 345–357.

Neri, C. (1995 [2005⁷]). *Group*. London: Jessica Kingsley. 1998.

Neri, C. (2005). What is the function of faith and trust in psychoanalysis? *Int. J. Psycho-Anal.*, *86*: 79–90.

Neri. C. (2007), Des pensées sans penseur, In: Bokanowski T., Guignard F. (sous la direction de), *Actualité de la pensée de Bion*, Paris: Éditions In Press.

Nicolò, A.M. (2002). Interpretare il legame nella coppia analitica. In: Berti Ceroni, G. (Ed.), (2005), *Come cura la psicoanalisi*? Milano: Franco Angeli.

Nissim Momigliano, L. (1984). Two people talking in a room: an investigation on the analytic dialogue. In: Nissim Momigliano, L., Robutti, A. (Eds.),

Shared Experience: The Psychoanalytic Dialogue. London: Karnac Books, 1992.

Ogden, T.H. (1997). *Reverie and Interpretation, Sensing Something Human*. New York: Rowman and Littlefield Pub Inc.

Ogden, T.H. (1999). The Analytic Third: An Overview. In: Mitchell S., Aron L. (Eds.), *Relational Psychoanalysis: The Emergence of a Tradition*. Hillsdale, NJ: Analytic Press.

Perrotti, P. (1983). *Eclissi dell'Io nel gruppo terapeutico*. In: La processualità nel gruppo, Roma: Bulzoni.

Pichon-Rivière, E. (1955–1972). *Del psicoanálisis a la psicologia social*. Buenos Aires: Galerna.

Pichon-Rivière, E. (1979). *Teoría del vínculo*. Buenos Aires, Ediciones Nueva Visión.

Puget, J. & Berenstein, I. (1997). *Lo vincular: clinica y técnica psicoanalítica*, Buenos Aires: Paidós.

Riolo, F. (1986). Dei soggetti del campo: un discorso sui limiti. *Gruppo e Funzione Analitica, VII*(3): 195–203.

Riolo, F. (1997). Il modello di campo in psicoanalisi. In: E. Gaburri (Ed.), *Emozione e interpretazione*, Torino: Boringhieri.

Searle, J.R. (1992). *The Rediscovery of the Mind*. Cambridge MA: The MIT Press.

Rouchy, J.C. (1998). *Le Groupe, espace analytique. Clinique et théorie*. Ramonville Saint-Agne: Éditions Érès.

Rushdie, S. (2005). *Shalimar the Clown*. London: Jonathan Cape.

Schafer, R. (1983). *The Analytic Attitude*. New York: Basic Books.

Schafer, R. (1992). *Retelling a Life*. New York: Basic Books.

Strozier, C.B. (2001). *Heinz Kohut. The Making of a Psychoanalyst*. New York: Farrar, Straus and Giroux.

Viderman, S. (1970). *La construction de l'espace analytique*. Paris: Gallimard.

CHAPTER FOUR

Adolescence as a dynamic field

Luis Kancyper

> "In brief, it is exciting that adolescence has become vocal and active, but the adolescent striving that makes itself felt over the whole world today needs to be met, needs to be given reality by an act of confrontation.
> Confrontation must be personal.
> Adults are needed if adolescents are to have life and liveliness.
> Confrontation belongs to containment that is non-retaliatory, without vindictiveness, but having its own strength.
> [...] Let the young alter society and teach grown-ups how to see the world afresh; but, where there is challenge of the growing boy or girl, there let an adult meet the challenge. And it will not necessarily be nice. In the unconscious fantasy these are matters of life and death".
>
> D.W. Winnicott (1972); G. Rosolato (1981)

Introduction

The confrontation between generations is an essential process for the acquisition of identity.

Its main condition is the presence of neither a soft nor arbitrary other who allows the tension of difference between opposites, while both parts admit that being an opponent is not equivalent to being an enemy.

Without this arch of tension, the dialectics of identification, disidentification and re-identification, which extend throughout our life span but are most present adolescence—which is in turn characterised by mentally letting go of the parents by overcoming the Oedipus complex and the end of sexual development—are paralysed.

Just as parents are much needed in accessing the Oedipus complex, they are equally important in enabling it to be left behind, so that the child can choose neither incestuous nor parricidal sexual objects and have access to new vocational interests beyond parental mandates.

This is a long, difficult, and tortuous path where many stop before the finish line.

F. Dolto points out that adolescence is a movement full of strength, of life promises, of expansion and that there is no such thing as an adolescent without problems, without suffering; it is perhaps the most painful period of life. It is, at the same time, the period in which joy is at its most intense (Dolto, 1985). It also represents a period of most intense grief, anxiety and joy for the adolescent's parents who, because of the sometimes tragic reactivation and resignification of their own long gone adolescence at a time coinciding with menopause and ageing, must go through a complex psychical working over.

Relinquishing the narcissistic desires of immortality and completeness invested in the child by the parents, the pygmalionic desires (Kancyper, 1990a) related to fantasies of making and modelling an other in the Maker's own image so as to exercise an absolute and omniscient power over the product fathered by them, causes anxiety and demands to be mourned. Moreover, parents must admit the child's blooming sexuality and the difference in developing strength between the child who is growing up and the parents who are getting old.

Parents must wage several battles on different fronts at the same time, in order to be able not only to demystify the Narcissus, Pygmalion and Oedipus who take shelter in different degrees in every parent's soul, but they must also dismantle Cronos, who devours his own offspring.

It is a painful and complex task for the adolescent's parents, aimed at admitting the inexorable irreversibility of the arrow of time, as well as the final prohibition of the devouring reappropriation of our children.

However, what happens when the father of the adolescent cannot let go of his own adolescence and in consequence, when he cannot carry out his paternal function? Or when he can neither go through all these mourning processes, characterised by a complex, multiple causality?

The difference between generations fades and the necessary oedipal rivalry becomes a tragic narcissistic struggle. Instead of confrontation, provocation, avoidance or disavowal of the generation gap are installed, hindering the process of identity.

Confrontation between generations and dynamic field

The confrontation between generations requires consideration as a whole, as a product of an intersubjective relationship in which parents and their children define each other, involved as they are in a dynamic field.

The field is a different structure from the sum of its parts—just as a melody is different from the sum of its notes—and it gives rise to a basic unconscious fantasy which, being a field product, is rooted in each of the members' unconscious (Baranger, 1992).

But why introduce the concept of dynamic field into the description of the act of confrontation between generations?

The concept of field has antecedents in Gestalt psychology and in Kurt Lewin's work; it was later reformulated by Merleau—Ponty in order to establish a psychology of man 'in situation', that is to say, a man able to notice and to understand psychical facts by means of their significance in the context of intersubjective relations.

Baranger (1961–62) and later Baranger et al. (1978) incorporated this concept to view the analytic situation as a bi-personal field.

"The analytic field is a shared ground between patient and analyst that gives rise to original phenomena, different both from what can be observed in each of the members and from the sum of what each of them contributes to it.

In this perspective, the object of study is neither the patient, nor his interaction with the analyst, but the field of the analytic situation as a producer of original phenomena and pathologies.

In consequence, we aim at revealing the movements that take place in this field, mostly unconsciously, and which shall be the starting point of our clinical and theoretical formulations" Baranger (1961–62).

In this paper, I shall be extending the concept of field out of the analytic situation and into the dynamics of the confrontation between parents and children and between siblings as well.

We cannot describe or understand parent-child and siblings relationships when involved in the act of confrontation as isolated individuals, but as a structured totality, whose dynamics result from the interaction of the members with each other and from the situation over both in a reciprocal causation within the same dynamic process.

This other view makes a better understanding of growing complexity possible, which can be ascribed to the progressive and regressive phenomena that appear in the generation interweaving, and to the dynamics originated between intrasubjectivity, intersubjectivity and their effects on the structuring-destructuring of each of the members' psychical agencies.

The functionality of the field of generational confrontation demands a radical asymmetry between paternal and filial functions. But both the parents and the child are required to go through different and complex processes of psychical working over:

1. Mourning processes in the narcissistic, oedipal and pygmalionic dimensions (Kancyper, 1995).
2. Mourning for the temporal irreversibility, including, in the same movement, the ageing parents' progressive loss of immortality and omnipotence and their admission of the new generation's growing strength as well as the latter's questioning of previous certainties and of dominating relationships within the family, institutions and society.
3. Gradual and paroxystic disidealisation of the child's image of wonderful parents and of the wonderful child who can manage to fulfil parental ideals (Kancyper, 1985).
4. Processes of reorganising of identifications and of resignification both in the parents and in the child.

The concept of field allows the approach to many problems in the generational confrontation as manifestations of the presence of pathology specific to that structure where both parents and children take part in different degrees and complementarily.

This intergenerational dynamic field depends, on the one hand, on the effects emerging from parental and filial narcissistic systems, which are not symmetrical, together with their fantasmatic configurations of immortality, omnipotence, idealisation and of the double; and on the other hand, on the incestuous, parricidal and filicidal fantasies belonging to the Oedipus complex, and of the furtive excommunication and confraternity fantasies belonging to fraternal complexes. I would like to emphasise that the fraternal complex is not a mere consequence of the Oedipal complex, rather, it has its own specificity and can or cannot be articulated with the nodular complex of neurosis (Winnicott, 1993).

We can enumerate different distortions in the dynamic field of generational and fraternal confrontation according to the predominance of the: a) stifling b) disavowal c) paralysis d) inversion e) avoidance of generational interweaving (Baranger, 1992).

These different dynamic fields are conditioned by the singular simultaneous interaction displayed between the child's peculiarities and the parents' characteristics: a) "do-all" b) "pendeviejos"[1] c) authoritarian d) soft e) parent-sibling f) "blind-eyed" and g) servile.

Dynamic field pathology in the generational and fraternal confrontation

I give the term "field" to the structure created between parents and the child, or between siblings, which allows the development of generational and fraternal confrontation.

This field includes three aspects: formal, dynamic and functional.

I. A formal aspect or rule of the game (the presence of a differentiated other who allows the tension between opposites).
II. A dynamic aspect: the evolution of parent-child and fraternal relationships as the different changes and conflicts inherent to different evolutionary stages start to appear.
III. A functional aspect, as its dynamics allow the recognition of the difference, as well as the display and the evolution of the collating between generations and between siblings.

A dynamic field that isn't working is perhaps one in which the confrontation process is paralysed or has been partially replaced, hindering the identity process.

Perversion is established within the field of generational and fraternal confrontation when the structuring aim of confrontation has essentially become a perverse activity that puts aside the main objective of the act of confrontation which is to tend to the growing assumption of similarity, difference and complementarity between participants.

This takes place when confrontation is experienced and administered in such ways that gratify perverse traits of the parent-child or fraternal couples by means of a thanatic defiance leading to pseudo-individuation.

The perverse trait in sadomasochistic or voyeuristic-exhibitionistic fields is often intellectualised by parents and their children or among siblings (for example, see the theory that extols the virtues of tolerance and altruism so as to smother masochistic, self-sacrificing satisfaction; or that other theory in which the entrenchment of liberating spontaneity and transparency masks a perverse exhibitionistic satisfaction; both find support in theoretical approaches which at the same time consolidate the crystallisation of the 'bulwark').

"The 'bulwark' is an immobilised structure which hinders or paralyses the process.

None of the participants are ever aware of it as this structure manifests itself by indirect effects: it stems from the complicity between both participants in unawareness and in silence in order to protect a bond that must not be disclosed. This situation culminates in the partial crystallisation of the field, in a neo-formation built around a shared fantasmatic set-up where important aspects of the histories of both participants are involved, and which assigns each a stereotyped imaginary role.

Sometimes the bulwark remains as a static alien body while the process apparently follows its course. At other times, the whole field becomes pathological as the bulwark completely invades the field and removes all functionality from the process" (Baranger et al, 1978).

I consider that Baranger's concept of field tends to be wrongly seen as an equivalent to the mere existence of transference in the analysand and of countertransference in the analyst. It does not amount to just that; the field creates an original fantasmatic whole: a basic unconscious fantasy. This concept awakens ample resistance among analysts. But in which way is this fantasy different from others?

This fantasy emerges within the analytic process created by the field situation and events follow through it. It is not the consequence of unconscious communication, nor of a mechanical interweaving of projective and introjective identifications, rather it is the condition of these identifications. The basic unconscious fantasy is an original production, it originates in the field and its dynamics are structured through it. It includes important aspects of each of the members' personal history, and each assumes a stereotyped imaginary role.

This fantasy does not exist clearly outside the field situation, although it is rooted in each of the members' unconscious.

Starting from this field unconscious fantasy, the psychical functioning and the intra-subjective history of each of the members can begin to be unravelled.

From intersubjectivity to intrasubjectivity. From *'hic et nunc'* to the past and the future. From this apparently atemporal precipitate to the temporality of resignification.

Admission of the status of the field basic unconscious fantasy is conditioned by the overcoming of several obstacles:

a. This concept inflicts a new wound upon the analyst's narcissism and power because he loses once again the illusion of omnipotence and self-sufficiency. In the relationship with the other and with others, the fantasy created in and because of the field situation "spreads its wings", it is autonomous and exercises its own influence over the individuals, like the unconscious which has its own rules and psychodynamics independent of rational and conscious control.
b. Accepting the presence of this concept in every stable and long-term relationship demands the inevitable assumption of complex and extra work. The analyst cannot go on maintaining his position as a passive observer of a situation that is unfairly alienating and frustrating him, rather, he is required to shift his position. Through his own psychical functioning, conditioned by his own complemental series, the analyst too has a part, in asymmetrical degrees, in the outcome of the relationship's trophic or destructive destinies.

c. The extra psychical work imposes the relinquishing of an automatic tendency to place in others the torrent of projections and projective identifications, or, onto oneself, the massive return of these, in order to admit that, in the end, each of the participants of the field has a part in the production of the intersubjective fantasy, which, furthermore, is original and originated by that particular field situation.

The fruitfulness of this concept opens up new paths: the advent of oneness, correlative to the consolidation of otherness; it allows the revision of the individual's own history as well as the other's, and the admission of points of similarity, difference and complementarity between participants (Kancyper, 1995).

Narcissism and sadomasochism

Sadomasochistic relationships between parents and their children give rise to a perverse dynamic field where confrontation and confirmation are replaced by acts of provocation.

This provocation holds back the field participants in a thanatical defiance which blocks the separation-individuation processes as well as the complementary support between generations.

These relationships present a bi-directional movement.

In the vast majority of cases the accent of sadistic polarity falls on authoritative parents, however, due to the exercise, use and abuse of asymmetrical relationship of control conditioned by the biological, psychical and social dependence of the child, in other cases the children themselves—independent of their real ages—are the ones acting as domestic tyrants to their parents, who ultimately become mere servile-slaves of their master-children within a relationship of sadistic complementarity.

I shall describe three distinct categories of parents who satisfy their own sadomasochistic and narcissistic drives whilst carrying out their parental functions.

From a clinical point of view they present remarkable differences to each other. According to the perspective of the dynamics of narcissism and its link to the masochistic component and to the establishing of the different kinds of fields they constitute along with their children, I shall classify them in: servile parents, parents who 'turn a blind eye', and 'do-all-sur-dying' parents.

Servile parents

Servile parents satisfy in a privileged way their own masochistic needs for punishment and they obtain a narcissistic gain through the fulfilment of an ideal governed by the logic of the tragic hero's sacrifice.

They are self-denying and long-suffering parents who can put up with anything and who besides intellectualise their excessive unconditional service with the entrenchment of an ideology that extols the virtue of unlimited altruism, but which in fact masks an economic gain of suffering in their parent-child relationships. The more they suffer, the better they feel they are as parents both before themselves and before others: the narcissistic secondary gain of parental masochism.

Servile parents usually suffer from 'delusions of insignificance', exactly as Freud describes the *Selbstgefühl* of the melancholic in "Mourning and Melancholy". They consider themselves unworthy of any respect or consideration on their children's part. They suffer from several outstanding debts which drive these guilt-ridden parents to acts of compulsive reparation, and their children often take advantage—either consciously or unconsciously—of the feelings of anxiety and guilt of these 'parents at fault', assuming the complementary role of home-executioners and predators who ill-treat the self-sacrificing parents.

The "servile parents" morally and/or erotogenically bring to fruition, through their children's sadism, their own masochistic fantasies from "A child-parent being beaten".

They operate as unconditional servants, carrying out strict ceremonials: genuflection, courtesy rules and preferring various gifts, offered in order to win their wonderful children's favour and ill-treatment: the princes and counts who live at the mansion enjoying every privilege and facing no duties. A pathology of the dynamic field comes into being: the perverse sadomasochistic field.

Parents who 'turn a blind eye'

Parents who 'turn a blind eye' constitute a pathological field along with their children. They make with the latter a 'pact of silence' which turns out to be the sub-product of a narcissistic collusion between the parents and the children.

An alliance is established between both of them, in order not to speak, not to listen and not to see. The main mechanism of this dynamic field is not indifference but ignorance as an active mechanism.

What prevails is not so much guilt as anxiety, which often manifests itself through severe symptoms in each of the participants.

Both servile and 'blind-eyed' parents are gagged before their own children. But there is a remarkable difference between them with regard to the act of intergenerational confrontation.

While with the former confrontation is replaced by the act of provocation that subjugates and ill-treats each of the participants of the perverse field through a thanatic defiance (Dora's case history) (Freud, 1901), with the latter—'blind-eyed' parents—we can witness the paralysis of the act of confrontation.

The bi-personal basic fantasy in the dynamic field formed by 'blind-eyed' parents and children is "escape and flight" (for example: 'I don't say anything because if I do I'll lose my self-control or I'll hit or kill him, or he'll kill me in retaliation'), and children tend to experience this parental inhibition as if it was carelessness on their part, while parents in turn often suffer anxiety because they cannot break the wall of silence. In cases such as these, a field of extreme avoidance can even be established that paralyses the generational confrontation.

Let us remember that in the case of homosexuality in a woman described by Freud in 1920, the adolescent "retired in favour" of her mother and her brother and "turned away" from her father; instead of confronting them she tried, by means of revenge—and through sadomasochism—to provoke her father and run away from the 'blind-eyed' mother who was narcissistically competing with her own daughter.

It could be said that what had taken shape between them was a particular field phenomenon and, moreover, a bi-personal fantasy rooted in each of the participants' unconscious, the fantasy of "retiring in favour of someone else".

> *"The girl we are considering had, in any case, altogether little cause to feel affection for her mother. The latter, still youthful herself, saw in her rapidly developing daughter an inconvenient competitor; she favoured the sons at her expense, limited her independence as much*

> *as possible, and kept an especially strict watch against any close relationship between the girl and her father. A yearning from the beginning for a kinder mother would, therefore, have been quite intelligible.*
>
> *The mother herself still attached great value to the attentions and to the admiration of men. If, then, the girl became homosexual and left men to her mother (in other words, 'retired in favour of' her mother), she would remove something which had hitherto been partly responsible for her mother's dislike"* (Freud, 1920).

In another paragraph belonging to the same case history, Freud points out:

> *"The mother was tolerant, as though she appreciated her daughter's 'retirement' as a favour to her; the father was furious, as though he realised the deliberate revenge directed against himself.*
>
> *Furiously resentful and embittered, she turned away from her father and from men altogether.*
>
> *After this great reverse she forswore her womanhood and sought another goal for her libido"* (Freud, 1920).

Freud points out in a footnote of this article the essential role that generational and fraternal confrontation have in constructing the adolescent's identity. He underlines that "retiring in favour of someone else" instead of confronting the parents on the one hand, and siblings on the other, discloses very complicated conditions in the mind which take part not only in erotic choice, but also in the sphere of vocational interests.

> *"As retiring in favour of someone else has not previously been mentioned among the causes of homosexuality, or in the mechanism of libidinal fixation in general, I will adduce here another analytic observation of the same kind which has a special feature of interest. I once knew two twin brothers, both of whom were endowed with strong libidinal impulses. One of them was very successful with women and had innumerable affairs with women and girls. The other went the same way at first, but it became unpleasant for him to be trespassing on his brother's preserves, and, owing to the likeness between them, to be mistaken for him on intimate occasions; so he got out of the difficulty by becoming homosexual. He left the women to his brother and thus*

> *retired in his favour. Another time I treated a youngish man, an artist, unmistakably bisexual in disposition, in whom the homosexual trend had come to the fore simultaneously with a disturbance in his work. He fled from both women and work together. The analysis, which was able to bring him back to both, showed that fear of his father was the most powerful psychical motive for both the disturbances, which were really renunciations. In his imagination all women belonged to his father, and he sought refuge in men out of submission, so as to retire from a conflict with his father. Such a motivation of the homosexual object-choice must be by no means uncommon; in the primeval ages of the human race all women presumably belonged to the father and head of the primal horde.*
>
> *Among brothers and sisters who are not twins this retiring plays a great part in other spheres as well as in that of erotic choice. For example an older brother studies music and is admired for it; the younger, far more gifted musically, soon gives up his own musical studies, in spite of his fondness for it, and cannot be persuaded to touch an instrument again. This is only one example of a very frequent occurrence, and investigation of the motives leading to this retirement rather than to open rivalry discloses very complicated conditions in the mind* (Freud, 1920).

In this case history we can see a pathology in the field dynamics: a perverse field through the revengeful provocation of the father ("to turn away from the father") and a "blind-eyed bulwark" along with the mother and the brother ("to retire in favour of someone else").

The pact of silence between the homosexual's mother and her daughter was an obstacle to the act of generational confrontation. It stemmed from the collusion between certain traits of the mother and corresponding aspects in the daughter's unconscious. A sphere of unawareness had been created in which both participants took part, as if they had agreed not to see what was going on with the daughter. It could be said that between them a 'link' had been created, an intersubjective 'blind-eyed bulwark'. Even if the concept of bulwark described by the Barangers, as I mentioned earlier, refers to an artificial formation and is a sub-product of analytic technique, it can also be extended to the bi-personal field between parents and their children and among siblings.

The 'do-all-sur-dying' parents (Kancyper, 1994)

The 'do-all' parents position themselves at the same time in a narcissistic and masochistic dimension. They are chronic debtors before the ideal agencies of their own personality: Ideal Ego-Ego Ideal-Superego. They adopt an attitude of sacrifice before their children: they offer themselves as a magical substance that can resolve any conflict, but at the same time they block in the other the origination and development of true desire, cancelling, furthermore, the essential function of anxiety as signal-affect to detect danger.

This signal of anxiety is a device put into action by the ego, as if it were a sensory organ specialised in perceiving internal and external realities; this function needs to be exercised and developed by each individual. But 'do-all' parents tend to assume this function in their children's name, depriving them of this alarm bell which alerts and organises, similar to the symbolic function of thought that allows the weighing up of tensions in the external and internal worlds.

These parents conceal behind an apparent omnipotence their own acute anxieties which stem from imaginary situations of uncertainty, from the potential dangers of their children abandoning them because of catastrophic fatalities: illness, accident, kidnapping or death. Due to the interchanging of roles, certain children often exercise an abusive power that exploits precisely those manifest and latent anxieties and feelings of guilt in their all-powerful parents, who become beggars subjected to the tyranny of their own creations.

'Do-all' parents are also 'sur-dying' because they build their view of the world on the defensive foundations of escape, control and attack mechanisms in order to protect themselves from castration-death; because, in this family environment, anxieties and feelings of guilt are the central axes of the members' psychical life. They live to save themselves through a permanent reassurance in order not to suffer. But they pay their right to existence through a constant amount of suffering, *dolo ergo sum*; they prefer to avoid displeasure rather than to seek pleasure, but they cannot stop suffering (Kancyper, 2000).

And it is precisely this tension of uncertainty, which stems from the mortification caused by the action of uncanny anxieties, that protects them from the absolute lack of tension characteristic of the Nirvana principle. To paraphrase the poets: 'Dying life, living death'.

'Do-all-sur-dying' parents generate addictive relationships with their children and they enslave each other, creating a retaliating pendulum that keeps itself up thanks to the validity of this link between uncanny anxiety and power.

One of the ways in which these parents exercise their power is by means of 'spells' and fascination techniques and through compulsive offerings: material, verbal and affective, in order to keep the threats stemming from their own anxieties neutralised, with the aim of guaranteeing the unconditional presence of their children-objects so that they will never leave.

The 'do-all-sur-dying' parents position themselves as deities who perfectly assist their children, fulfilling every *Ananké*. They are placed in a phallic position and consider their child as a helpless anti-anxiety object who is always there in order to guarantee the presence of a mirror-like and marvellous other, so that, when the father mirrors himself in his own 'work', he reflects his own omnipotence as the "Maker", the pygmalionic father who models and creates his own creature. The repetition of these parental anxieties turns 'do-all' parents into domestic slaves, into unconditional servants to demanding children, although wrapped—in their eyes and in others'—in the disguise of 'demi-god' parents.

In this aspect, 'do-all-sur-dying' parents are different from the other parents described earlier because they occupy the place, from the very beginning, of the Ideal-Ego, of the all-powerful parents: the "Three Wise Men" who magically provide a world without conflicts, struggling to combine infantile narcissistic perfection with their facile denial of a world which is, in reality, quite unpleasant, and the psychical existence of destructive and self-destructive drives which are essentially incompatible with narcissistic happiness.

The 'do-all' parents' need to feel they are above everyone else is so intense that it allows them to disavow the very high costs of suffering and displeasure that result from their masochistic behaviour, so as to keep sustaining narcissism's phallic logic in the relationship with their children. I propose to apply the term "masochistic dimension of parental narcissism" to the relationship between narcissism and the thanatic component between 'do-all-sur-dying' parents and their children, whereas "narcissistic dimension of parental sadomasochism" applies to the relationship between servile and 'blind-eyed' parents and their children (Kancyper, 1998).

From subjection to generational confrontation. The fathers of silence

Bezoari and Ferro point out with regard with the unconscious fantasy organising the analytic field described by the Barangers: 1) That it is a bi-personal fantasy that cannot be reduced to the classic conception of unconscious fantasy (for example, that of S. Isaacs), that is to say, as the expression of the individual's instinctual life; and 2) That the unconscious bi-personal fantasy is formed by the interweaving of groups of projective identifications in which the analyst as well as the analysand are involved (Bezoari, 1990).

"Assuming this radically bi-personal model, that of projective identification, also produces important changes in the conception of transference and countertransference dynamics. According to the Barangers, what is classically conceived of as transference-neurosis (or psychosis) shall have to be considered within the notion of field as transference-countertransference neurosis (or psychosis), that is to say, as a function of the couple. The patient's pathology does not enter the field as such, but only in relation to the analyst, who in turn actively contributes (although, it is to be hoped, to a lesser degree) to the constitution of that field pathology which shall be the objective of analytic working over" (Ferro, 2001, 2002).

In the same line of thought, we can study the obstacles in the process of generational confrontation as a dynamic field involving, as a whole, mourning processes and the reordering of identifications and resignifications, both in the growing child and in the ageing parents. Between them a field phenomenon is created, one which could only be created between that child and those parents. Metaphorically speaking, a precipitate is formed between these interacting elements, and a blocking or a paralysis of the field dynamics occurs.

I shall now present a clinical case so as to illustrate the 'blind-eyed' silence between Jackie and her teenage daughter.

Clinical case: the "blind-eyed" bulwark

Jackie is 49. She is a successful professional and an attractive and elegant woman. Physical "aesthetics" have a significant relevance in the discourse of this family. Nancy, the daughter, is 18 and she excels intellectually, but she is 20 kilos overweight.

The fragments of the sessions I am about to quote belong to the third year of Jackie's own psychoanalytical process, after she had attended a jazz dance show, "kindly" invited by her daughter, towards whom she felt a wave of rejection and shame which resignified her own adolescence as well as her unresolved narcissistic and oedipal conflicts.

> —*I play the mother—I am not the mother—because I perform all the duties, I carry out all the gestures, I perform the tea-time ceremony but I do not drink/have the tea. Just like geishas who do everything for others though I don't know if they are really into it.*
>
> *I sometimes have this feeling about Nancy, that I come and go, I do things, but I feel something more visceral is lacking.*
>
> *Last night, after I had seen her on stage I couldn't sleep.*
>
> *I was in bed, feeling anxious, I felt a pain in my stomach. I feel I can't get closer to her. The aesthetic thing about her weight is too strong for me. It is as if I can only bond with Nancy intellectually. I am a very good mum intellectually, but I can't cope with her body. There is something incompatible between her body and mine. This happened at the time Nancy kind of exploded. Her breasts grew out of all proportion and she started getting fatter and fatter.* (Pause)
>
> *I also think there is something between Juan and me: we were expecting a very pretty, perfect girl, but she wasn't the baby of our dreams and now we have the burden of her weight.*
>
> *These extra kilos destroy an idea of perfection and this is what I find most painful.*
>
> *It's not her extra kilos but my own idea of perfection that makes me feel guilty. I reject my own idea of perfection and it makes me angry.*

Analyst: You can't leave behind the idea of a perfect mother and a perfect daughter.

> —*In my head I have this idea of what a perfect mum should be. Between the heavenly mum I wish I were and the mum I really am, I sometimes feel there is an abyss. It pains me, both for her and for myself. I've never been a mum that is there for her.*

Analyst: Perhaps your pain has partly to do with the rejection you feel towards your daughter and with the rejection that your mother used to feel towards you when you were an adolescent, according to what you remembered last week.

> *—Absolutely. It hurts me to be repeating the same history. It's a kind of blind alley—to repeat what one went through.*
>
> *I cannot be different from the way my own mother was with me. It's terrible. As if it were a twist of fate, I don't know ... something inevitable.*
>
> *I think her fatness is aimed at me, dedicated to me. I think it's a rebellion against me. If I didn't care so much for physical appearance, it would be less evident.*
>
> *I don't think we can go on turning a blind eye. I have responsibilities and so does Juan. But I think he goes to the opposite extreme. He is really mad about what's going on with Nancy but he lets it pass. Whereas I cannot look at her except with that hypercritical look which is so scary. But I don't tell her anything.*

Analyst: That is to say that there is a pact of silence between your husband, your daughter and yourself. There is silence in the words but not in the looks.

> *—In the looks I am just like my mum. It's terrible, but that's how it is.*

Resignification in the adolescent and in the adolescent's parents

> What is hushed up during childhood generally cries out during adolescence.
>
> Kancyper, L. (1998)

During adolescence, the pathogenic consequences of certain "posthumous primary processes" manifest themselves. That is to say, those experiences, impressions and mnemonic traces from childhood which have remained in the psyche without forming trauma—in the sense that they have not produced pathogenic effects—are resignified only in this phase. Adolescence is characterised by the re-commencement of sexual development due to organic maturation, drive increase, restructuring of the psyche's agencies and the new demands from the social world.

These new adolescent events are linked to infantile outlines in a time in torsion and allow the deferred manifestation of psychical effects.

We are not just dealing with deferred action, with a cause that remains latent during childhood until the opportunity comes of manifesting itself during adolescence, but with a retroactive causation: from the present onto the past. The introduction of *Nachtraglichkeit* pinpoints the time in which Freud left behind the model of mechanical causality and linear temporality, according to the past-present vector, in order to favour a dialectical view of causality where the future and the past condition each other to structure the present.

With regard to this we can verify how Freud's perspective is more structural than genetic and, in this sense, adolescence would represent a privileged process of the subsequent reaction (*Nachtraglichkeit*) (Kancyper, 1983).

The other significant period is represented by menopause, because of the eloquent restructuring that takes place at this time.

In "Analysis terminable and interminable" Freud points out that:

> *"Twice in the course of individual development certain instincts are considerably reinforced: at puberty, and, in women, at the menopause. We are not in the least surprised if a person who was not neurotic before becomes so at these times. When his instincts were not so strong, he succeeded in taming them; but when they are reinforced he can no longer do so"* (Freud, 1937).

And in this same article he describes the essential importance of the concept of ***a posteriori*** for our analytic practice: the subsequent correction (***Nachtraglich)*** of the original process of repression, which puts an end to the dominance of the quantitative factor, would thus be the real achievement of analytic therapy.

Baranger, Baranger and Mom hold that "causality and temporality are the concepts supporting the possibility of a therapeutic action specific to psychoanalysis; if this retroactivity did not have a part in the constitution of trauma (and I would add: in the constitution of identifications in two separate times), there would not be any chance of changing our history either" (Baranger et al, 1987).

Hence the importance historisation acquires in the treatment of adolescents, so as to re-integrate the elements of traumatic situations to those situations of the past where they belong, allowing access to a different temporal dynamic. All this in spite of the resistance adolescents generally show in remembering traumatic facts from childhood and their tendency to put into action the defensive technique of flight from their own origins. This is a frequent mechanism that drives them, instead, to look for and create a neo-spatiality and a neo-temporality which manifests itself through the planning of trips to material and psychic realities by means of geographic distance and/or drugs.

We have already stated that adolescence involves a period of turbulence not just for the child who is growing up but for the adolescent's parents who witness the resignification of their own infantile and adolescent history which has left as sequels—as historical precipitates—certain forgotten chapters of their relationships with their own parents and siblings and which are inexorably reanimated when the generational confrontation with the adolescent takes place.

These historical precipitates acquire and show their psychic effectiveness through the 'unpaid bills'—with high interest—that children demand from their parents, their siblings and by extension from society, because of all the narcissistic affronts and the traumatic situations suffered during childhood and which have since remained split and repressed through the latency period.

But certain parents also react during this stage with serious authoritarian counter-measures, in response to the effects of the growing powers of autonomy adolescents hold.

This rivalrous situation can even determine the resignification of unsolved oedipal and fraternal complexes in the parents' histories, by not allowing the generational confrontation and implanting instead an endless thanatical defiance between parents and children (Kancyper, 1994).

Session previous to Nancy's graduation trip

> *—Yesterday I spent the whole day feeling anxious.*
>
> *I was in bed, in pain. I had a terrible pain in my soul. And another thing is that I am torn between wanting to see her off and not. I use my job to make excuses. Something is going on and I am finding it hard to see her off. I hate saying goodbye, but I have this unbearable feeling of anxiety.*
>
> *I wish tomorrow were over—what I feel is that this trip to Bariloche will be good for Nancy.*

> *I wish I were a less demanding mother with the looks and not demanding with words. I try but I find it hard. It's a huge self-criticism I admit I must make and something which I have to change.*

Analyst: What are your feelings when you look at your daughter nowadays?

> *—I feel many things: it tortures me; I'm mad at her because she's fat. Lots of times I find it hard to get closer to her. I feel a bit of sadness and a bit of pity.* (Pause)
>
> *It's not clear to me where confrontation ends and where ill-treatment and aggression begin.*
>
> *There is a certain point where they get confused. In my mind confrontation has to do with putting someone down. That is why I avoid it.*
>
> *I feel I am afraid of my daughter. I am afraid of harming her. I remember my mother used to make me feel I was worthless, that I was horrible because I was plump, and that her friends' daughters were great.*
>
> *She had this way, I can't quite put my finger on it, of telling me things, instead of saying things nicely, she said them in a bad way. For example: "I've been talking to your father and to other people and I think that … ." As she couldn't cope with things by herself she had to share them, she used to talk to lots of people, we would end up fighting and I eventually used to feel I was rubbish and I didn't need to lose weight or take care of myself.*
>
> *So, in order not to let it go that far with my daughter, I don't confront her and I let it pass.* (Pause)
>
> *When I was her age I was 5 kilos overweight, but she is 20 kilos overweight and, in order not to irritate her, I choke with anger and I make a pact of silence, saying yes to everything. But then, it's the same as saying nothing to her, because I can't find the right limit with my daughter. I feel that there is a very fine line between getting angry at her and hurting her. Because if I say "no" there is a chance that she may feel bad, that I might lose my temper and say something really bad to her that could cause her such deep pain, just like my mother used to do with me.*
>
> *I always used to end up deeply hurt when I clashed with my mother and I used to be furious with her.*

The pact of silence between Jackie and her daughter put obstacles before the act of generational confrontation. It operated as a crystallised structure or an immovable way of relating between both participants. It came from the collusion between unconscious aspects of the mother and corresponding aspects in the daughter's unconscious (Nancy had her own psychoanalytic process). A zone of unawareness had been created, which both shared in a way that involved turning a blind eye.

This pact, a product of 'too well-mannered conversations' and at the same time one which turns a blind eye to the open manifestations of an affective compromise, is a compulsion to repeat concealed by Jackie's negative identification with her own mother taking the shape of a smothered contempt towards the daughter (Kancyper, 1985).

This contempt operates as a source of anxiety and guilt that inhibits the exercise of the maternal function, accompanied by a series of reproaches and complaints against herself which stems from her own superego, which in turn increases inhibition: "Eventually I end up choked in anger and silence".

This maternal inhibition causes the absence of a much needed 'other' so that the daughter can display the necessary confrontation.

Jackie had to go through a complex working over of processes during her psychoanalytic treatment in order to see Nancy as 'other' and to admit the differences between generations.

Establishing the limits between herself and her daughter required—as a necessary precondition—the discrimination and deciphering of the repetitive play of simultaneous identifications with the aggressor and with the aggressed, so as to manage to unravel her own history as an adolescent daughter affronted by her own mother. It was precisely this situation that was resignified at the time of Nancy's adolescence (Baranger et al, 1989).

There is an identification between Jackie's situations with her own mother and her daughter's identification with herself. Moreover, this double identification is negative, in the sense of rejecting the relationship with her own mother who used to devalue her and generated in her a hostile reaction towards her and against herself.

But at a deeper level, repetition is absolute (Baranger, 1994). When she compares her daughter on stage with other adolescents, she is ashamed of her and despises her viscerally: "I was in bed, feeling anxious, I felt a pain in my stomach. I feel I cannot get closer to her. The aesthetic thing about her weight is stronger than me".

Her daughter could have perceived the mother's contempt, just as Jackie had previously felt her own mother's scorn.

The progressive unlocking of identifications, of the overlapping between both histories, and the working through of dangerous situations Jackie associated with showing hostility towards her daughter, allowed us to discover the existence of an a 'esthetical' bulwark in the intrasubjective and intersubjective dimensions (Freud, 1937).

"To the analysand, the intrasubjective bulwark represents an unconscious shelter for powerful omnipotence fantasies. It is extremely diverse between one person and another but it is always there. The analysand does not want to display it because the risk of losing it would place him in a state of extreme helplessness, vulnerability, and hopelessness.

For some people, the bulwark can be their intellectual or moral superiority, their relationship with an idealised object or the idealisation of it, their fantasy of social aristocracy, their material goods, their profession, etc. The analysands' most frequent behaviour in defence of their bulwark consists in avoiding mentioning its existence.

The analysand can be very sincere regarding several problems and aspects of his life. But he becomes evasive, sly and even mendacious when the analyst comes close to a bulwark (Freud, 1937).

In Jackie's case we discovered that the daughter's adolescence resignified her own conflictive adolescence with her mother and the persistence of a bodily-aesthetic bulwark that revealed her conflictive sexual identity.

From the time she became aware of the existence of an intrasubjective and intersubjective bulwark, she started to free herself from her own masochistic and sadistic position. The session I am about to quote illustrates the particular time when the veil of silence started to fall away and the point from which the passage from subjection to generational confrontation became effective (Kancyper, 1991, 1992, 1994).

> *—Yesterday I finally had a real fight with my daughter. In the past I could not confront her because she wouldn't talk to me, she would lock herself up in her room. This time she cried, she was feeling anxious, and we yelled at each other, but nobody got hurt; quite the contrary, it was a relief for both of us.*
>
> *We have always been too silent, always engaged in too-well mannered conversations. This is a relief, the opportunity to have someone*

to fight with. I have someone who will answer back, there is no more muteness and besides, she doesn't reply with an intellectualisation.

This surprises me, but I liked it, although I was afraid at a certain time when she threatened to leave home if I kept on meddling in her life.

I pay attention to what is going on between her and her friends, who fill up her head with lies. I telephoned her friend's house to find out if she really did have a suspicious illness and was told not at all.

My daughter threatened me, saying her friendship would be broken because of me, and I told her that wasn't true. I don't feel like I meddled in her privacy, all I wanted was to talk mother to mother because these are serious things and parents have the right and the obligation to do something.

At night we had dinner at home and everything was fine, I was expecting my daughter to be resentful and it was just the reverse.

Final reflections

Generational confrontation requires consideration as a whole, as a product of an intersubjective relationship in which parents and their children define each other, involved as they are in a dynamic field.

As I have already pointed out, in this paper I extend the concept of field out of the analytic situation and into the confrontation between parents and children and between siblings as well.

We cannot describe or understand the parent-child and the siblings relationships when involved in the act of confrontation as isolated individuals but as a structured totality, whose dynamics result from the interaction of the members with each other and from the situation over both in a reciprocal causation within the same dynamic process.

This other view makes a better understanding of growing complexity possible, which can be ascribed to the progressive and regressive phenomena that appear in the generational interweaving.

The functionality of the field of generational confrontation demands a radical asymmetry between paternal and filial functions. But both the parents and the child are required to go through different and complex processes of psychical working over.

From a clinical point of view, the individuals can be grouped within three categories:

- Those who are unable to confront their parents and siblings.
- Those who perpetuate an endless confrontation through a thanatic defiance (the perverse field).
- Those who have put behind them the thanatic defiance and have managed to engage in a trophic challenge, obtaining all the structuring benefits for the construction of identity from the generational and fraternal confrontation.

Note

1. Untranslatable word which describes a middle-aged person who behaves as if he/she were an adolescent.

References

Baranger, W. & Baranger, M. (1961–62). "La situación analítica como campo dinámico", In: *Problemas del campo psicoanalítico,* Buenos Aires, Kargieman, 1993, p. 129.

Baranger, W., Baranger, M. & Mom, J. (1978). "Patología de la transferencia y contratransferencia en el psicoanálisis actual: el campo perverso", In *Revista de Psicoanálisis, XXXV,* 5.

Baranger, W., Baranger, M. & Mom, J. (1987). "El trauma psíquico infantil: de nosotros a Freud", In *Revista de Psicoanálisis, XLIV* (4): p. 771.

Baranger, W., Goldstein, N. & Goldstein, R. (1989). "Acerca de la desidentificación", In *Revista de Psicoanálisis, XLVI* (6): p. 895.

Baranger, M. (1992). "La mente del analista, de la escucha a la interpretación", In *Revista de Psicoanálisis, XLIX* (2): p. 225.

Baranger, W. (1992). *Los afectos en la contratransferencia,* XIV Congreso Psicoanalítico de America Latina, Buenos Aires.

Baranger, W. (1994). Personal Communication.

Bezoari, M. & Ferro, A. (1990). "Elementos de un modelo del campo psicoanalítico: los agregados funcionales", In *Revista de Psicoanálisis, XLIVII* (5/6): p. 852.

Dolto, F. (1985). *Palabras para adolescentes,* Buenos Aires, Atlántida, p. 19.

Ferro, A. (2001). *La sesión analítica,* Buenos Aires, Lumen, p. 193.

Ferro, A. (2002). "Desde la tiranía del Superyó a la democracia de los afectos", In: *revista de Psicoanálisis,* T. *LIX* (4): p. 861.

Freud, S. (1901). "Fragmento de análisis de un caso de histeria", AE, *VII*: p. 3.

Freud, S. (1920). "Sobre la psicogénesis de un caso de homosexualidad femenina", AE, *XVIII*.

Freud, S. (1937). "Análisis terminable y interminable", AE, *XXIII*.

Kancyper, L. (1983). "El baluarte en el sujeto y en el campo intersubjetivo en un caso clínico", presented at the Argentine Psychoanalytic Association, April 14.

Kancyper, L. (1985). "Adolescencia y a posteriori", In *Revista de Psicoanálisis, XLII* (3): p. 535.

Kancyper, L. (1990). "Adolescencia y desidentificación", In *Revista de Psicoanálisis, XLVII* (4): p. 750.

Kancyper, L. (1991). "Remordimiento y resentimiento en el complejo fraterno", In *revista de Psicoanálisis, XLVIII (1):* p. 120. Paper presented at the 37th International Congress of Psychoanalysis, Buenos Aires.

Kancyper, L. (1992). "Resentimiento y odio en la confrontación generacional", XX Internal Congress and XXX Symposium, APA, p. 173.

Kancyper, L. (1994). "Eros y Ananké en la confrontación generacional", Fourth Conference on Family and Couple Psychoanalysis, APA.

Kancyper, L. (1994). "Angustia y poder en la confrontación generacional", Córdoba, FEPAL.

Kancyper, L. (1995). "Complejo de Edipo y complejo fraterno", paper presented at the 39 International Congress of Psychoanalysis, San Francisco.

Kancyper, L. (1998) (comp.). *Volviendo a pensar con Willy y Madeleine Baranger*, Buenos Aires, Lumen, 1999, p. 13.

Kancyper, L. (2000). *La confrontación generacional*, Buenos Aires, Lumen, 2003, p. 125 [Italian version available under the title: *Il confronto generazionale*, Milan, F. Angeli, 2000, p. 101.].

Rosolato, G. (1981). "Culpabilidad y sacrificio", In *La relación de Desconocido*, Barcelona, Petrel, p. 115.

Winnicott, D. (1972). *Realidad y juego*, Buenos Aires, Granica, p. 193.

Winnicott, D. (1993). *El hogar, nuestro punto de partida*, Buenos Aires, Paidós, p. 192.

[Translated from Spanish by Valeria Muscio valeriamuscio@yahoo.co.uk]

CHAPTER FIVE

Las Meninas

Laura Ambrosiano and Eugenio Gaburri

Introduction

In Italy, the idea of an "Analytical Field" started from a particular connection that W. Bion had maintained between his experience with groups, the clinic and psychoanalytical theory (F. Corrao 1986).

The idea of the group remained, in fact, in Bion's thoughts when he wrote his work on "Thought and Maternal reverie". (One of his last works, 1970, "Attention and Interpretation" has a sub-title: "A Scientific Approach to Insight in Psychoanalysis and Groups").

When Bion speaks of groups he does not refer to a concrete phenomenon, he describes a mental space constituted to gather the transformations of meaning from multiple points of observation.

In group psychoanalysis, Bion explores not so much the affective transition between individuals who make up the group (ties, relationships, dynamics), but the weaving and the hybridisation that, starting from protoemotions and from protothought, allow the affective meaning of the experience in hand to emerge.

Bion (1961) describes two configurations: the Basic Assumption Group represents a level of meeting between non differentiated individuals, but amalgamated by emotive elements that urge to be not thinkable but assumed in their own right. The second configuration is the Work Group as a space for the meeting of differentiated people treading the same work path, to elaborate the emerging emotions and transform them into images and alpha elements, that are thinkable.

These two configurations that emerged from the therapeutic work with groups also constitute, for Bion, two different levels for the functioning of the psychic apparatus: that of the differentiated mind and that of a part of the non differentiated pre-individual mind. The two levels are not seen as milestones of development but are present throughout the whole of existence. Beside a singled out, specific personal thought, there is always (present) a pre-individual dimension prone to contagion by the valency present in the field of meeting (E. Gaburri, L. Ambrosiano 2003).

Therefore it is important to receive from a meeting with a group or just two people, the continuous transformative movements that are allowed to emerge from a pre-individual common background, something specific regarding the experience in motion, this being the matrix of knowledge.

The perspective of field develops the idea that the significance is polyhedral and facetted, so that in itself it can be approached from different points of view that hybridise the perception of the single individual with that of the group and its culture.

Two people that meet in the consulting room bring with them "two worlds", the two scenarios that Freud (1937) speaks of. From this encounter an energetic field is released that generates new meaning. This field crosses the emotive coordinates of the two interlocutors, the relationship that has been established, their theories about the world. In this dimension the margins between people are mobile and transient[1], like the margin between the conscious and the subconscious, between mind and body, between past and future … .

The request for therapy brought by the patient creates an a-symmetry on the basis of which the analyst is summoned to monitor the emotions, both his and those of the patient as well as the overall picture.

The analytical field

The notion of Field takes into account some pre-individual aspects of the analytical encounter, of the dimension of contact in which individuals are tangled together (Freud 1915 to Bion 1963), where for a certain time, the emotions are perceived as diffused, not clearly attributed to one or other partner. With the paradigm of Field, one takes into account that the position of the analyst, during the session, is not extra-territorial: he is involved as much as the patient, even if in a different way.

The paradigm of field does not mean so much a concept of force and power, but that of an energy that implies propagation and expansion. (F. Corrao 1986).

In this sense the Field indicates trans-personal space-and-time, crossed by energies of which the interlocutors may just be carriers.

The Analytical Field is a paradigm to describe a meeting of energies that propagate, expand, not vectorially, and change according to the combination of light and the position of the observer. Reality, in its own right, tends to be defined by the culture of the group. But the perception of reality depends on the modifications that intervene in the environment, the variation of light that falls upon an object: the alternating of areas of shade on the surface of the objects often allows for better identification of the structure.

The dimension of the Field is ample, but not infinite, in fact, thinking back, it becomes animated on the specificity of the encounter between individuals in that setting.

But the field does not coincide with the setting as a space for the encounter for therapy. Here, by setting we mean the stable framework of rules, but we are also referring to that live and mobile dimension described by Bleger (1967) as the third protagonist of the analytical encounter, in so for as being a depository of the patient's split aspects.

The Field does not even coincide with the analyst-patient relationship, it's not about a "dual-personal field" (Baranger M. and W. 1968), nor does it coincide with the concept of "ties", nor with the patients and the analyst's theories and mentality (group reference). All these levels are implied, often they are starting points, emotive themes that run to our aid while we allow ourselves to be captured by the meaning.

We could imagine the Field generating, expanding from the meeting of three factors: the setting, the relationship, the therapy. Above this triangular space we allocate the therapy request. As the field expands, new meanings emerge about the request for therapy over and above that which the patient formulates explicitly, as we shall see in the clinical scenes with Diletta and Gigi.

The encounter between two individuals in the psychoanalytical setting, summoned in the here and now by the request for therapy, generates emotive energy that expands significance over and beyond the coercion of repetition.

In this schematic definition, one needs to underline that in the paradigm of field a series of optional theories are included that range from the theory of thought (alpha elements, beta elements, alpha-reverie function) to Bion's concept of change, seen as tolerance of the no-thing, of shadows, of the absent, of the unknown.[2]

(E. Gaburri 1998).

In this contribution we would like to deepen the meaning of field as a dimension traversed by new thoughts that are looking for thinkers that will accept them and transform them (for further meanings of the same field paradigm please see the work of C. Neri in this volume).

The "unborn"

Paraphrasing the novel "Erewhon, or over the range" by Samuel Butler (1860), we could say that this special meeting, in the special setting that aims to cure psychic pain, activates a field of ideas and significance not yet born in anyone's mind. These unborn entities endlessly torment us until they manage to be received and be born as somebody's idea. The inhabitants of Erewhon, the imaginary universe described by Butler in the nineteenth century, believe that the unborn are nobody until a mind receives them, even if they do exist independently from the fact of being received ... the unborn ideas generate in the field without it being possible to say, straightaway, if they belong to the present, the past or the future ... they describe in an instant the incessant part of the experience and they reconstruct the whole.

For the analyst, a condition for being able to receive these ideas, thoughts without a thinker (Bion 1970), is not to oppose[3] an associative non linear course that allows the observing of the experience from different points of view.

To follow an associative course is the requisite of the psychoanalyst at work, the mental state for listening is fundamental to the setting imagined by Freud, and is a strong point in Bion's intuition when he invites us to suspend memory and be without desire. This suspension consents tolerating together with the patient that instant, filled with persecution, in which the new idea emerges, without falling into the trap of the compulsion to evacuate it.

As we know, associative thought is difficult, it creates a sense of vertigo, it expropriates our ideas and the sensation that it is we who have them. In the mental associative dimension, thoughts reach us, often filling us with wonder or catching us unaware, without us feeling that we have generated them; they were already there, we were just limited to receiving them … and thinking them.

Thoughts without a thinker describe to us the ongoing experience, they catch some aspects and transform them into scenes that give sense to our encounter with the patient's deep pain. But when, thanks to the alpha function, we put these thoughts into communicable shapes for the patient himself, so that he can see, touch and smell that which we are communicating (Bion 1963), they help in enlarging the mind towards another emerging scene.

This transformation is moved by the analyst's sudden intuition (or sometimes the patient's) that connects "phenomena apparently not linked to each other, in such a way that they assume a coherence and significance that they didn't possess before" (F. Corrao 1998, p. 83). The analyst's sudden intuition marks an auto-organisation of the field that expands to receive new aspects.

The psychoanalytical theories, the very same clinical reports, constitute a series of transformations in as much as they are representations that can be shared in an emotional experience never recognisable in itself. ("O"). We are not capable of defining through empiric observation what is happening in the analysis in that very moment, we can only let it emerge from the emotional tangle and, in the transformation it undergoes, give back to the patient new knowledge about his mental functioning.

We need to publish (Bion 1970) our approximations. Publication is an inescapable dimension of an analyst's work, for we need to communicate our intuitions and exchange our ideas with a group of colleagues. While we gather an associative course we, nevertheless, need the protection that theories offer us and the presence of a group of colleagues to share our passion for research (L. Ambrosiano 2006).

This helps us maintain a connection with the thought shared in common, sets down a barrier between the analyst and the risk, ever present, of auto referential drift, the risk of closing oneself off, together with the patient, in a universe made for two (L. Ambrosiano 1999). Communicating a clinical sequence is a transformation of the session and, as such, it implicitly includes a new perspective for both the analyst and the patient.

Diletta

Diletta asks me for an analysis after a previous attempt has been bitterly broken off.

For about a year, she says, she had suffered, not having been understood by her previous analyst; one of my colleagues, she tells me, without naming her, had treated her so badly.

In spite of her training (Diletta is a psychotherapist with several years' experience behind her), she does not know how an analysis is conducted, but does not think that an analysis includes being badly treated, by telling the patient she doesn't understand anything, that she's delusional, that she is presumptuous and omnipotent … … …

She had consulted another analyst who backed her idea of interrupting that analysis, giving her the names of some colleagues amongst which was mine.

After some months had gone by … . Diletta telephones me.

She appears to me to be a hurt and suffering person. But she speaks in a programmed way about her Catholic faith and her wish to find a Catholic analyst. But, she says, she had rapidly come to realise that "one can't ask" analysts if they are religious or not, therefore she has learnt not to do so. She is a devoted practicing Catholic and lives an intense spiritual life that also helps her to change, she says. From the analysis she expects some hints on how to be able "to make a synthesis" between her spiritual life and psychoanalysis!

Perplexed, I speak to her of the dimension of suffering that I seem to receive from her, though maybe only slightly perceived by her. But for Diletta the motivation for the analysis is not to find a cure. Notwithstanding this, she is very aware of the importance for her of resuming analysis.

We begin to see each other.

In the first sessions, the previous therapist stands out largely, Diletta goes on and on about what she said to her, how she was treated, how she humiliated her, without reason … the therapist seemed a bit similar to her mother, she comments, unpredictable and mortifying … .

In the meantime I find myself working out a hypothesis for myself on who this analyst might have been … I imagine one colleague after another who, I tell myself, might have functioned in this way … .

The patient's memories are fresh and burning, they invade the sessions … I think I must let Diletta purge all her bitterness and also her violent unrecognised rage.

After about a month from the start of the analysis Diletta recounts a dream for the first time: "I was here in a session, but you were sitting in front of me instead of behind … I asked you why and you said: because you are so rich, so interesting, so full of things, I don't want to lose anything … then it turned out that you told me that you were also a believer, that you went to a nearby church every evening and that you prayed for your patients … you then said you were Orthodox … not Catholic. … who knows why Orthodox of all things … ."

While in my mind Moscow Churches unfold with their exotic images, icons and the smell of wax from the candles … Diletta is saying that the previous analyst didn't even notice when she was crying, she had to tell her … the analyst continued to speak and speak and speak so much … without even noticing that she was crying … .

I tell her the dream maybe starts to answer the question we asked ourselves the other day: why does she want to be analysed at this time?

… the dream seems to say that she needs an analyst who looks at her … that looks at her and not her own prejudices or theories … that appreciates her and backs her self-confidence; that is sufficiently similar to herself … but that some differences may be allowed to enter the field … .

Diletta reacts vivaciously saying how much she likes to imagine an exchange that is not interrupted by the differences between people … but it's so difficult for this to come about … not a chance with the previous analyst … it's also impossible with the friend that she had mentioned to me, the friend who pursues her own way of thinking with an iron logic and does not admit to anything else … it's even difficult to discuss work matters, she is aware of sometimes being a bit of a school mistress, in explaining to colleagues those things she had learnt in her greatly varied training, but it's hopeless … …

Unexpectedly another scenario presents itself to my mind, but I am reluctant to abandon the exotic panorama which I felt I had been invited to enter, I find it hard to leave the perfume of the candles and the shade of the Orthodox churches, then I say to her: Even now if we look at things from this point of view maybe it will turn out that you imagine that I, as an SPI analyst (Società Psicoanalica Italiana) am Orthodox, whilst you are Heterodox, that you have explored different approaches, have trained in different fields … ."

Diletta: "Yes, that's where the word Orthodox originates from! … but it is not a negative thing, one can be Orthodox yet not be narrow minded or have preconceived ideas". In the next session the patient begins to speak of the previous analysis once more, she relates episodes that she has already mentioned, that I seem to know about … .

But, all of a sudden, these stories seem to describe an internal leak, an "inner crazed object". An object that to Diletta appears destructive, untrustworthy, unreliable, that one can only try to tame or keep at bay, through the spiritual Catholic devotion, I think to myself.

My impression is to now understand Diletta's need for therapy, the help she seeks regarding this split dimension until now "personified" by the previous therapist. (E. Gaburri 1986). I also have the sensation that the dream constituted an invitation on her part, an invitation that she felt I handled well.

The willingness to move around the mental space, to change vertex, not letting go of the dynamic background figure; perhaps maybe this transmitted to her the possibility that two scenarios might meet. Maybe she has diffused in the field the possibility of nearing this crazed object without being too frightened.

In this sense Diletta's dream has been a precious message that emerged from her inner world, for the commencement of this analytical journey.

"The dreamer who dreams the dream is the ineffable subject of being, who, as an archivist of pain, dissatisfaction and sense of insecurity, cries out in the shape of messages represented and projected into that container which is the dreamer that understands the dream, whose reverie, as that of the mother to her child, gathers the torment and transforms it into meaning."(J.S. Grotstein 2000 p. 46). The container that is the mother and her reverie, once internalised, becomes the dreamer who understands the dream. Fear of the Unknown.

Thoughts do not need a thinker. Lies need a thinker to shape and demonstrate them. New thoughts emerge from the emotional context of the field, rather than from the minds of the subjects involved. It's about imagining a continuous and changing surfacing of new thoughts, and all we are able to do is to simply receive them, without claiming to have generated them. In the encounter with Diletta, for example, the almost delusional theme of orthodoxy and religious belonging changes its sense and becomes the matrix of a new field of significance.[4]

This manner of proceeding finds an obstacle in our fear of the unknown.

The need for security pushes us into avoiding the perturbations of the field by constructing anti-anxiety lies: explanations to which we attribute absolute truths, assumptions to which we relegate the task of making us feel protected against the unknown. Around this fear of the unknown individuals and institutions develop elaborate systems of reassurance, as Freud (1921) and Bion (1970) have described so well.

In short, we are talking about the difficulty that individual human beings have in tolerating what Freud called the impersonality of destiny which leaves us like gnats lost in the universe.

Over and above the privations imposed by a civilisation of which he, together with other men, is a member of, man succumbs to the damage that destiny inflicts upon him, states Freud (1927 p. 446). It is difficult to be entirely aware of destiny as an impersonal and casual force, it would mean feeling oneself crushed by total impotence. It is not only about the total impotence that we are born with, but being aware of our irrelevance in the universe.

"It was only by the narrowest of chances that man was not man, life was not life, and the world was not the world. You wonder at this matter, mixed haphazardly, at the mercy of fate, how it was able to constitute man, seeing as so many things were necessary to construct him. Are you not aware that a hundred million times, this raw matter, whilst it was producing man, halted to produce here a stone there a piece of lead, here a coral, there a flower, here a comet (Calvin 1988 Voyage dans la Lune. American lessons. Garzanti, Milano).

So as not to feel like gnats lost in the universe we need to seek The Truth and so it happens that we are transformed into many Saint Georges hunting for cruel dragons to subjugate or eliminate. It's worth saying that we search for a personification of destiny, of those elements which offer us the illusion of being able to anticipate it, tame it, of having remedies to oppose it with (E. Gaburri 2007).

The human individual is exposed to an unpredictable world, with weak and inadequate equipment for thought and knowledge, constructed like a fisherman's net to catch bits of truth, to capture fish-thoughts with which to nourish his mind.

To fish fresh thoughts to make sense of his experiences man lays himself bare before those emotions that he feels he cannot dominate, he shows himself with only light-weight luggage filled with acquired experiences, so as not to saturate his mind (the negative capacity).

But man tends to run away from new thoughts that pursue him, as described by S. Butler in the novel previously mentioned, they disturb him, often they pursue him because they continuously pose questions that he wanted to consider closed once and for all (L. Ambrosiano 1999). They drag him back into contact with the unknown.

A friend says to me: I've read the book you recommended to me, beautiful! But it has left confusion in two or three "drawers" in my wardrobe of knowledge, those very ones that I thought I had really put in order! This is the adventure of human knowledge, of psychoanalytical work and of Bion's work that underlines the chaotic muddle from which our knowledge stems (ever emersed in the dynamic PS-D).

The mind does not perceive single impressions, but correlations that give sense to the whole. The experiences are woven one into the other, the meaning is not univocal, its appearance does not follow a linear logic nor the cause and effect one. For this reason the paradigm of Field suggests to us that analysts must not be in too great a hurry with meanings, and not saturate the therapeutic encounter with meanings too greatly defined (A. Ferro 2005). We must encourage the willingness to change vertex, to also look at things from another view point, and to allow oneself to be caught off guard, too, by what emerges on it's own and which often has implicit therapeutic consequences that are much more efficacious than a well constructed interpretation. This availability often allows one to reach areas in semi-darkness, pre-ambivalent aspects that have not yet been verbalised, pre-individual dimensions that have not yet touched on the differences.

New thoughts emerge from the situational context of the field, we have said, and these thoughts occasionally create a space for the split dimensions of the patient's experience and self. The split dimensions are drawn closer once more so they can stay in the field awaiting the transformative moments; or so that they can exist silently beside more aware elements, without any expectation of a forced and non authentic integration for the patient (A. Ferro 1996).

Gigi

In the first meetings, Gigi tells me a familiar, dramatic personal story; in his fragile identity and jumbled, elaborate defence strategies, I seem to glimpse a "child who is trying to be born".

We begin analysis.

The analysis has been going on for almost a year, when I notice, with amazement and a certain amount of perturbation, that I'm not getting very involved in Gigi. It seems to me what I feel towards this patient is just a "normal" professional interest. I have often asked myself, privately, the reasons for this lukewarm involvement, without finding any real answers.

The existence of my lukewarm interest in Gigi was quite clear to me away from the sessions, while, when I subsequently met him, I was interested in him and empathised with him.

In one session Gigi speaks of his relationship with his girl, she, too, he says, is rather lukewarm sexually … but he understands her and justifies her because the girl, when little, was abused and that has left an open wound. This fact on the other hand, leaves him, too, wounded and impotent in his sexual relationship with her … .

He had already often spoken to me about this situation, but now I am struck by his attitude to the girl which seems hyper-protective and justifying. After a while I say to him that his attitude makes me think of "Saint George and the Dragon", the painting by Paolo Uccello … Saint George throws himself heroically to defend the girl kept prisoner by the dragon, but the girl is tied with such a slender, thin cord that one gets the impression that it is she who is holding the dragon on a lead and not vice-versa … .

After the session I was surprised by this association, apparently out of the field; I was also struck by the fact that, while listening to what in many ways was a repetitive discourse, a painting should have come into my mind that, for personal reasons, is very dear to me … . At the time I was only aware of a metaphoric intention to cure my patient from a situation of auto-idealisation. Only in the next session would I arrive partially in understanding where, unawares, the emotive situation in the field had led me.

Gigi arrives at the next session saying straightaway that he has had a nightmare. He woke up at five in the morning and then he stayed in bed tormenting himself with problems at work. He says a colleague has been promoted instead of him, and, in his drowsy state, he finds that a strong intention has taken hold of him to protest to the director, a thing he normally would have been reluctant to do ... .

Then he recalls that, yesterday, after the session, he went searching for the Paolo Uccello painting on the Internet, and all the Saint George iconography ... that evening, at first his girl friend was sexually inviting towards him, but after that she remained passive and finally she fell fast asleep ... Gigi thought that his partner was actually quite lazy to hell with old wounds and abuse! ... immediately after, he describes his dream of the previous night: he and his partner were busy on a very important, mysterious task. While carrying it out he found himself alone in a very bright hyper-tech supermarket, he's in a queue to buy a bufala mozzarella like the ones from his home town, but, while he waits, he notices that the shop assistants, between serving one client and another, are devouring an enormous quantity of mozzarella. Anyway, he manages to get his mozzarella wrapped and leaves the supermarket to reach the parking lot where he has parked his car. He doesn't remember his car very well, but a distinguished gentleman comes close to him to point it out; his is a small prestigious car that his father had given him when he was eighteen. The gentleman informs him with authority that the front tyre was turn up and that he had taken it upon himself to substitute it. The gentleman goes away ... here, interrupting his description of the dream, Gigi says that the distinguished gentleman reminded him of his analyst ... but ... As the gentleman is moving away, Gigi becomes aware that the driver's seat in the car is burning. He tries to call the gentleman back to ask for help, but can't see him any more ... then he thinks that maybe it's his fault, he may have burnt it with a cigarette, but he can't find the butt, he tries to put out the fire with a hose that he sees there, it's very long, he can't find it's nozzle ... but from a hole in the tube a rivulet of water comes out and with it he tries to put out the fire ... continuing to look at the car seat, he notices with mounting horror that an abyss is forming there, at the bottom of which there is a spark of fire that is not fully extinguished ... .

Many are the elements of the dream: a project in common (the coming wedding? the analysis itself?), or the sensation of finding himself alone; an unappeased hunger in the presence of the shop keepers, the abusive devourers of mozzarella; the ever giving, ever generous presence of the father/analyst who repairs the car wheel, but then vanishes; the relative indifference that I had noted in myself vis-à-vis Gigi—his impotence and his guilt for having smoked hashish in the past; the confusion between anus and mouth ... between hunger and persecution ... .

While I pursue these threads of thought there appears before me the image of the inflamed abyss on the car seat, like the jaws of a fire spitting dragon ... .

Gigi's mouth as a child. Suddenly I remember something that Gigi had told me during one of our first meetings.

When he was being weaned, Gigi had suffered a serious intoxication from food gone bad that forced him to stay in hospital for weeks on end with the risk of dying.

This story had remained in the shade until this moment of analysis. Now I am struck by the fact that the analyst, the "gentleman who repaired the wheel", might bring into the field the mother of the weaned child, an absent mother who had left Gigi alone before facing the "function" that should have been tackled together ... .

I limit myself to saying that for Gigi maybe the burning abyss is his mouth, hungry for the good mozzarella from back home; the analyst, I may add, would be well advised not to leave him alone to face this fire.

From here began some delicate and careful work to placate Gigi's burning and hunger without mortifying him. My counter transference feeling, up to that point lukewarm, became warm in re-evoking the traumatic event that has now found its place in the analytical field.

The dimension of relative passivity had allowed me to adhere to "let me not to the marriage of true minds admit impediments" to the transformation of the scene that was taking place before my eyes: from a Gigi/Saint George who faces the dragon which keeps the woman hostage, to a hungry Gigi, defenceless and terrorised by his mouth in flames, which he risks being sucked into.

An inversion of the meaning of the analyst's own proposed metaphor is produced when he was at a quite different vantage point.

How come, I thought, after all these months does he now seem able to tell me of an event that he certainly has no memory of? ... but the dreamer of the dream, to say it in unison with Grotstein (2000 op. cit.), speaks of the sensation of having his mouth full of flames, terrible burning, dryness in the oral cavity going right to the bottom of the stomach, that must have accompanied an experience that remained wordless ... .

The analyst, like the polite gentleman in the dream, might well have passed the fire without seeing it, occupying himself as he does with the tyre ... . But, the evocation of the painting by Paolo Uccello tells us that the analyst had, subconsciously, caught hold of something burning and on fire.

The analyst's manifest rendering let this fire stay in the background. Only in the next session, thanks to the dream, does it become a presence, taking up a position in the background as a painful and representational nucleus. The pain, until that moment, had remained without a place to live in or be thought in.

An emotive and such catastrophic experience that, in the dream dreamt the patient, the analyst himself risks leaving it all behind. A literally intolerable thought from the past, through the work of the dream, now finds a space and an affection able to be present during the work of the couple.

"Las Meninas"

In 1994 the Italian Society for Psychoanalysis promoted a congress on the theme of the analytical field ("The analyst's answer and the transformations of the field"). On that occasion, to illustrate the paradigm of Field we used as a metaphor the Velasquez painting "Las Meninas". Rivers of ink were consumed by critics to "explain" the technique with which Velasquez succeeded in obtaining this perturbing effect that is similar to a continuous and multiple reversal of *gestalt*.

The painting has been the object of a variegated decomposition by Picasso. Captured by the mystery of this painting, Picasso tried to transform it, painting, in the course of a few months, fifty eight different versions that portray the numerous perspectives that are intersected in Velasquez's work of art. Picasso's restless curiosity seems to place it into a temporal sequence which, in Velasquez's work, is a togetherness of spatial vertex.

The Velasquez painting, repainted by Picasso, is for us a good metaphor for some psychoanalytical elements included in the function of the Field.

The painting has an unprecedented breadth and depth: one can look at it as a portrait of the Infanta of Spain, as the painter's self portrait, as a painting of Spain's Royalty, as a scene of an intruder who enters the painter's studio through a door at the back, as a play of mirrors, a conversation with the spectator … .

In the painting the Infanta of Spain, her family history, the images of her parents appear evoked in a mirror that reflects them, leaning on the wall at the back.

A mysterious courtier also appears, in a very light coloured panel beside the mirror that reflects the Infanta's parents, an enigmatic figure descending a stairway … . Both the royals and the mysterious courtier are enigmatic images because they seem to be placed outside the painting, as if they were in the place of the spectator. They appear as ghosts or persons in the analytical chamber, not present in the here and now of the sitting, but evoked by the exchange taking place. The Infanta of Spain is surrounded by a group around her: ladies in waiting that are looking after her, a dwarf, a small child, and, beside him, a big dog … .

The restlessness of the painting in its polyphonic tangle, the energy in the expansion that gives the sensation of "becoming"; the spaces, the lights, the dark, the clarity, increase the sense of the unsaturated that the painting leaves with the spectator.

The spectator remains nonplussed and, normally finds himself feeling a slightly *unheimlich* sentiment, because he has the impression of watching a scene through a one-directional mirror. But the spectator is also present "in the painting" and "called to witness".

The painting seems to launch our mind towards thoughts not yet thought that, in the course of analysis, compel the analyst and the patient to face the unpredictable angles of pain, of life and the future.

Like the painting, the structure of the analytic encounter is proposed as a spatial-temporal field in which the objects, the characters, the stories and dreams are go-betweens, so that the patient and the analyst engage in a transformative course on psychic pain.

Pain does not follow a plot, it is not the effect of a cause, one doesn't catch its meaning by following a logical line, not even the traumatic one. Pain is not a point in time and space (Ferenczi 1932), it is a complexity of inner scenes (and outer ones) continually modified and re-told, in which each scene is covered by another scene (the remembrance of coverings that Freud speaks of), or is revealed in pauses and narrative obstacles … … ...

Let's consider Diletta who sees her analyst at the foot of her bed watching her while something different is about to take place, a discarding between the two of them who belong to different mentalities (Catholic and Orthodox). In the dream the setting is apparently upset (the analyst is at the foot of the bed), but the scene described in the dream is functional to the therapy of the patient who needs to be observed beyond the shield behind which she has hidden herself: the belonging to the Catholic faith being an identity factor. The narration of the dream places the analyst in a point in space, the analyst's interpretation springs from the point that the patient has placed him in. It's not a Sherlock Holmes interpretation, but an interpretation that gushes from analytical facts while they are happening (A. Ferro 2004).

For us the Velasquez painting is fertile with references and we'd like to stop for a moment to examine some of its aspects.

The first of which refers to the dimension of the patient's story, to the there and then.

The emotive vicissitudes of the patient's past history are in the session's field on various levels of figurativeness and representation. We consider that the "there and then" of the patient's story is expressed, in the session, by its mental functioning, in the here and now. With the paradigm of field the reconstruction of the past is translated into the exploration of psychic functioning, of the patient and the analytical field in its togetherness. The quality of the resources for the containing of the patient becomes important, the possibility of making the most of the transformative movements opened up by the dynamic container-contained.

Let's agree with the hypothesis that, when in therapy, the interpretation verges principally on transference and counter-transference in the here and now, without undergoing a reconstruction of the traumatic experience, the most dramatic valency of this experience risks not being reached. (W. Bohleber "Memory, trauma and collective memory. The battle to remember in psychoanalysis" The principal report in the XLV Congress of the International Psychoanalytic Association in Berlin 2007). But let us consider that the traumatic experience finds expression in the auto-protective defence organisation of the patient, in the defences that occlude thought and exploration, or they are channelled towards predefined spaces. Gigi had narrated his trauma to the analyst in the first encounters but then had put it to one side, as a not thinkable area. In an analogous way Diletta places her religious beliefs in a not thinkable niche. These niches tend to become hardly visible, not thought about in fact, by the analyst himself, who for a time, adopts a similar mental functioning to that of the patient. Analogous but not the same or identical, the analyst has developed a more complex mental functioning.

With Gigi the analyst for a while brushes close to the not thinkable trauma without gathering it up, he follows his patient's vicissitudes in their, let us say, most adult aspect: work, marriage, conflict with his father ... working on trying to put these matters right on this level (the broken car tyre). We arrive thus at another aspect that we wish to highlight.

The analyst-patient encounter goes beyond the dynamics of co-transference. In fact we conceive that some areas in the minds of both partners are attracted by basic assumptions functioning.

It is a functioning that calls upon the patient and analyst to share some basic assumptions, not as distinct and separate individuals, but in a pre individual element of an undifferentiated agglomerate.

A mental functioning on a basic level spreads in the entire field of the encounter, it defines for both protagonists the areas to be explored, because believed to be possible for thought, and those not to be explored, because they are open to nameless terror, to the paranoia cry, to the disappearance of words.

This mental functioning of the basic assumption permeates the field of the encounter, halts in it by the side of other more evolved analyst and patient functioning.

The fire in the mouth, a trace of primitive trauma, is not reached thanks to an analysis of co-transference, but is gathered thanks to the apparently casual association of a new metaphor for both participants.

And here we reach the third aspect that we intend to highlight. There is also another dimension that intersects the Velasquez painting: the first, in close up, is the back of a painting that we do not see, it seems an allusion to the halo of the unknown that things are surrounded by. While we see the painter at work, the transformation that is being brought about remains obscure.

Something analogous is presented in the Theo Anghelopulos film "Lo Sguardo di Ulisse" (Ulysses' gaze). In the film, having accompanied the protagonist in his long and doleful search for some lost reels of cinema film, as Corel (2004) mentions, at the end we spectators don't actually see what he has found again. The director offers us a blank screen, while the protagonist looks at the retrieved reels and weeps.

In the analytical scene, too, there is a painting that's not visible: the no thing. This notion was introduced by Bion (1970) to describe the halo of darkness that surrounds knowledge, and to distinguish the psychotic functioning of the mind (the impossibility to tolerate the unknown) from the (non psychotic) situation in which to live and to represent it is possible in virtue of this very limited knowledge.

The re-found traumatic narration does not assume a fetishistic value, but, as in the atmosphere in the Anghelopulos film, the finding in itself becomes the factor for development.

In fact, it shows the dependence of the subconscious: the presence of an inner thinker unknown, that follows paths that are not linear or associative and throws some suggestions into the field. We as aware thinkers can welcome these suggestions and explore new territories. The inner thinker is analogous to the dreamer who dreams the dream that Grotstein speaks of (op. cit.), and in fact plays a dream function in the state of wakefulness. (Ferro 1996) deals with this.

The association with Saint George and the Dragon occurred to the analyst by chance, it wasn't created by him, even though he thinks so. The surprise with which the analyst plucks out this association shows that in the field there are other subconscious protagonists who interact, so to speak, without our knowledge.

The analyst's inner thinker can, in the a state of wakefulness, dream about the patient, allow figurative messages to emerge that are turned to the conscious thinker who, with his reverie, receives them, transmits them to the patient, modulating the psychic pain.

This inner thinker is a representation of internalised analytical containment.

The association of the inner thinker has generated, with Gigi, the patient's dream discourse, and the figurative discourse dreamed by the patient has made sense of the analyst's association.

Only through this exchange between the dream of the night and the day dream was it possible to understand the quality of the patient's primary experience that would have, for the moment, escaped if the analyst had halted at summits more familiar to him: abandonment, masochism, homosexuality, idealisation etc.

From the image of the suffering dragon transformations have started to take place in the field.

As a result of these transformations the analyst was able to make sense of his counter-transference, in which he had averted an affective distance from his patient. And again as a result of the exchange the analyst was able to contain the impulse that might have pushed him, like a new Saint George, to feed the patient with hyper saturated interpretations.

From the height of the exchange undertaken, patient and analyst can look at and see the abyss of the dry throat of a suffering baby-dragon left alone.

An abyss that is seen as an inflamed hole where there was once a breast. The split pain was hidden behind Saint George's shining armour. The armour held Gigi in a constraint of guilt and a need to remedy, to feel guilty and try to please. Like all constraints, this one, too, puts at the individual's disposal a space with a very narrow diameter, the way Bion describes it (1997), that does not permit us to meet the suffering child.

Francesca's dream

Francesca is afraid of getting old, of dying, of getting ill. She has hypochondriac thoughts that fill her days with anxiety. She is married with children, works, but inside her she is full of nostalgia for her early youth, for Andrea, her then fiancee. Andrea when he was just a little over thirty died in an accident, a few years after they had left each other ... but Francesca continues to think about him ... At the fifth year of a good analysis, years in which she felt lifted from her anxiety and was more present in her life, at the end of the summer holidays Francesca seemed to precipitate into a vortex of anxiety, rush and hypochondria ... I don't seem to be able to reach her ... she seems in permanent flight when she brings a dream ... .

Francesca narrates the dream as soon as she lies down on the couch: "As often happens, I dreamt of Andrea, we met, we had an appointment and I was very nervous ... wondering what to wear ... that sort of thing ... he was just like then, thin, young, a boy, I thought how is it possible! With all the years that have gone by ... he was walking me through a neglected sort of garden, the sort of place you go to have a roll in the hay ... and he guides me to a slope full of yellow, autumnal leaves ... he says: remember that today is March 23rd ... I think—what should this date remind me of? It is the start of Spring ... but we are now in Autumn ... we descend and I see a clearing full of dry leaves, and in the centre there are white tulips, very beautiful, fresh as though placed in a subterranean vase ... I think it looks like a tomb ... I wake up ... yes, it did seem a tomb ... tulips are my favourite flowers ... a few days ago I gave some to a friend who was giving a party ... I always planted tulips in a pot by my window with my mother when I was a little girl ... and I would always go in Spring to see if they had opened ... then one day I planted them on my own ... I was quite little ... they didn't blossom out ... my mother looked under the earth and noticed that I had planted them head first .... "

Francesca, in the previous sessions had spoken about her terrible character, that she felt she was now discovering; she had always imagined she was good ... now she noticed she was brusque and cold ... even on her wedding anniversary, she had bought no present for her husband, through sheer forgetfulness ... ...

I, too, found her unbearable in those days ... she arrived at sessions out of breath, she began to enumerate in a great hurry her tasks for the day, what with accompanying the children, the home chores ... I had spoken to her of her desire to wear me out, skipping sessions, arriving late ... as if she felt an impulse in being brusque and—yes, distracted ....

But after the session, while I was carrying out a few chores at home, I thought that Francesca in this manner was saying: now I work, now I am an adult, and this is the way adults behave, they do what they want, they don't listen to reason, and now it's my turn, I'll get my own back on you all ....

I thought how tyrannical the analytic times might seem, I decide on the holidays, the length of the session ... it's like the mother who, "to find herself" had left the family to go and work in another city when she was seven years old ....

When Francesca recounts her dream I sense something good ... in fact, I feel that by the end of the session the field between us has changed ... I rediscover my ties to her ... find different rhythms in myself ... life and death are so mixed up together ....

This is what Francesca's dream is all about: life and death mixed up. There is no way of tracing neat boundaries. The very fact of their being all mixed up bears an ineffable beauty, Freud would say (1916).

For the very fact that they are mixed up it is not important to notice the obstacles, the defences, the artifices of mere survival. What is needed is to gather and give value to the future, what is not yet there, what has been advancing, even though unnoticed, for a long time. "In some part of the analytical situation, buried under masses of neurosis, psychosis and so on, there is a person fighting to be born. It seems to me that the function of the analyst is not to demonstrate the neurotic and psychotic mechanisms, or only as an accidental fact in the course of the work in liberating the patient ... to free the procedures that remind us of real life ... helping the child find the adult that is latent in him". (Bion 1987 p. 48)

The Field paradigm for us alludes to just this. The "task in common" between the patient and the analyst is to walk along a slender confine guided by pain and by a sense of something being born. Francesca's dream helped both the analyst and patient to face this shared task.

Conclusive considerations

The field is constituted when two people meet for a therapy, and it generates and transforms meanings. We have imagined the Field as a space that is generated between the vertex of the setting, the relationship, the therapy. The request for therapy characterises it immediately, perhaps before the first meeting and the first telephone call. As the work proceeds new meanings emerge for the request for therapy that go beyond those that the patient had explicitly formulated just think of Diletta and Gigi.

As we said, the paradigm of field includes/entails the concepts of propagation and expansion, it is traversed by vectors of significance that, often, remain subconscious for a period of time.

One could reduce the concept of field to a simple question of counter transference, but it isn't so. In fact the analyst, to receive new thoughts, needs to collocate himself into the same mental place inhabited by the patient. In this way the analyst finds himself momentarily sharing the patient's undifferentiated mental states, the Basic Assumptions implicit of his psychic functioning.

To draw close to the primordial and undifferentiated areas of the mind allows for the patient's potential specificity to emerge.

But to come close to these dimensions the patient must first inhabit with the analyst an area in common, without being submerged by the fear of the undifferentiated. In this way it is possible to make contact anew with infantile dimensions that have been silenced by the reassuring dynamics of that which is already known, and that which still, in the here and now, risks being hushed up.

From the moment in which analyst and patient inhabit a common space, (in common) the interaction is still anchored to the pre-individual states of mind, while in the field possible thoughts are circling round by way of characters, scenes, traumatic tales, symptoms … .

These thoughts, still at a figurative level, introduce themselves even before being thinkable or representational.

Diletta's religious faith, before the dream, could not have been the object of any pertinent interpretation, but, through the dream, it emerges from the world of the known significance and turns into a new idea.

In an analogous way, Gigi's infantile trauma was present as a fact in the mind of the patient and analyst, but seeing the inflamed abyss gave them back the depth of the live pain.

We have highlighted the meaning of the field as a dimension traversed by new thoughts searching for thinkers to receive and transform them.

New thoughts render us aware that in the session there are other people present, the inner thinkers and dreamers that send us mysterious precious messages for exploration in the analysis.

One condition for being able to receive these ideas, the thoughts without the thinkers (Bion 1970), is to "let me not to the marriage of true minds admit impediment", not to oppose a non linear associative course that allows for the observance of experiences coming from various summits, just the way we observe the Meninas painting.

Anyway letting oneself follow an associative course is a psychoanalyst's prerequisite at work, it is the basis of the setting imagined by Freud. The associative course is also Bion's chief advice when he invites us to be without memory and without desire.

Francesca's dream, with its reference to the impotence and anguish of death, indicates the possible start of an integrative course: the anguish of death (nameless terror) that activates the repetition compulsion and finds a place, a name, to become thinkable and representational.

The analyst himself, understandably, hesitates in venturing into these border territories. Death is frightening, and, even more, death leads to anguish regarding aspects that have never been "born".

To face these aspects with even an admittedly rich theoretical psychoanalytical load/preparation is not all. To set out, listening to the subconscious unknown thinker that is in us, makes us feel we are in a situation of dependence and keeps in the fear of the unknown in the field, the fear of the limits in our psychoanalytical knowledge.

Bion considered the diameter in psychic functioning. One takes refuge in the narrow diameter to keep the fear of death at bay, the fear of going insane. The field psychoanalytical therapy tends to enlarge the diameter into a visible and thinkable space that is tolerable to the fragile human mind and that doesn't let in too much fear.

The Ego comes into being, we notice its transformations when they have already taken place. For that reason there is a need that we, as analysts, look inside the patient for the person that is fighting to be born, that we try to glimpse in him that which he is not yet.

The analytical exploration is possible thanks to the tolerance of "no-things", that which is not yet explored, but that remains in the background as thoughts being born: the future … .

The back of a painting that is not visible in the Velasquez painting, is postponed to a moment in the future, to the amount of work that the patient has accomplished and will be able to carry forward even after the analysis has ended.

This indicates a priority task for us, that of containing as best we can the frightened part of ourselves, which, because of our fear becomes, in fact, arrogant and intolerant, and dares to reduce the unknown into "nothing".

When we are able to contain fear we can venture into discovering the subconscious, a discovery that, in curing mental pain, "enlarges the space it explores".

Notes

1. Several Analysts from different theoretical vertex have shown interest in this transience of confines. We will limit ourselves in remembering J. Bleger (1967), H. Loewald (1970), S. Mitchell (1988). However little these analysts quote Bion, and are in turn not quoted by him, they nevertheless explore very similar dimensions, each giving a coherent and fascinating theoretical vision. Ogden's (1989–2004) work verges on analogous mental territories and merits a full treatment, which alas is not possible in this presentation.
2. The close examination of this dimension of the field is concerned with Bion's "nameless terror" and it normally presents itself in the field as a death anxiety derived from the "psychotic" side of the personality. In the Basic Assumption groups a mental state comes about in which the no-thing and the nothing become isomorphous.
3. This particular formulation that we propose as the background for the analyst's mental setting is the principal change that distinguishes him from the classic "neutrality" of the analyst's classical position. This formulation is inspired by the analyst's "negative" function, capable of tolerating and elaborating the persecution ('see W. B. Yates by R. Bion). "Do not admit impediments" (at the

arrival of unborn thoughts), it could be linked to Shakespeare's famous sonnet: "Let me not to the marriage of true minds/Admit impediments, love is not love/Which alters when it alteration finds/or bends with the remover to remove/… … .

4. One could link this event as a crossing from a Basic Assumption Group to a Working Group.

References

Ambrosiano, L. (1998). Il complesso intreccio tra teoria ed esperienza clinica [The complex interweaving of theory and clinical experience]. *Riv Psicoanal 44*: 41–66.

Ambrosiano, L. (1999). Tra clinico e istituzionale: nessi possibili [From clinical to institutional: possible links]. *Riv Psicoanal 45*: 475–92.

Ambrosiano, L. (2006). The analyst: His professional novel. *Int. J. Psychanal.* 2005; *86*: 1611–26.

Baranger, M. e W. (1968). La situazione analitica come campo dinamico Cortina Milano.

Bion, W.R. (1967). Second throughts (Selected papers of psychoanalysis), London: Heinemann.

Bion, W.R. (1961). *Experiences in groups*. New York: Basic Books.

Bion, W.R. (1962). *Learning from experience*. London: Heinemann.

Bion, W. R. (1963). *Elements of Psychoanalysis*. London: Heinemann.

Bion, W.R. (1965). *Transformations* London: Heinemann.

Bion, W.R. (1970). *Attention and interpretation: A scientific approach to insight in psychoanalysis and groups.* London: Tavistock.

Bion, W.R. (1987). *Clinical Seminars and four Papers* 1987, trad. it. "Seminari clinici Brasilia e San Paolo" Milano Raffaello Cortina 1989.

Bion, W.R. (1992). *Cogitations*. Karnac Books, London.

Bion, W.R. (1997). Taming wild thoughts H. Karnac Books, London.

Bleger, J. (1967). *Psicoanalisis del encuadre psicoanalitico. Rev. de psychan.* 24(2): pp. 241–258.

Bleger, J. (1967). *Symbiose et ambiguité: étude psychanalitique*. Paris: Presses Univ. de France.

Calvino, I. (1988). Voyage dans la lune Lezioni americane. Garzanti Milano.

Corel, A. (2004). Theo Anghelopulos: Lo sguardo di Ulisse. *I.J.P.* 2004.

Corrao, F. "Il concetto di campo come modello teorico". In *Orme Contributi alla psicoanalisi.* (Tracks. Contributions to the psychoanalysis) Milano Cortina.

Ferenczi, S. (1932). Confusion of tongues between adults and the child. J. XXX 225, Milano Cortina vol. *IV*.

Ferro, A. (1996). *In the analyst's consulting room*. Hove: Brunner-Routledge. 2002.

Ferro, A. (2004). Seeds of illness and seeds of recovery: The genesis of suffering and the role of psychoanalysis. Hove: Brunner-Routledge. p. 122 [(2002). Fattori di malattia. Milan: Cortina.].

Ferro, A. (2005). Theoretical and clinical observations. IJPA 2005, *86*: 1535–42.

Freud, S. (1916). On transience. S.E. 14, pp. 305–7.

Freud, S. (1915). Instincts and their vicissitudes. S.E. 14.

Freud, S. (1921). "Group psychology and the analysis of the Ego". S.E. 18.

Freud, S. (1927). The future of an illusion S.E. 21.

Freud, S. (1937). "Constructions in analysis". S.E. 23.

Freud, S. (1938). "An outline of psychoanalysis". S.E. 23.

Gaburri, E. (1986). Dal gemello immaginario al compagno segreto [From the imagined twin to the secret friend]. *Riv Psicoanal*, *32*: 509–20.

Gaburri, E. (1992). Emozioni, affetti, personificazioni [Emotions, affects, personifications]. *Riv Psicoanal*, *38*: 325–52.

Gaburri, E. (1998). "Il campo gruppale e la non cosa" In: "Il campo gruppale" G. Rugi & E. Gaburri (a cura di). Borla Roma.

Gaburri, E., Ambrosiano, L. (2003). Ululare con i lupi. Conformismo e reverie [Howling with wolves. Conformism and rêverie]. Turin: Bollati Boringhieri. p. 152.

Gaburri, E. (2007). La promesse délirante et les flutes magiques. Revue Française de Psychanalyse ottobre LXXI, 979–997.

Grotstein, J.S. (2000). *"Who is the Dreamer Who Dreams the Dream. A Study of psychic Presences" The Analytic Press. Inc. Hillsdale*, New Jersey, USA.

Loewald, H.W. (1970). *Papers on Psychoanalysis* Yale University.

Mitchell, S. (1988). *Relational concepts in psychoanalysis. An integration.* Harvard University Press, Cambridge, Mass London, trad. it. Bollati Boringhieri 1993.

Napolitano, F. (2006). *Sete. Appunti di filosofia e psicoanalisi sulla passione di conoscere. (Thirst. Philosofic and psychoanalytic notes on passion for knowledge.).* Quodlibet Macerata Italy.

Ogden, T. (1989). *The primitive edge of experience.* Jason Aronson Inc.

Ogden, T. (2004). *An Introduction to the Reading of Bion. Int. J. Psychoanal. 85*(2): pp. 285–300.

CHAPTER SIX

The dynamic field of psychoanalysis: A turning point in the theories of the unconscious

Carlos Sopena

In this paper I will refer to the theoretical and clinical model of the dynamic field of psychoanalysis, created by Madeleine and Willy Baranger in 1961–62. I will focus on the concept of unconscious which derives from such model and which differs from the traditional model. The authors state that the field's unconscious is neither the analysand's nor the analyst's and is shaped up during the session. This is, in my judgement, a turning point in the theories of the unconscious, because it anticipates further concepts that will acknowledge the role of intersubjectivity in the formations of the unconscious.

Description of the field, its structure

The authors indicate that the dynamic field is structured according to the basic functional configuration contained in the initial agreement made by the participants, where their roles are explicitly defined. Other important aspects of the analytical framework, such as spatial and time arrangements are quite stable, for instance, the agreed terms on sessions' duration and frequency and interruptions. This belongs to the pre-conscious registry of the field.

A characteristic of the field is that even if the basic configuration is bipersonal on the level of perceptive reality, such dualism is transcended because there is a third one absent or in the discourse. Rather than a character, the third one is the place of the absent one, a symbolic rather than imaginary place. This corresponds to the core oedipical configuration of neurosis, as defined by the authors in another paper, and which may vary and become dual or even fusional at regressive moments, but the triangle is the central situation where all other situations are composed from (Baranger, 1964).

The field is essentially structured by an unconscious phantasy, but which is not created solely by the patient but by both of them and not by either one of them individually considered. Nor can it be conceived as the sum of two internal situations because it is something that is created by both of them within the unit they become at the session, something different from what they are on their own Baranger (1961–62).

According to the authors, this unit is created by the mechanism of reciprocal identifications, and they explain that if the projective identification process has the general scope identified by M. Klein, it would not be surprising that it played a decisive role in structuring any couple. The couple is created by an intergame of projective and introjective identifications, with its corresponding corollary of counteridentifications. They also explain that the projective identification of the analytical couple must work under special characteristics because it must be very limited on the analyst's side.

The concept of field meant a significant change in the manner of conceiving the therapeutical relationship since it recognized that the analyst may not only be affected by countertransference but be included in the field he or she analyzes, as well. It is about two individuals who are linked and involved in creating and elucidating this relationship, where none of them is intelligible without the other.

This also allowed understanding the transfer-countertransference relation more accurately. The latter is no longer conceived as a lineal response to transference because it results from something created in the field by both of them: *The so called countertransference is the bipersonal field as seen from the point of view of the analyst when he or she is included in the field* (Baranger, 1969).

These changes in clinical practice are based on a different concept of unconscious underlying the structure and the functioning of the field. We could say that like transference, which is at the same time a place and the contents displaced to it, the field is simultaneously the producer and the atopic place of the unconscious. The field's unconscious is neither the analysand's nor the analyst's, nor the sum of them both but the session's which includes both; this by-two unconscious which transcends individuals, is not just something given because it is only fully configured when the analytical dialogue takes place during the session.

The authors present a different unconscious, which they relate to the unconscious of therapeutical groups, particularly the basic assumptions introduced by Bion who detected the existence of unconscious formations shared by the group but which do not belong to any particular member. The field's unconscious, which is not explained enough, brings forward further psychoanalytical developments, where the participation of the other in the configuration of the unconscious will be recognized.

We will recap this issue further on.

A further redefinition of the psychoanalytic field

In 1969, W. Baranger published "Contradictions between the analytical theory and technique" where he substantially modified the definition of the dynamic field by introducing a new dimension. It reads as follows: *The specific object of study of psychoanalysis is the intersubjective field of language in the analytical situation. The field is created neither by the analysand nor by the analyst. It is created when they meet; it is a new fact which is beyond them both.*

And he adds: *The interpretation not only reflects or puts the field into words but also contributes to a great extent to its formation and orientation.*

The analytical process is the modification of the intersubjective field by means of words (Baranger, 1969).

This is a crucial change. Although the basic structure of the field as defined in 1962 is kept, the core of the interest in crossed projective identifications has shifted towards the intersubjectivity of a language field where the analytical object will be configured when both discourses meet. The field is structured in a symbolic order with its own laws and demands, which discriminates functions and places of differentiated subjects and which belongs to a registry other than imaginary projections; the latter accounts for the promotion of symmetric links which operate in the field but cannot organize it.

In 1966 Lacan's Ecrits had been published and this may have exerted an influence on W. Baranger for him to prioritize the symbolic universe of the dynamic field. This means hierarchizing the place of the Other, discriminating it from the dual ego to ego relationship. In a word field, the analysand addresses to the analyst and through him, to an impersonal Other which is the place of significants.

The concept of field and the context of previous ideas

At the end of the 40s and beginning of the 50s, H. Racker and P. Heinmann had assigned a new role to countertransference which was no longer considered an obstacle to be surmounted but a technical instrument which opened a gateway to the analysand's unconscious.

Many years before, in 1918 in his work on psychoanalytical technique, S. Ferenczi had described the analyst's resistance to his or her countertransference, which impeded keeping it under control and limited his or her capability to understand the patient. Three decades later, an essential change took place when the analytical process was recognized not to be something that only occurred inside the analysand and which the analyst tried to unveil but something that implied the unconscious of both participants. As a result, a series of theoretical-technical developments have been carried out in connection with the new role of the psychoanalyst during the healing process.

The concept of dynamic field is part of these developments. The authors have borrowed the concept of field from Gestalt psychology (Kurt Lewin) and from M. Merleau-Ponty's oeuvre, where in Phenomenology of Perception he had explained: *During the experience of dialogue a common ground is created between the other and myself, my thought and his or hers make up a single tissue, my sayings and the interlocutor's are required by the state of the discussion and are inserted in a common operation whose creator is neither of us* (Merleau-Ponty, 1945).

The French philosopher maintained that before the subject and the object bifurcate, there is a certain kind of relation with the world that will not cease to secretly determine this relation. M. and W. Baranger have considered that this common ground, this new tissue knit during dialogue is applicable to the situation created between the analysand and the analyst, at least at a descriptive level.

The changes we have been referring to derive from intrinsic factors of the psychoanalytical environment, i.e., from clinical experience and from reflecting on it. Other changes which are no less important derive from other disciplines and synthesize the influence of the culture of our times which psychoanalysis cannot afford to disregard. In this particular case, there is no doubt the influence the French philosophical and psychoanalytical approach have had on M. and W. Baranger, especially if we take into account that when they settled on either margin of the River Plate—Buenos Aires and Montevideo—they already had a solid philosophical and humanist background.

An influence to be considered, I believe, is philosopher Georges Politzer's, who questioned Freud's interpretation of dreams, arguing that he had reduced dreams to a simple figurative, regressive and mechanical translation of thoughts and to preexisting phantomatic and latent representations, which could be brought back to consciousness after overcoming the forces of resistance.

Politzer objected to how the distinction between manifest content and latent content was made. He maintained that if the latter was conceived to be something that had existed a priori as a previously assigned meaning which determined the appearance of the manifest content, it would be turned into a psychological entity. Therefore, he criticized an objectifying tendency in the way of conceiving the unconscious. In his critique of inner life, this author recognized it is very difficult to get rid of a psychology which has inherited the cult of the soul, and according to which inner life has managed to become part of the set of values (Politzer, 1927).

Politzer's critique was well founded and was the result of having carefully read Freud's oeuvre. But it is only fair to recognize that what Freud actually meant by studying dreams, was to put forth a methodological solipsism. To sieve the unconscious, he had to hierarchize the intrapsychic, telling it from information coming from the outer world and from consciousness, carrying out a theoretical exclusion. Dreams take place in an environment closed to external input, so the outer world is set aside in order to be able to study the unconscious. This results in the creation of a specific psychic place which is the most subjective phenomenon anyone can think of.

Years later, solitary, inner life's questioning was intensified. In 1936, J.P. Sartre published "Ego's transcendence", where he questioned the inwardness of consciousness. Based on Husserl' phenomenology, he wrote as follows: *The ego can neither be formally nor materially found in consciousness; it is outside, it is a world being like the other's ego. My self is no more certain than the self's consciousness of the other fellow beings; it is simply more intimate.* This accounts for the radical criticism to introspection, self knowledge and inner life (Sartre, 1936). To know oneself it is necessary to get out of oneself and to project oneself into the world.

For existentialism, the being is defined by how it is within the world. Men are, above all, a project; they are not what they are but what they are about to be. The situations in which this relation is shaped up by the world may be analyzed only in terms of possibilities, since this is something future orientated. These ideas are against XIX century romanticism, when the importance of inwardness as well as so called spiritual values were extolled as opposed to material and worldly issues.

Bringing up to date the concept of dynamic field

a) Its essential ambiguity

It is essential for the analytical procedure that each thing or event in the field be at the same time something else. If this ambiguity is lost, so is the analysis Baranger (1961–62). Ambiguity is what is not fully determined or defined.

Without ambiguity analytical listening would not take place. The analyst does not respond to the manifest discourse; taking into account the non-congruence between words and the thing, he decentralizes the analysand's discourse, often hears something different to what is being said, he stops on one word or on a discourse mishap, trying to allow the other discourse, the unconscious' discourse, to emerge.

This ambiguity takes place in the language field where words are subject to the test of double registry listening which dismantles the manifest discourse in order to bring it to life. It is crucial to release language from having a single meaning, from rigid designations, from the wall of logical discourse. The best example is free association. The dynamic field tends towards mobility and diversity; this explains why discourse changes provide the most tangible evaluation of the effects of analysis.

Analysts' main task, specially in the case of certain patients, is to try to put into words contents which bear a strong emotional load, deprived of words and images and which are, therefore, reticent to any symbolization. But it is not always a question of putting into words; according to poet Roberto Juarroz, in "Vertical Poetry", it is necessary to "unbaptize the world,/sacrifice the name of things/to gain their presence".

As to the object, resistance may struggle to compose a defined object once and for all by means of categorical designations which deny its changing variables. Then, it is a question of progressively dismantling the image which is trying to be imposed on us, to retrieve the plural changing, unpetrified object. It is a disfiguration deconstruction task, an issue that Derrida has rigorously developed. The analysis challenges certainties; to this end it produces a constant movement of figuration and disfiguration as recreation to rerouse the living forms that offer resistance against the immobility of images and labels.

There are two sides to the object: the representation side (the fellow being) and the side of the unrepresentative, which is not prone to being seized by means of a description (the stranger) and whom identifying with is not possible. The rigid designator has the effect of dissipating uncertainty; it aims at sieving not only a character trait or attribute, but the very otherness of the other. But the other as otherness does not lend itself to being described but in a very imperfect manner, because there is always a resisting remnant.

The dead-alive described by W. Baranger, and the impossibility of going through mourning, I believe, are related to the impossibility of recognizing the radical otherness of the object. This explains why the melancholic person does not know what he or she has lost when he or she loses the object.

b) Temporal structure of the field

M. and W. Baranger had an early interest in how time was dealt with in terms of past, present and future, both in the analysis and the dialectic process. By focusing on the prospective temporal aspect of interpretation, they were bringing forward an issue that was not being dealt with at that time. In the paper we have been referring to, they say that the temporal aspect of the field does not look like the time lived in common situations. The process not only tries to reconstruct the past, but to move towards the construction of the future.

Analytic time is at the same time a present, a past and a future time. It is a present time because it is a new situation, such as relating with someone who adopts a different attitude from the objects' of the analysand's history. This is why traumatic situations which are resumed in the analysis may be re-elaborated and re-integrated within a different temporal perspective.

This drive towards the future has led us to consider that the dynamic field is inhabited by temporal pulsations which are responsible for bringing it to life. The field, in its prospective aspect is not a mere repetition but a potential field open to transformations.

The prospective aspect of listening and interpretation is nothing new, at present. The hierarchization of the past is similar to the archeological attitude of the beginning of psychoanalysis, which focused on the historical reality of the patient. Nowadays, there are different viewpoints among analysts; in the patient's discourse, some of them hear the repetition of an original text, which would be their referral, others prioritize what is open to something new in the discourse, i.e., open to the possibility of generating new, particular and concrete significances. There is a shift between recalling what was already there and the psychic working out of what is created a posteriori. In this case, it would be both a question of creating new memories as well as recalling forgotten ones (Rodriguez Parodi, 2005).

In temporal dialectics, the past is not really an explanation of the present, but something (re)constructed from what is actualized in the transference, the same as future projection. The historization of the past is produced a posteriori in the present; it is a past to-come.

c) The impasse and the second look

From the clinical point of view, the most important thing is the field's mobility or its crystallization. The immobilized structure which paralyzes the dialectic process is called bastion by the authors, and it is defined as an unconscious neoformation built around a shared fantasy set-up which attributes an imaginary stereotyped role to each of them. *The bastion is an unconscious refuge of phantasies of omnipotence, jointly created by the patient and the analyst*. Bastions' mobilization is what allows the restitution of the therapeutical process dynamics.

This issue has been reconsidered and developed in "Process and non-process in the analytic work". There they write that the bastion, whose aim is to avoid anxiety, gives rise to interferences in the base structure's functioning. At that moment, the basic dissymmetry and the ternary structure are lost; a dual, more symmetrical structure takes over, where the unconscious attachment between analyst and analysand becomes an involuntary complicity against the process (baranger et al, 1983). From being something alive, dynamic and potential, the field becomes something repetitive and unproductive.

It is then necessary to give a second look to enable the analyst to change his or her perspective and stay outside the field so that he or she can contact its unconscious configuration. This is how the analyst rescues his or her function, which refers to a term beyond the relation between the two of them. It is of utmost importance to allow this third one to remain, so that the relation is kept open to a symbolic place where the interpretation may come from.

The field plays a crucial role when it becomes a symptom of the relation and an obstacle for the development of the process. Under these circumstances, countertransference may cause uneasiness. When the analyst's mental functioning feels threatened, what Pontalis has called "to put countertransference to death" occurs: It refers to the death of the intellect as a result of the lack of representations made from words or thinking processes. The patient has a direct impact, which is not mediated by words, on the analyst's psychic-body.

It is not a question of getting rid of our emotional responses but to work them out because they are the result of our receptivity to the patient's unconscious conflict. This author states that it is the unpleasant feeling experienced in countertransference which moves the analyst's psychic work (Pontalis, 1977). In other words, that the look on the field is not always a calm look, even if the analyst is generally used to going through paths where there is no signalling. It is what Bion calls negative capability. This second look on the field is a task the analyst carries out with his or her own psychic functioning and his or her symbolizing capability which will eventually result in interpretation.

d) The unconscious and the other

As we said before, the session's unconscious is neither the analysand's nor the analyst's. It is an interpsychic product which is generated when both discourses meet. The transmissions that take place occur at two levels: one is at the level of thoughts and fantasies, i.e., of symbolic elements at preconscious level; the other one, which happens simultaneously, is not a representable material exchange and it is experienced in a more direct manner at body level.

It is a verifiable fact that, from the very beginning, the analyst and the analysand have unconscious perceptions of each other. This communication between both unconscious is a complex issue and, naturally, the manner it is conceived depends on our concept of the unconscious. If we think that they are two separate and independent unconscious, it will not be easy for us to explain how representations circulate between them. We should conceive an unconscious open to the effects generated by somebody else's unconscious, which is the support of intersubjective transmissions, especially all those which exceed linguistic communication.

It should be taken into account that all communications involve different levels of functioning of the psychic apparatus and that there are constant passages taking place between them. It is practically impossible to have no involvement of the pre-conscious, so it would be more accurate to say that the processes we are referring to take place in the border between the unconscious and the pre-conscious rather than at pure unconscious level (Arfouilloux, 1997). This is how the possibilities of symbolization of what is being transmitted are preserved. Thanks to the cooperation of the pre-conscious, it is possible for the analyst to be not only the receptor but the transformer of the patient's communications as well.

In the unconscious relationship with the other, the latter is prior to the subject. Perhaps, it would not be far fetched to think that in a way, the most inaccessible Freudian unconscious already included the other. In a paragraph of The Ego and the Id, Freud defines the id as "that other"; therefore, the unconscious is not a double of oneself but that other thing inside of me which divides and separates me.

In his "Brief treaty of the unconscious", Laplanche states that the unconscious' formation begins with the enigmatic message of the other. He believes that the original seduction has a structuring function which is at the base of the formation of the unconscious. The small human being has no unconscious, and he is confronted with messages, invaded by the unconscious of the other. This author uses a translation model to explain the repression and the unconscious' configuration. This process is developed in three moments.

1) The mother's caresses are messages sent to the child and they are first inscribed by means of a simple implantation which requires no translation; 2) Such caresses are perceptive elements and are enigmatic messages the meaning of which is partially sexual. They tell something to the child he or she cannot understand and which is ignored by the mother herself. It should be borne in mind that the mother has an adult sexuality and that caresses are a source of pleasure for her; 3) What is found at unconscious level is not the "enigmatic significant" of the beginning. To be unconscious, messages have to go through a reorganization process during which a translation process also takes place on some of their aspects but it is denied to others and they become unconscious. These unconscious significants are significants which have been deprived of their significance (Laplanche, 1993).

This remainder, which has not been translated and is beyond determination, is destined to be repeated in the phantasy.

e) The unconscious on focus

The present heyday of intersubjetivism in psychoanalysis may unfortunately result in including the analytical relation within the most ample register of interpersonal relations with standardized roles, thus losing its specificity. What I actually mean to say is that the dynamic field should be differentiated from this trend.

The psychic reality takes place at a dimension other than the place where interactive phenomena happen. If the analyst's priority is the vicissitudes derived from person to person interaction, he or she will establish an imaginary dual relation with the analysand, and the central place of the unconscious, beyond personal exchanges, will be dodged. It would be more adequate to the analytical method, to have an intesubjectivity knit by language itself, with a mediating function between speakers so that the perspective change due to the second look may give rise to an interpretation which would undo the imaginary weave of intersubjectivity.

Green warns that the emphasis placed on intersubjectivity may end up wiping out the intrapsychic. According to the field's theory, the articulation between the intersubjective and the intrapsychic takes place as follows. In the analytical experience, first comes the field emerging unconscious structure, created by the analysand and the analyst during the session. The intrapsychic is built as something differentiated stemming from the intersubjective. *Second*—according to W. Baranger—*we can formulate something related to the internal world of the analysand. We misrepresent reality when we consider the analysand's unconscious fantasy the cause of what takes place in the analytical situation* (Baranger, 1969).

We have to take into account that the blurred frontier between the intersubjective and the intrapsychic is a limit which is not easily distinguished and that the unconscious elaborated during the session ends up in a subjective integration movement. The intrapsychic has to go through the Other—symbolic place—in order to be able to unfold and be recognized as such.

Our theory and practice are based on the reference we make to the unconscious, and to be consistent we have to know what unconscious we are talking about. In this sense, I believe the most remarkable feature of the field model is that it makes us reconsider the concept of the unconscious, for it has introduced a new configuration of the unconscious which results from therapeutical encounter and goes beyond the individual level. Unlike what was thought until then, the analyst is not outside the analytical experience, or the unconscious of the session or resistance. I believe this is an issue that today's psychoanalysis is working on.

The unconscious is a permanently evolving concept which has been theorized in different manners since it was discovered or invented by Freud. The first one to do so was Freud himself when he introduced the second topic. If the unconscious of the first topic, which is made up by repression, is organized as a network of representations of drives which accounts for the existence of articulated thoughts, in the chaotic id of the second topic, there are only drives which are not linked within an articulated group of representations.

Recognizing that not all psychism belongs to the representation level makes it necessary to consider not only the repressed, i.e., the represented, but that which cannot be represented and has effects on the ego as well. In other words, it is a question of thinking the unthinkable, to which end the analytical work does no longer stop at lifting repressions but goes beyond them into dark regions.

As from Freud, all the analytical orientations have different concepts behind the same "unconscious" word. After the unconscious' objectivity was questioned as to whether it was something intrapsychic and pre-existing, its concept has been gradually losing sharpness. Lacan defines the unconscious as the Other's discourse, so it occurs outside. Even if it belongs to a certain subjectivity, it has a social character because it can only appear with respect to the other, so it is inseparable from transference.

This unconscious is not something material articulated to the past, deeply buried like Pompeii. While the Freudian unconscious is continuous, Lacan conceives an unconscious which is characterized by discontinuity; this is why he introduces the existence of a logical temporality of the unconscious which appears in order to disappear later, which opens in order to close again. The unconscious is ontically evasive and unpredictable because we can only have a glimpse of it. It is not what it is but what it is about to be, or something which insists on being without being.

Madeleine Baranger says *we are caught between an impossible ontology and the threat of interpretative arbitrariness.* And she adds: *To imagine that the analyst seeks a latent content that exists behind the manifest content would be to reify something dynamic. The unconscious is not behind but elsewhere* (Baranger, 1993).

Throughout this paper I have been wondering how to explain the production of the unconscious in the intersubjective field of language. I could make the following assumption: Everything starts when two discourses meet in a secondary process, where the primary process starts, as a remainder of the manifest speech which translation has being denied to. This is how we are able to understand the construction of a "dual construction two" unconscious, a place which is detached from them but which links them at the same time. The unconscious creates bonds that strengthen the transferencial link. From this perspective, the field would be the place where the unconscious register is fixed and which produces and supports the unconscious analyst-analysand relation.

The concept of dynamic field does not belong to the past; analysts from different geographical areas are working on this concept and exploring its potential. Contemporary analysts' recognition of the intersubjective nature of the analytical process has raised the interest on the Barangers' work, who were pioneers in this issue. It is meaningful that the paper on dynamic field will be published in English, in the International Journal of Psycho-Analysis, for the first time. Thus, the dynamic field keeps spreading in time and space.

Summary

The author considers the concept of the dynamic field of psychoanalysis presented by M. and W. Baranger in 1962 a turning point in the theories of the unconscious because they conceived that the unconscious of the field is neither the patient's nor the analyst's but the session's which includes both. This unconscious generated between the two of them transcends individuals and is not limited to something given, but is something which is about to be, and it is configured when they meet at every session. This moment of change is placed in the context of both the psychoanalytical and philosophical ideas that came before it as well as the further conceptions of the unconscious, until the most recent ones.

References

Arfouilloux, J.C. (1997). "Relation d`inconnu, seduction, transfert de pensée". *Transmission, transfert de pensée, interprétation.* (Ed.), du Monde Interne, Puteaux.

Baranger, M. & Baranger, W. (1961–62). "La situación analítica como campo dinámico". *Revista Uruguaya de Psicoanálisis*, T.IV, No. 1.

Baranger, M. & Baranger, W. (1964). "El insight en la situación analítica". En *Problemas del campo analítico.* (Ed.), Kargieman, Bs.As. 1969.

Baranger, M., Baranger, W. & Mom, J. (1983). "Process and Non-Process in Analytic Work". *Int. J. Psycho-Anal, 64*: 1.

Baranger, M. (1993). "The mind of the Analyst: From Listening to Interpretation". *Int. J. Psycho-Anal, 74*: 15–24.

Baranger, W. (1969). "Contradicciones entre la teoría y la técnica analíticas". En *Problemas del campo analítico.* (Ed.), Kargieman, Bs.As. 1969.

Laplanche, J. (1993). "Court traité de l'inconscient". *Nouvelle Revue de Psychanalyse*, No. 48.

Merleau-Ponty, M. (1945). *Fenomenología de la percepción*. Fondo de Cultura Económica, México, 1957.

Politzer, G. (1927). *Crítica de los fundamentos de la psicología y el psicoanálisis.* (Ed.), Dávalos/Hernández, 1964.

Pontalis, J.B. (1977). "A partir du contre-transfert: le mort et le vif entrelacés". En *Entre le rêve et la douleur.* (Ed.), Gallimard, Paris.

Rodríguez Parodi, M.E. (2005). "Acerca de las construcciones en el análisis". *Presented at the APM in October 2005.*

Sartre, J.P. (1936). *La trascendencia del ego.* (Ed.). Síntesis, Madrid, 2003.

CHAPTER SEVEN

Working with and in the basic layer of the interpersonal field: Opportunities and dangers

Rudi Vermote

Abstract

The psychic experience of the basic layer of the interpersonal field is apprehended by linking it with several known concepts. Pathology within this basic zone is described. The particular psychoanalytic attitude in working from within this basic layer is delineated. Finally some of the dangers of this transformative approach are stressed.

The basic layer of the interpersonal field

The interpersonal field was originally defined by the Barangers (1983) and further elaborated by Ferro (1992, 1996). The concept of the interpersonal field refers to an immaterial reality. I would like to focus on a very basic and vital aspect of it, the basic layer of the interpersonal field. This text is a trial to give some form to it. The experience of such a basic layer is a psychic phenomenon that is touched upon by several authors, but not dealt with specifically in psychoanalytic literature. By its basic nature it is difficult to define it. My approach is to link several known concepts to give an impression of this peculiar psychic experience, which most readers will certainly recognise and probably put in other words and concepts. The aim of this text lies more in the recognition of this psychic experience and finding a way not to close it and trying use its forces than in delineating a clear cut concept and definition.

The basic layer of the interpersonal field has the characteristics of a feeling, and is undifferentiated. Hence it is difficult to locate it in the analyst or in the analysand, it is clearly inbetween. In this sense it corresponds to what Winnicott named the transitional space. You can connect to it, you cannot own it. It is a psychic place of vital importance where we can retreat and relax (Winnicott, 1971). One feels a link with the 'incommunicado self' or the 'true self' which corresponds as well to an indefinable feeling in contrast with the false self which is a clear and distinct entity but with defensive qualities and experienced as inauthentic (Winnicott, 1960).

As a feeling the basic layer shows the properties that Matte-Blanco (1988) defined as infinite. It is basic in the sense that it is the most undifferentiated layer of the interpersonal field. The dimension undifferentiation—differentiation, infinite-finite is probably what characterises it most. There seems to be a complex relation with separation-individuation. Paradoxically, being in contact with the basic layer seems to help to tolerate separation, while individuation is rather at a representational differentiated finite level of the interpersonal field.

The basic layer is more related to being than to doing and in this way it bears feminine and even maternal characteristics. In this way it corresponds as well with the notion of the primary mother (Kohut, 1971), the good internal object (Klein, 1935), which is not one between many internal objects but the primary internal object. The basic layer has a quality of rest, safety. In the basic layer (zone) the tone is tempered and quiet. It touches on the notion of the background experience of safety (Sandler, 1960), and felt security (Sroufe, 1996). Meltzer & Williams (1988) tried to apprehend it in their notions on 'aesthetic experience and conflict'.

There seems to be a link as well between being in contact with the basic layer of the interpersonal field and the phenomenon of positive regression (Meissner, 1996).

From a neurophysiologic point of view, the psychic experience of the basic layer of the interpersonal field is probably related to mesolimbic and prefrontal zones which are activated in attachment and in religious feelings as they are as well generalised, non-differentiated basic feelings.

Experimental approach

This basic layer of the interpersonal field seems of paramount importance in the psychoanalytical process. In an empirical process outcome study it was shown that changes in this basic layer were very significantly related with positive outcome in symptoms and personality measures (Vermote, 2005). This seems corroborated with the finding of Sandell (2005) who found that the difference between analysands who considered the results of their analyses as positive versus analysands who considered their analysis as having a negative result consisted particularly in the ability to return in times of distress to this feeling, or layer that was built up in their analysis.

Pathology and the basic layer of the interpersonal field

We owe to Balint the powerful description of the failing of this basic layer, which he called the basic fault referring to the geological phenomenon of the fault, the discontinuity in the earth's crust caused by the friction of tectonic plates. However Balint's description is maybe overly located in one person, while by its undifferentiated nature the basic layer is a psychic experience which cannot be located in or outside the person. In this it reminds us of Ogden's 'the analytic third'. Therefore the word "zone" is maybe a more evocative word than layer. It expresses perhaps better the dynamic, permeating quality of the experience. You can be in contact with the zone, be connected to it, be in it.

As Balint described, the fault in the experience of this basic layer or zone is explicit in people with a borderline personality structure (in other words: personality disorders) and in psychotics. People with a clinical borderline syndrome are very sensible to the experience of the basic layer of the interpersonal field while narcissistic patients are very often closed to it when they start therapy. Once people are in touch with people with the experience of a fault in the basic layer of the interpersonal field, they often desperately cling to the experience of this zone of psychic functioning. Like plants who are dried out and cling to revitalising water. They feel relieved when entering this zone. But as they have difficulty in finding the experience themselves, they want to own it. They mistake the analyst for the basic layer of the interpersonal field or the zone that is created in the encounter.

Working from within the basic layer of the interpersonal field

Although Bion did not describe this zone, he seemed to have been sensible to it. His notion of containment points to it for instance. But even without mentioning the basic layer explicitly, he described particularly well how to work in this undifferentiated zone, which he calls infinity. Relying on mathematical models he points out the dynamics that occur when finite psychic objects evolve from the undifferentiated zone. He describes how they take form in the finite psychic elements which he categorised in his Grid (Bion, 1965). The mental attitude that goes along with these transformations he described as being in infinity (Bion, 1970). All finite feelings and thoughts may arise in the interpersonal field with the basic zone as a background; this is further elaborated by Ferro as the alphabetisation that takes place in the interpersonal field. Of the many finite feelings and thoughts that take form in the interpersonal field, as analysts in a psychoanalytic session, we focus mostly on the finite transference—countertransference feelings and thoughts about self and other. We see them evolve in the sessions and dreams and hear in stories how they are at work in daily life. However also the zone itself can emerge as a representation. In my experience it is often, but not necessarily, in images with water, lakes and the sea. Examples from my practice are a pontoon bridge in a lake, a good and caring fisherwoman, a whale with beautiful eyes, a lake in a cave etc. Patients are mostly deeply moved when these images arise and experience it as something with great transformative value.

Difficulties and dangers in working with the basic layer of the interpersonal field

The effects of the contact with the zone or basic layer of the interpersonal field can be great and therefore its side-effects are great as well. Although most psychoanalysts see free association and free floating attention as the hallmark of psychoanalysis, the experience of the undifferentiated basic layer may be closed involuntary by the analyst in trying to understand and looking for cause-effect relations in the material of the sessions. Borderline patients usually react strongly against this attitude as they do not feel that their most basic needs have been met. However, more neurotic and narcissistic patients can collude with this approach and strengthen their defence.

Indeed the number of differentiated thought versus undifferentiated interventions seems to make a difference in this contact with the basic layer. In the beginning of a psychoanalytic therapy or psychoanalysis, some patients do not even accept some simple finite questions and feel they are losing contact with the basic layer, feeling excluded from it by such differentiated reactions. It creates terrible feelings of loss, of having no psychic base.

The number of sessions seems to play a great role. Experiencing the basic layer of the interpersonal zone happened mostly in psychotherapies of three times a week and in psychoanalyses. Changes in the number of sessions or even in the time schedule of the sessions illustrate well the importance of this variable. A patient preferred not to have a session than rescheduling one that could not take place. Otherwise it was like a false note in a piece of music as he put it. Another patient, being bombarded with beta-elements (A6 elements from Bion's Grid), kept her psychic equilibrium with excessive running. When she could bring these beta-elements in the interpersonal field, a richer psychic life developed until she was in touch, by sophisticated thoughts and dreams, with what was happening inside her (C-D row elements). However a temporary diminishing of the number of sessions from 4 to 3 because of circumstances, brought her out of the basic layer. After a period in which she could not dream, she reported a dream in which everything was floating in space without gravity, even the toilet seat which was no longer attached to the toilet. When the number of sessions could be changed again from three to four, she reported a dream in which she was in a peaceful lake in a cave. Some sessions later she could dream of Nazi figures and horrible insects and link this with memories in feelings and childhood experiences. In psychotherapies with frequencies of one or two times a week, the basic layer of the interpersonal field can be an important dimension as well, but in my experience these therapies tend to be extended over a much longer period than psychoanalyses or psychotherapies with a higher frequency.

The use of the couch facilitates the contact with the basic layer or zone of the interpersonal field, and the great forces this relieves may be a reason not to use it in some patients like borderline patients so that this contact can be dosed. Dosing can also be done by a deliberate use of differentiated interventions (column 1 & 2 in Bion's Grid), but with a danger of closing the contact with the basic layer of the interpersonal field.

It is peculiar that in working with the zone, viewed over the limited number of patients in a psychoanalytic practice, a more than expected number of patients explored spontaneously their creative possibilities and started to paint or write.

One of the dangers of an open attitude towards the basic layer of the interpersonal field is falling in love, because an opening of the contact with the basic layer or zone of the interpersonal field can be experienced as seductive and the analyst must be well aware of this. One of the reasons is probably that the zone irradiates in an undifferentiated non-verbal way and has to do as well with trust, presence, voice, smell, gaze, rhythm. Dimensions which are predominant as well in the dynamics of falling in love (see e.g., Objet a, Lacan, 1978). There is however a great difference between falling in love and the psychoanalytic contact with the basic zone. In the condition of falling in love there is desire and very finite pre-occupations—which are the opposite of the non-generalised safe and infinite feelings that characterise the basic layer of the interpersonal field which is in this sense close to what Bion advocated as being without memory, desire and understanding.

In falling in love and longing for a concrete love relationship, there is often a confusion between the concrete figure of the analyst and the experience of the basic zone that is evoked by the psychoanalytic functioning within the psychoanalytic setting.

In some patients there is a creation of separate fictional lives, a phantasy world where the zone is evoked. Living in such a world, which is in fact an extension of the interpersonal field, can have intense near psychotic and paranoid features. It can become addictive and coloured with sexual excitement.

In the same vein, there are patients who are more able to experience the in-between characteristic of the contact with the basic layer of the interpersonal field but tend to recreate it in a semi-concrete way. This can be seen as a transitional phase before introjecting the experience. Examples are a patient renting an apartment where she could retire from time to time to evoke the 'scent', the zone of the session. Another patient did so in walking in a specific area of the town, a kind of prolongation of the contact with the zone in the sessions, in this way recreating for herself a transitional place to retreat and relax.

The greatest danger comes when the analyst is identifying himself with this zone which is evoked in the sessions, and becomes a kind of apprentice magician, playing with these great forces out of his own narcissistic needs and wishes. A deep respect for the psychoanalytic frame, which makes the manifestation of the basic zone possible, is probably the best guarantee for the psychoanalyst.

Working within the basic zone of the interpersonal field may give the impression that negative feelings and transference is precluded or split off. In my experience it is rather the contrary. Against the background of safety of the basic layer of the interpersonal field, cruel and very negative feelings and objects emerge and can be dealt with. There may however be a difference: despite negative transferences, the therapeutic alliance seems to be strong when working from within the basic layer. In the destruction of the analyst-object as Winnicott (1969) described, the basic layer is not touched. This basic zone is of another level than the bundle of projections of the negative transference.

The psychic reality of the basic zone of the interpersonal field explains why patients with a basic fault tend to have prolonged analyses. In certain phases of their analysis holidays are often felt as disastrous and patients stop living, going into a kind of hibernation until the holiday is over. My experience is that it can be important to work from within the zone on tolerating separation, so that gradually the experience that the basic layer does not disappear with the separation is anchored. This is work that needs to be done a great deal at an unconscious phantasy and dream level.

If this work is not done, some patients run the risk of going into a false analysis producing analytic material solely to keep the analysis and the contact with the basic zone going. This danger is greater if the frequency of the sessions is not high enough. For some patients it may however be necessary to share the basic zone for a very long time in the sessions before they have the capacity to hold the contact with the basic layer of the interpersonal field without the presence of the analyst.

As previously mentioned, the contact with the basic zone requires that the analyst adopts an attitude not of understanding or constructing, but of being in infinity with a restoration of the Great Mother (Bion, 1970). It is evident that this does not preclude working at another finite level, however it is important to keep in contact with the undifferentiated, infinite basic zone of the interpersonal field and the spontaneous dynamics between the two levels as described by Bion.

In conclusion

The basic zone of the interpersonal field is a vital undifferentiated experience which is mostly latent. Within the artificial psychoanalytic frame it becomes manifest and with a specific attitude of the analyst—working from the infinite—the analytic couple can work with and within it until the analysand does not need the analyst any longer to be connected to this vital psychic layer. This kind of work is of paramount importance in patients with a basic fault, but is, at the same time, dangerous in this kind of patient.

References

Balint, M. (1968). *The Basic Fault. Therapeutic Aspects of Regression.* London: Tavistock Publications.

Baranger, M. & Baranger, W. et al. (1983). Process and non-process in analytic work. *Int. J. Psychoanal.*, *64*: 1–15.

Ferro, A. (1992). *The Bipersonal Field: Experiences in Child Analysis.* London: Routledge.

Ferro, A. (1996). In the Analyst's Consulting Room. London: Brunner-Routledge, 2002.

Bion, W.R. (1965). *Transformations*. London: H. Karnac Books.

Bion, W.R. (1970). *Attention and Interpretation*. London: H. Karnac Books.

Klein, M. (1935). A contribution to the psychogenesis of manic-depressive states. In: Klein, M., *The Writings of Melanie Klein. Volume I: Love, Guilt and Reparation*. (pp. 262–289). London: Hogarth Press.

Kohut, H. (1971). *The Analysis of the Self.* New York: International University Press.

Lacan, Jacques (1978). *The Four Fundamentals of Psychoanalysis*, translated by Alan Sheridan. New York: W.W. Norton & Company, Inc.

Matte-Blanco, I. (1988). *Thinking, Feeling and Being.* London and New York: Routledge and the Institute of Psycho-Analysis.

Meissner, W.W. (1996). *The Therapeutic Alliance.* New Haven: Yale University Press.

Meltzer, D. & Harris Williams, M. (1988). The apprehension of beauty: The role of aesthetic conflict in development, art and violence. Perthshire, Scotland: Clunie Press [Buenos Aires: Spatia, 1990].

Sandell, R. (2005, March). *Learning From the Patients Through Research.* Paper presented at the 18th Conference of the European Psychoanalytical Federation. Vilamoura, Portugal. (reference to be completed, published by now I expect).

Sandler J. (1960). The background of safety. *International Journal of Psychoanalysis, 41*: 352–356.

Sroufe, L.A. (1996). *Emotional Development: The Organization of Emotional Life in the Early Years.* New York: Cambridge University Press.

Vermote, R. (2005). *Touching Inner Change: Psychoanalytically Informed Hospitalization-Based Treatment of Personality Disorders: A Process-Outcome Study.* Leuven, Belgium: Catholic University Press.

Winnicott, D.W. (1960). Ego distortion in terms of true and false self. In: Winnicott, D.W., *The Maturational Processes and the Facilitating Environment.* (pp. 140–152). London: Hogarth Press.

Winnicott, D.W. (1969). The Use of an Object. *International Journal of Psychoanalysis, 50*: 711–716.

Winnicott, D.W. (1971). *Playing and Reality.* New York: Basic Books.

CHAPTER EIGHT

The analytic third: Working with intersubjective clinical facts

Thomas H. Ogden

Abstract

In this paper, two clinical sequences are presented in an effort to describe the methods by which the analyst attempts to recognise, understand and verbally symbolise for himself and the analysand the specific nature of the moment-to-moment interplay of the analyst's subjective experience, the subjective experience of the analysand and the intersubjectively-generated experience of the analytic pair (the experience of the analytic third). The first clinical discussion describes how the intersubjective experience created by the analytic pair becomes accessible to the analyst in part through the analyst's experience of 'his own' reveries, forms of mental activity that often appear to be nothing more than narcissistic self-absorption, distractedness, compulsive rumination, daydreaming and the like. A second clinical account focuses on an instance in which the analyst's somatic delusion, in conjunction with the analysand's sensory experiences and body-related fantasies, served as a principal medium through which the analyst experienced and came to understand the meaning of the leading anxieties that were being (intersubjectively) generated.

And he is not likely to know what is to be done unless he lives in what is not merely the present, but the present moment of the past, unless he is conscious, not of what is dead, but of what is already living (T. S. Eliot, 1919, p. 11).

On this occasion of the celebration of the 75th anniversary of the founding of The International Journal of Psycho-Analysis, I shall endeavour to address an aspect of what I understand to be 'the present moment of the past' of psychoanalysis. It is my belief that an important facet of this 'present moment' for psychoanalysis is the development of an analytic conceptualisation of the nature of the interplay of subjectivity and intersubjectivity in the analytic setting and the exploration of the implications for technique that these conceptual developments hold.

In this paper, I shall present clinical material from two analyses in an effort to illustrate some of the ways in which an understanding of the interplay of subjectivity and intersubjectivity (Ogden, 1992a), (1992b) influences the practice of psychoanalysis and the way in which clinical theory is generated. As will be seen, I consider the dialectical movement of subjectivity and intersubjectivity to be a central clinical fact of psychoanalysis, which all clinical analytic thinking attempts to describe in ever more precise and generative terms.

The conception of the analytic subject, as elaborated in the work of Klein and Winnicott, has led to an increasingly strong emphasis on the interdependence of subject and object in psychoanalysis (Ogden, 1992b). I believe that it is fair to say that contemporary psychoanalytic thinking is approaching a point where one can no longer simply speak of the analyst and the analysand as separate subjects who take one another as objects. The idea of the analyst as a neutral blank screen for the patient's projections is occupying a position of steadily diminishing importance in current conceptions of the analytic process.

Over the past fifty years, psychoanalysts have changed their view of their own method. It is now widely held that, instead of being about the patient's intrapsychic dynamics, interpretation should be made about the interaction of patient and analyst at an intrapsychic level (O'Shaughnessy, 1983, p. 281).[1]

My own conception of analytic intersubjectivity places central emphasis on its dialectical nature (Ogden, 1979), (1982), (1985),

(1986), (1988), (1989). This understanding represents an elaboration and extension of Winnicott's notion that '"There is no such thing as an infant" [apart from the maternal provision]' (quoted in Winnicott, 1960, p. 39, fn.). I believe that, in an analytic context, there is no such thing as an analysand apart from the relationship with the analyst, and no such thing as an analyst apart from the relationship with the analysand. Winnicott's statement is, I believe, intentionally incomplete. He assumes that it will be understood that the idea that there is no such thing as an infant is playfully hyperbolic and represents one element of a larger paradoxical statement. From another perspective (from the point of view of the other 'pole' of the paradox), there is obviously an infant and a mother who constitute separate physical and psychological entities. The mother—infant unity coexists in dynamic tension with the mother and infant in their separateness.

Similarly, the intersubjectivity of the analyst—analysand coexists in dynamic tension with the analyst and the analysand as separate individuals with their own thoughts, feelings, sensations, corporal reality, psychological identity and so on. Neither the intersubjectivity of the mother—infant nor that of the analyst—analysand (as separate psychological entities) exists in pure form. The intersubjective and the individually subjective each create, negate and preserve the other (see Ogden, 1992b, for a discussion of the dialectic of oneness and twoness in early development and in the analytic relationship). In both the relationship of mother and infant and of analyst and analysand, the task is not to tease apart the elements constituting the relationship in an effort to determine which qualities belong to each individual participating in it; rather, from the point of view of the interdependence of subject and object, the analytic task involves an attempt to describe as fully as possible the specific nature of the experience of the interplay of individual subjectivity and intersubjectivity.

In the present paper, I shall attempt to trace in some detail the vicissitudes of the experience of being simultaneously within and outside of the intersubjectivity of the analyst—analysand, which I will refer to as 'the analytic third'. This third subjectivity, the intersubjective analytic third Green's [1975] 'analytic object'), is a product of a unique dialectic generated by (between) the separate subjectivities of analyst and analysand within the analytic setting.[2]

I will present portions of two analyses which highlight different aspects of the dynamic interplay of subjectivities constituting the analytic third. The first fragment of an analysis focuses on the importance of the most mundane, everyday aspects of the background workings of the mind (which appear to be entirely unrelated to the patient) in the service of recognising and addressing the transference—countertransference.

The second clinical vignette provides an opportunity to consider an instance in which the analytic third was experienced by the analyst and analysand largely through the medium of somatic delusion and other forms of bodily sensations and body-related fantasies. I shall discuss the analyst's task of using verbal symbols to speak with a voice that has lived within the intersubjective analytic third, has been changed by that experience, and is able to speak about it, in his own voice, as analyst to the analysand (who has also been a part of the experience of the third).

Clinical illustration: The purloined letter

In a recent meeting with Mr L, an analysand with whom I had been working for about three years, I found myself looking at an envelope on the table next to my chair in my consulting room. For the previous week or ten days, I had been using this envelope to jot down phone numbers retrieved from my answering machine, ideas for classes I was teaching, errands I had to attend to, and other notes to myself. Although the envelope had been in plain view for over a week, until that moment in the meeting I had not noticed that there was a series of vertical lines in the lower right-hand portion of the front of the envelope, markings which seemed to indicate that the letter had been part of a bulk mailing. I was taken aback by a distinct feeling of disappointment: the letter that had arrived in the envelope was from a colleague in Italy, who had written to me about a matter that he felt was delicate and should be kept in strictest confidence between us.

I then looked at the stamps and for the first time noticed two further details. The stamps had not been cancelled, and one of the three stamps had words on it that to my surprise I could read. I saw the words 'Wolfgang Amadeus Mozart' and realised after a moment's delay that the words were a name with which I was familiar and were 'the same' in Italian as in English.

As I retrieved myself from this reverie, I wondered how this might be related to what was currently going on between myself and the patient. The effort to make this shift in psychological states felt like the uphill battle of attempting to 'fight repression' that I have experienced while attempting to remember a dream that is slipping away on waking. In years past, I have put aside such 'lapses of attention' and endeavoured to devote myself to making sense of what the patient was saying, since, in returning from such reveries, I am inevitably a bit behind the patient.

I realised that I was feeling suspicious about the genuineness of the intimacy that the letter had seemed to convey. My fleeting fantasy that the letter had been part of a bulk mailing reflected a feeling that I had been duped. I felt that I had been naïve and gullible, ready to believe that I was being entrusted with a special secret. I had a number of fragmentary associations, which included the image of a mail sack full of letters with stamps that had not been cancelled, a spider's egg sac, Charlotte's Web, Charlotte's message on the cob-web, Templeton the rat, and innocent Wilbur. None of these thoughts seemed to scratch the surface of what was occurring between Mr L and myself: I felt as if I were simply going through the motions of countertransference analysis, in a way that seemed forced.

As I listened to Mr L, a 45-year-old director of a large non-profit-making agency, I was aware that he was talking in a way that was highly characteristic of him—he sounded weary and hopeless, and yet was doggedly trudging on with his production of 'free associations'. During the entire period of the analysis, Mr L had been struggling mightily to escape the confines of his extreme emotional detachment both from himself and from other people. I thought of his description of his driving up to the house in which he lives and not being able to feel it was his house. When he walked inside, he was greeted by 'the woman and four children who lived there', but could not feel they were his wife and his children. 'It's a sense of myself not being in the picture and yet I'm there. In that second of recognition of not fitting in, it's a feeling of being separate, which is right next to feeling lonely.'

I tried out in my own mind the idea that perhaps I felt duped by him and taken in by the apparent sincerity of his effort to talk to me; but this idea rang hollow to me. I was reminded of the frustration in Mr L's voice as he explained to me again and again that he knew that he must be feeling something, but he did not have a clue what it might be.

The patient's dreams were regularly filled with images of paralysed people, prisoners, and mutes. In a recent dream he had succeeded, after expending enormous energy, in breaking open a stone, only to find hieroglyphics carved into the interior of the stone (like a fossil). His initial joy was extinguished by his recognition that he could not understand a single element of the meaning of the hieroglyphics. In the dream, his discovery was momentarily exciting, but ultimately an empty, painfully tantalising experience that left him in deep despair. Even the feeling of despair was almost immediately obliterated upon awakening and became a lifeless set of dream images that he 'reported' to me (as opposed to telling to me). The dream had become a sterile memory and no longer felt alive as a set of feelings.

I considered the idea that my own experience in the hour might be thought of as a form of projective identification in which I was participating in the patient's experience of despair at being unable to discern and experience an inner life that seemed to lie behind an impenetrable barrier. This formulation made intellectual sense, but felt clichéd and emotionally lacking. I then drifted into a series of narcissistic, competitive thoughts concerning professional matters, which began to take on a ruminative quality. These ruminations were unpleasantly interrupted by the realisation that my car, which was in a repair shop, would have to be collected before 6:00 p.m., when the shop closed. I would have to be careful to end the last analytic hour of the day at precisely 5:50 p.m. if there were to be any chance at all of my getting to the garage before it closed. In my mind, I had a vivid image of myself standing in front of the closed garage doors with the traffic roaring behind me. I felt an intense helplessness and rage (as well as some self-pity) about the way in which the owner of the garage had shut his doors at precisely 6:00 p.m., despite the fact that I had been a regular customer for years and he knew full well that I would need my car. In this fantasised experience, there was a profound, intense feeling of desolation and isolation, as well as a palpable physical sensation of the hardness of the pavement, the smell of the stench of the exhaust fumes, and the grittiness of the dirty glass garage-door windows.

Although at the time I was not fully conscious of it, in retrospect I can better see that I was quite shaken by this series of feelings and images, which had begun with my narcissistic/competitive ruminations and had ended with the fantasies of impersonally ending the hour of my last patient of the day and then being shut out by the owner of the garage.

As I returned to listening in a more focused way to Mr L, I laboured to put together the things that he was currently discussing: his wife's immersion in her work and the exhaustion that both he and his wife felt at the end of the day; his brother-in-law's financial reversals and impending bankruptcy; an experience while jogging, in which the patient was involved in a near accident with a motor-cyclist who was riding recklessly. I could have taken up any one of these images as a symbol of the themes that we had previously discussed, including the very detachment that seemed to permeate all that the patient was talking about, as well as the disconnection I felt both from him and from myself. However, I decided not to intervene, because it felt to me that if I were to try to offer an interpretation at this point I would only be repeating myself and saying something for the sake of reassuring myself that I had something to say.

The phone in my office had rung earlier in the meeting and the answering machine had clicked twice to record a message before resuming its silent vigil. At the time of the call, I had not consciously thought about who might be calling, but at this point in the hour I checked the clock to see how much longer it would be before I could retrieve the message. I felt relieved to think of the sound of a fresh voice on the answering-machine tape. It was not that I imagined finding a specific piece of good news; it was more that I yearned for a crisp, clear voice. There was a sensory component to the fantasy—I could feel a cool breeze wash across my face and enter my lungs relieving the suffocating stillness of an overheated, unventilated room. I was reminded of the fresh stamps on the envelope—clear, vibrant in their colours, unobscured by the grim, mechanical, indelible scarring of machine-made cancellation marks.

I looked again at the envelope and noticed something that I had been only subliminally aware of all along: my name and address had been typed on a manual typewriter—not a computer, not a labelling machine, not even an electric typewriter. I felt almost joyous about the personal quality with which my name had been 'spoken'. I could almost hear the idiosyncratic irregularities of each typed letter: the inexactness of the line, the way in which each 't' was missing its upper portion above the bar. This felt to me like the accent and inflection of a human voice speaking to me, knowing my name.

These thoughts and feelings, as well as the sensations associated with these fantasies, brought to mind (and body) something that the patient had said to me months earlier, but subsequently had not mentioned. He had told me that he felt closest to me not when I said things that seemed right, but when I made mistakes, when I got things wrong. It had taken me these months to understand in a fuller way what he had meant when he had said this to me. At that point in the meeting, I began to be able to describe for myself the feelings of desperateness that I had been feeling in my own and the patient's frantic search for something human and personal in our work together. I also began to feel that I understood something of the panic, despair and anger associated with the experience of colliding again and again with something that appears to be human, but feels mechanical and impersonal.

I was reminded of Mr L's description of his mother as 'brain dead'. The patient could not remember a single instance of her ever having shown any evidence of feeling anger or an intense feeling of any sort. She immersed herself in housework and 'completely uninspired cooking'. Emotional difficulties were consistently met with platitudes. For example, when the patient, as a 6-year-old, was terrified each night that there were creatures under his bed, his mother would tell him, 'There's nothing there to be afraid of'. This statement became a symbol in the analysis of the discord between the accuracy of the statement, on the one hand (there were, in fact, no creatures under his bed), and, on the other, the unwillingness/inability of his mother to recognise the inner life of the patient (there was something he was frightened of that she refused to acknowledge, identify with or even be curious about).

Mr L's chain of thoughts—which included the idea of feeling exhausted, his brother-in-law's impending bankruptcy, and the potentially serious or even fatal accident—now struck me as a reflection of his unconscious attempts to talk to me about his inchoate feeling that the analysis was depleted, bankrupt, and dying. He was experiencing the rudiments of a feeling that he and I were not talking to one another in a way that felt alive; rather, I seemed to him unable to be other than mechanical with him, just as he was unable to be human with me.

I told the patient that I thought that our time together must feel to him like a joyless obligatory exercise, something like a factory job where one punches in and out with a time card. I then said that I had the sense that he sometimes felt so hopelessly stifled in the hours with me that it must have felt like being suffocated in something that appears to be air, but is actually a vacuum.

Mr L's voice became louder and fuller in a way that I had not heard before as he said, 'Yes, I sleep with the windows wide open for fear of suffocating during the night. I often wake up terrified that someone is suffocating me as if they have put a plastic bag over my head'. The patient went on to say that when he walked into my consulting room, he regularly felt that the room was too warm and that the air was disturbingly still. He said that it had never once occurred to him to ask me either to turn off the heater at the foot of the couch or to open a window, in large part because he had not been fully aware until then that he had had such feelings. He said that it was terribly discouraging to realise how little he allowed himself to know about what was going on inside of him, even to the point of not knowing when a room felt too warm to him.

Mr L was silent for the remaining fifteen minutes of the session. A silence of that length had not previously occurred in the analysis. During that silence, I did not feel pressured to talk. In fact, there was a considerable feeling of repose and relief in the respite from what I now viewed as the 'anxious mentation' that had so often filled the hours. I became aware of the tremendous effort that Mr L and I regularly expended in an effort to keep the analysis from collapsing into despair: I imagined the two of us in the past frantically trying to keep a beach ball in the air, punching it from one to the other. Toward the end of the hour, I became drowsy and had to fight off sleep.

The patient began the next meeting by saying that he had been awakened by a dream early that morning. In the dream he was underwater and could see other people, who were completely naked. He noticed that he too was naked, but he did not feel self-conscious about it. He was holding his breath and felt panicky that he would drown when he could no longer hold his breath. One of the men, who was obviously breathing underwater without difficulty, told him that it would be okay if he breathed. He very warily took a breath and found that he could breathe. The scene changed, although he was still underwater. He was crying in deep sobs and was feeling a profound sadness. A friend, whose face he could not make out, talked to him. Mr L said that he felt grateful to the friend for not trying to reassure him or cheer him up.

The patient said that when he awoke from the dream he felt on the verge of tears. He said he had got out of bed because he just wanted to feel what he was feeling, although he did not know what he was sad about. Mr L noticed the beginnings of his familiar attempts to change the feeling of sadness into feelings of anxiety about office business or worry about how much money he had in the bank, or other matters with which he 'distracts' himself.

Discussion

The foregoing account was offered not as an example of a watershed in an analysis, but rather in an effort to convey a sense of the dialectical movement of subjectivity and intersubjectivity in the analytic setting. I have attempted to describe something of the way in which my experience as an analyst (including the barely perceptible and often extremely mundane background workings of my mind) are contextualised by the intersubjective experience created by analyst and analysand. No thought, feeling or sensation can be considered to be the same as it was or will be outside of the context of the specific (and continually shifting) intersubjectivity created by analyst and analysand.[3]

I would like to begin the discussion by saying that I am well aware that the form in which I have presented the clinical material was a bit odd, in that I give almost no information of the usual sort about Mr L until rather late in the presentation. This was done in an effort to convey a sense of the degree to which Mr L was at times quite absent from my conscious thoughts and feelings. My attention was not at all focused on Mr L during these periods of 'reverie' (I use Bion's term reverie to refer not only to those psychological states that clearly reflect the analyst's active receptivity to the analysand, but also to a motley collection of psychological states that seem to reflect the analyst's narcissistic self-absorption, obsessional rumination, day-dreaming, sexual fantasising, and so on).

Turning to the details of the clinical material itself as it unfolded, my experience of the envelope (in the context of this analysis) began with my noticing the envelope, which, despite the fact that it had been physically present for weeks, at that moment came to life as a psychological event, a carrier of psychological meanings, that had not existed prior to that moment. I view these new meanings not simply as a reflection of a lifting of a repression within me; rather, I understand the event as a reflection of the fact that a new subject (the analytic third) was being generated by (between) Mr L and myself, which resulted in the creation of the envelope as an 'analytic object' (Bion, 1962); (Green, 1975). When I noticed this 'new object' on my table, I was drawn to it in a way that was so completely ego-syntonic as to be an almost completely unselfconscious event for me. I was struck by the machine-made markings on the envelope, which again had not been there (for me) up to this point: I experienced these markings for the first time in the context of a matrix of meanings having to do with disappointment about the absence of a feeling of being spoken to in a way that felt personal. The uncancelled stamps were similarly 'created' and took their place in the intersubjective experience that was being elaborated. Feelings of estrangement and foreignness mounted to the point where I hardly recognised Mozart's name as a part of a 'common language'.

A detail that requires some explanation is the series of fragmentary associations having to do with Charlotte's Web. Although highly personal and idiosyncratic to my own life experience, these thoughts and feelings were also being created anew within the context of the experience of the analytic third. I had consciously known that Charlotte's Web was very important to me, but the particular significance of the book was not only repressed, but had also not yet come into being in such a way that it would exist in this hour. It was not until weeks after the meeting being described that I became aware that this book was originally (and was in the process of becoming) intimately associated with feelings of loneliness. I realised for the first time (in the following weeks) that I had read this book several times during a period of intense loneliness in my childhood, and that I had thoroughly identified with Wilbur as a misfit and outcast. I view these (largely unconscious) associations to Charlotte's Web not as a recollection of a memory that had been repressed, but as the creation of an experience (in and through the analytic intersubjectivity) that had not previously existed in the form that it was now taking. This conception of analytic experience is central to the current paper: the analytic experience occurs on the cusp of the past and the present, and involves a 'past' that is being created anew (for both analyst and analysand) by means of an experience generated between analyst and analysand (i.e., within the analytic third).

Each time my conscious attention shifted from the experience of 'my own' reveries to what the patient was saying and how he was saying it to me and being with me, I was not 'returning' to the same place I had left seconds or minutes earlier. In each instance, I was changed by the experience of the reverie, sometimes only in an imperceptibly small way. In the course of the reverie just described, something had occurred that is in no way to be considered magical or mystical. In fact, what occurred was so ordinary, so unobtrusively mundane, as to be almost unobservable as an analytic event.

When I refocused my attention on Mr L after the series of thoughts and feelings concerning the envelope, I was more receptive to the schizoid quality of his experience and to the hollowness of both his and my own attempts to create something together that felt real. I was more keenly aware of the feeling of arbitrariness associated with his sense of his place in his family and the world, as well as the feeling of emptiness associated with my own efforts at being an analyst for him.

I then became involved in a second series of self-involved thoughts and feelings (following my only partially satisfactory attempt to conceptualise my own despair and that of the patient in terms of projective identification).[4] My thoughts were interrupted by anxious fantasies and sensations concerning the closing of the garage and my need to end the last analytic hour of the day 'on time'. My car had been in the garage the entire day, but it was only with Mr L at precisely that moment that the car as analytic object was created. The fantasy involving the closing of the garage was created at that moment not by me in isolation, but through my participation in the intersubjective experience with Mr L. Thoughts and feelings concerning the car and the garage did not occur in any of the other analytic hours in which I participated during that day.

In the reverie concerning the closing of the garage and my need to end the last analytic hour of the day 'on time', the experience of bumping up against immovable mechanical inhumanness in myself and others was repeated in a variety of forms. Interwoven with the fantasies were sensations of hardness (the pavement, glass and grit) and suffocation (the exhaust fumes). These fantasies generated a sense of anxiety and urgency within me that was increasingly difficult for me to ignore (although in the past I might well have dismissed these fantasies and sensations as having no significance for the analysis except as an interference to be overcome).

'Returning' to listening to Mr L, I was still feeling quite confused about what was occurring in the session and was sorely tempted to say something to dissipate my feelings of powerlessness. At this point, an event that had 'occurred' earlier in the hour (the phone call recorded by the answering machine), occurred for the first time as an analytic event (that is, as an event that held meaning within the context of the intersubjectivity that was being elaborated). The 'voice' recorded on the answering-machine tape now held the promise of being the voice of a person who knew me and would speak to me in a personal way. The physical sensations of breathing freely and suffocating were increasingly important carriers of meaning. The envelope became a still different analytic object from the one that it had been earlier in the hour: it now held meaning as a representation of an idiosyncratic, personal voice (the hand-typed address with an imperfect 't').

The cumulative effect of these experiences within the analytic third led to the transformation of something the patient had said to me months earlier about feeling closest to me when I made mistakes. The patient's statement took on new meaning, but I think it would be more accurate to say that the (remembered) statement was now a new statement for me, and in this sense was being made for the first time.

At this point in the hour, I began to be able to use language to describe for myself something of the experience of confronting an aspect of another person, and of myself, that felt frighteningly and irrevocably inhuman. A number of the themes that Mr L had been talking about now took on a coherence for me that they had not held before: the themes now seemed to me to converge on the idea that Mr L was experiencing me and the discourse between us as bankrupt and dying. Again, these 'old' themes were now (for me) becoming new analytic objects that I was encountering freshly. I attempted to talk to the patient about my sense of his experience of me and the analysis as mechanical and inhuman. Before I began the intervention, I did not consciously plan to use the imagery of machines (the factory and the time clock) to convey what I had in mind; I was unconsciously drawing on the imagery of my reveries concerning the mechanical (clock-determined) ending of an analytic hour and the closing of the garage. I view my 'choice' of imagery as a reflection of the way in which I was 'speaking from' the unconscious experience of the analytic third (the unconscious intersubjectivity being created by Mr L and myself). At the same time, I was speaking about the analytic third from a position (as analyst) outside of it.

I went on in an equally unplanned way to tell the patient of an image of a vacuum chamber (another machine), in which something that appeared to be life-sustaining air was, in fact, emptiness (here, I was unconsciously drawing on the sensation-images of the fantasised experience of exhaust-filled air outside the garage and the breath of fresh air associated with the answering-machine fantasy).[5] Mr L's response to my intervention involved a fullness of voice that reflected a fullness of breathing (a fuller giving and taking). His own conscious and unconscious feelings of being foreclosed from the human had been experienced in the form of images and sensations of suffocation at the hands of the killing mother/analyst (the plastic bag [breast] that prevented him from being filled with life-sustaining air).

The silence at the end of the hour was in itself a new analytic event and reflected a feeling of repose that stood in marked contrast to the image of being violently suffocated in a plastic bag or of feeling disturbingly stifled by the still air in my consulting room. There were two additional aspects of my experience during this silence that held significance: the fantasy of a beach ball being frantically kept aloft by being punched between Mr L and myself, and my feeling of drowsiness. Although I felt quite soothed by the way in which Mr L and I were able to be silent together (in a combination of despair, exhaustion and hope), there was an element in the experience of the silence (in part, reflected in my somnolence) that felt like faraway thunder (which I retrospectively view as warded-off anger.)

I shall only comment briefly on the dream with which Mr L opened the next hour. I understand it as simultaneously a response to the previous hour and the beginnings of a sharper delineation of an aspect of the transference—countertransference, in which Mr L's fear of the effect of his anger on me and of his homosexual feelings toward me were becoming predominant anxieties (earlier on, I had had clues about these, which I had been unable to use as analytic objects, e.g., the image and sensation of roaring traffic behind me in my garage fantasy).

In the first part of the dream, the patient was underwater with other naked people, including a man who told him that it would be alright to breathe, despite his fear of drowning. As he breathed, he found it hard to believe he was really able to do so.

In the second part of Mr L's dream, he was sobbing with sadness while a man, whose face he could not make out, stayed with him but did not try to cheer him up.

I view this dream as in part an expression of Mr L's feeling that in the previous hour the two of us had together experienced and begun to better understand something important about his unconscious ('underwater') life and that I was not afraid of being overwhelmed (drowned) by his feelings of isolation, sadness and futility, nor was I afraid for him. As a result, he dared to allow himself to be alive (to inhale) that which he formerly feared would suffocate him (the vacuum breast/analyst). In addition, there was a suggestion that the patient's experience did not feel entirely real to him in that, in the dream, he found it hard to believe he was really able to do what he was doing.

In the second portion of Mr L's dream, he represented more explicitly his enhanced ability to feel his sadness in such a way that he felt less disconnected from himself and from me. The dream seemed to me to be in part an expression of gratitude to me for not having robbed the patient of the feelings he was beginning to experience, i.e., for not interrupting the silence at the end of the previous day's meeting with an interpretation or otherwise attempting to dissipate or even transform his sadness with my words and ideas.

I felt that, in addition to the gratitude (mixed with doubt) that Mr L was experiencing in connection with these events, there were less-acknowledged feelings of ambivalence toward me. I was partly alerted to this possibility by my own drowsiness at the end of the previous hour, which often reflects my own state of defendedness. The fantasy of punching the beach ball (breast) suggested that it might well be anger that was being warded off. Subsequent events in the analysis led me to feel increasingly convinced that the facelessness of the man in the second portion of the dream was in part an expression of the patient's (maternal transference) anger at me for being so elusive as to be shapeless and nondescript (as he felt himself to be). This idea was borne out in the succeeding years of analysis as Mr L's anger with me for 'being nobody in particular' was directly expressed. In addition, on a more deeply unconscious level, the patient's being invited by the naked man to breathe in the water reflected what I felt to be an intensification of Mr L's unconscious feeling that I was seducing him into being alive in the room with me in a way that often stirred homosexual anxiety (represented by the naked man's encouraging Mr L to take the shared fluid into his mouth). The sexual anxiety reflected in this dream was not interpreted until much later in the analysis.

Some additional comments

In the clinical sequence described above, it was not simply fortuitous that my mind 'wandered' and came to focus on a machine-made set of markings on an envelope covered by scribblings of phone numbers, notes for teaching and reminders about errands that needed to be done. The envelope itself, in addition to carrying the meanings already mentioned, also represented (what had been) my own private discourse, a private conversation not meant for anyone else; written on it were notes in which I was talking to myself about the details of my life. The workings of the analyst's mind during analytic hours in these unselfconscious, 'natural' ways are highly personal, private and embarrassingly mundane aspects of life that are rarely discussed with colleagues, much less written about in published accounts of analysis. It requires great effort to seize this aspect of the personal and the everyday from the unself-reflective area of reverie for the purpose of talking to ourselves about the way in which this aspect of experience has been transformed such that it has become a manifestation of the interplay of analytic subjects. The 'personal' (the individually subjective) is never again simply what it had been prior to its creation in the intersubjective analytic third, nor is it entirely different from what it had been.

I believe that a major dimension of the analyst's psychological life in the consulting room with the patient takes the form of reverie concerning the ordinary, everyday details of his own life (that are often of great narcissistic importance to him). In this clinical discussion, I have attempted to demonstrate that these reveries are not simply reflections of inattentiveness, narcissistic self-involvement, unresolved emotional conflict, and the like; rather, this psychological activity represents symbolic and proto-symbolic (sensation-based) forms given to the unarticulated (and often not yet felt) experience of the analysand as they are taking form in the intersubjectivity of the analytic pair (i.e., in the analytic third).

This form of psychological activity is often viewed as something that the analyst must get through, put aside, overcome, etc., in his effort to be both emotionally present with and attentive to the analysand. I am suggesting that a view of the analyst's experience that dismisses this category of clinical fact leads the analyst to diminish (or ignore) the significance of a great deal (in some instances, the majority) of his experience with the analysand. I feel that a principal factor contributing to the undervaluation of such a large portion of the analytic experience is the fact that such acknowledgement involves a disturbing form of self-consciousness. The analysis of this aspect of the transference—countertransference requires an examination of the way we talk to ourselves and what we talk to ourselves about in a private, relatively-undefended psychological state. In this state, the dialectical interplay of consciousness and unconsciousness has been altered in ways that resemble a dream state. In becoming self-conscious in this way, we are tampering with an essential inner sanctuary of privacy, and therefore with one of the cornerstones of our sanity. We are treading on sacred ground, an area of personal isolation in which, to a large extent, we are communicating with subjective objects (Winnicott, 1963); (see also Ogden, 1991). This communication (like the notes to myself on the envelope) are not meant for anyone else, not even for aspects of ourselves that lie outside of this exquisitely-private/mundane 'cul-de-sac' (Winnicott, 1963, p. 184). This realm of transference—countertransference experience is so personal, so ingrained in the character structure of the analyst, that it requires great psychological effort to enter into a discourse with ourselves in a way that is required to recognise that even this aspect of the personal has been altered by our experience in and of the analytic third. If we are to be analysts in a full sense, we must self-consciously attempt to bring even this aspect of ourselves to bear on the analytic process.

The psyche-soma and the analytic third

In the following section of this paper, I will present an account of an analytic interaction in which a somatic delusion experienced by the analyst, and a related group of bodily sensations and body-related fantasies experienced by the analysand, constituted a principal medium through which the analytic third was experienced, understood, and interpreted. As will become evident, the conduct of this phase of the analysis depended on the analyst's capacity to recognise and make use of a form of intersubjective clinical fact manifested largely through bodily sensation/fantasy.

Clinical illustration: The tell-tale heart

In this clinical discussion, I shall describe a series of events that occurred in the third year of the analysis of Mrs B, a 42-year-old, married lawyer and mother of two latency-aged children. The patient had begun analysis for reasons that were not clear to either of us; she had felt vague discontent with her life, despite the fact that she had 'a wonderful family' and was doing well in her work. She told me that she never would have guessed that she would have 'ended up in an analyst's office'; 'It feels like I've stepped out of a Woody Allen film'.

The first year-and-a-half of analysis had a laboured and vaguely unsettling feeling to it. I was puzzled by why Mrs B was coming to her daily meetings and was a bit surprised each day when she appeared. The patient almost never missed a meeting, was rarely late and, in fact, arrived early enough to use the lavatory in my office suite prior to almost every meeting.

Mrs B spoke in an organised, somewhat obsessional but thoughtful way: there were always 'important' themes to discuss, including her mother's jealousy of even small amounts of attention paid to the patient by her father. Mrs B felt that this was connected with current difficulties such as her inability to learn ('take things in') from female senior partners at work. Nonetheless, there was a superficiality to this work and as time went on it seemed to require greater and greater effort for the patient to 'find things to talk about'. The patient talked about not feeling fully present in the meetings, despite her best efforts to 'be here'.

By the end of the second year of analysis, the silences had become increasingly frequent and considerably longer in duration, often lasting fifteen to twenty minutes (in the first year, there had rarely been a silence). I attempted to talk with Mrs B about what it felt like for her to be with me in a given period of silence. She would reply that she felt extremely frustrated and stuck, but was unable to elaborate. I offered my own tentative thoughts about the possible relationship between a given silence and the transference—countertransference experience that might have immediately preceded the silence or perhaps been left unresolved in the previous meeting. None of these interventions seemed to alter the situation.

Mrs B repeatedly apologised for not having more to say and worried that she was failing me. As the months passed, there was a growing feeling of exhaustion and despair associated with the silences and with the overall lifelessness of the analysis. The patient's apologies to me for this state of affairs continued, but became increasingly unspoken and were conveyed by her facial expression, gait, tone of voice, etc., In addition, at this juncture in the analysis, Mrs B also began to wring her hands throughout the analytic hours, and yet more vigorously during the silences. She pulled strenuously on the fingers of her hands and deeply kneaded her knuckles and fingers to the point that her hands became reddened in the course of the hour.

I found that my own fantasies and day-dreams were unusually sparse during this period of work. I also noticed that I experienced less of a feeling of closeness to Mrs B than I would have expected. One morning while driving to my office, I was thinking of the people I would be seeing that day and could not remember Mrs B's first name. I rationalised that I had recorded only her last name in my appointment book and never addressed her by her first name—nor did she ever mention her first name in talking about herself, as many patients do. I imagined myself as a mother unable to give her baby a name after its birth as a result of profound ambivalence concerning the birth of the baby. Mrs B had told me very little about her parents and her childhood. She said that it was terribly important to her that she tell me about her parents in a way that was both 'fair and accurate'. She said that she would tell me about them when she found the right way and the right words to do so.

During this period I developed what I felt to be a mild case of the 'flu, but was able to keep my appointments with all of my patients. In the weeks that followed, I noticed that I continued to feel physically unwell during my meetings with Mrs B, experiencing feelings of malaise, nausea and vertigo. I felt like a very old man and, for reasons I could not understand, I took some comfort in this image of myself, while at the same time deeply resenting it. I was not aware of similar feelings and physical sensations during any other parts of the day. I concluded that this reflected a combination of the fact that the meetings with Mrs B must have been particularly draining for me and that the long periods of silence in her meetings allowed me to be more self-conscious of my physical state than I was with other patients.

In retrospect, I am able to recognise that during this period I began to feel a diffuse anxiety during the hours with Mrs B. However, at the time I was only subliminally aware of this anxiety and was hardly able to differentiate it from the physical sensations I was experiencing. Just before my sessions with Mrs B, I would regularly find things to do, such as making phone calls, sorting papers, finding a book, etc., all of which had the effect of delaying the moment when I would have to meet the patient in the waiting room. As a result, I was occasionally a minute or so late in beginning the hours.

Mrs B seemed to look at me intently at the beginning and end of each hour. When I asked her about it, she apologised and said that she was not aware of doing so. The content of the patient's associations had a sterile, highly controlled feeling to it and centred on her difficulties at work and worries about the emotional troubles that she felt her children might be having—she brought her older child for a consultation with a child psychiatrist because of her worry that he could not concentrate well enough in school. I commented that I thought Mrs B was worried about her own value as a mother just as she was worried about her value as a patient (this interpretation was partially correct, but failed to address the central anxiety of the hour because, as I will discuss, I was unconsciously defending against recognising it).

Soon after I made the intervention concerning the patient's self-doubts concerning her value as a mother and analysand, I felt thirsty and leaned over in my chair to take a sip from a glass of water that I keep on the floor next to my chair (I had on many occasions done the same thing during Mrs B's hours, as well as with other patients). Just as I was reaching for the glass, Mrs B startled me by abruptly (and for the first time in the analysis) turning around on the couch to look at me. She had a look of panic on her face and said, 'I'm sorry, I didn't know what was happening to you'.

It was only in the intensity of this moment, in which there was a feeling of terror that something catastrophic was happening to me, that I was able to name for myself the terror that I had been carrying for some time. I became aware that the anxiety I had been feeling and the (predominantly unconscious and primitively symbolised) dread of the meetings with Mrs B (as reflected in my procrastinating behaviour) had been directly connected with an unconscious sensation/fantasy that my somatic symptoms of malaise, nausea and vertigo were caused by Mrs B, and that she was killing me. I now understood that for several weeks I had been emotionally consumed by the unconscious conviction (a 'fantasy in the body', Gaddini, 1982, p. 143) that I had a serious illness, perhaps a brain tumour, and that during that period I had been frightened that I was dying. I felt an immense sense of relief at this point in the meeting as I came to understand these thoughts, feelings and sensations as reflection of transference—countertransference events occurring in the analysis. In response to her turning to me in fright, I said to Mrs B that I thought she had been afraid that something terrible was happening to me and that I might even be dying. She said that she knew it sounded crazy, but when she heard me moving in my chair she became filled with the feeling that I was having a heart attack. She added that she had felt that I had looked ashen for some time, but she had not wanted to insult me or worry me by saying so (Mrs B's capacity to speak to me about her perceptions, feelings, and fantasies in this way reflected the fact that a significant psychological shift had already begun to take place).

While this was occurring, I realised that it was me whom Mrs B had wanted to take to see a doctor, not her older child. I recognised that the interpretation that I had given earlier in the hour about her self-doubt had been considerably off the mark, and that the anxiety about which the patient was trying to tell me was her fear that something catastrophic was occurring between us (that would kill one or both of us) and that a third person (an absent father) must be found to prevent the disaster from occurring. I had often moved in my chair during Mrs B's hours, but it was only at the moment described above that the noise of my movement became an 'analytic object' (a carrier of intersubjectively-generated analytic meaning) that had not previously existed. My own and the patient's capacity to think as separate individuals had been co-opted by the intensity of the shared unconscious fantasy/somatic delusion in which we were both enmeshed. The unconscious fantasy reflected an important, highly-conflicted set of Mrs B's unconscious internal object relationships, which were being created anew in the analysis in the form of my somatic delusion in conjunction with her delusional fears (about my body) and her own sensory experiences (e.g., her hand-wringing).

I told Mrs B that I felt that not only was she afraid that I was dying, but that she was also afraid that she was the direct and immediate cause. I said that just as she had worried that she was having a damaging effect on her son and had taken him to a doctor, so she was afraid that she was making me so ill that I would die. At this point, Mr B's hand-wringing and finger-tugging subsided. I realised then, as Mrs B began to use hand movements as an accompaniment to her verbal expression, that I could not recall ever having seen her hands operate separately (i.e., neither touching one another, nor moving in a rigid, awkward way). The patient said that what we were talking about felt true to her in an important way, but she was worried that she would forget everything that had happened in our meeting that day.

Mrs B's last comment reminded me of my own inability to remember her first name and my fantasy of being a mother unwilling to acknowledge fully the birth of her baby (by not giving it a name). I now felt that the ambivalence represented by my own act of forgetting and the associated fantasy (as well as Mrs B's ambivalence, represented in her anxiety that she would obliterate all memory of this meeting) reflected a fear, jointly held by Mrs B and myself, that allowing her 'to be born' (i.e., to become genuinely alive and present) in the analysis would pose a serious danger to both of us. I felt that we had created an unconscious fantasy (largely generated in the form of bodily experience) that her coming to life (her birth) in the analysis would make me ill and could possibly kill me. For both our sakes, it was important that we make every effort to prevent that birth (and death) from occurring.

I said to Mrs B that I thought I now understood a little better why she felt that, despite every effort on her part, she could not feel present here with me and had increasingly not been able to think of anything to say. I told her that I thought she was attempting to be invisible in her silence, as if she were not actually here and that she hoped that in so doing she would be less of a strain on me and keep me from becoming ill.

She responded that she was aware that she apologised to me continually and that at one point she had felt so fed up with herself that she felt, but did not say to me, that she was sorry that she had ever 'got into this thing' (the analysis) and wished she could 'erase it, make it never have happened'. She added that she thought that I would be better off too, and she imagined that I was sorry that I had ever agreed to work with her. She said that this was similar to a feeling that she had had for as long as she could remember. Although her mother repeatedly assured her that she had been thrilled to be pregnant with her and had looked forward to her birth, Mrs B felt convinced that she had 'been a mistake' and that her mother had not wanted to have children at all. Mrs B's mother had been in her late thirties and her father in his mid-forties when the patient was born; she was an only child and, as far as she knew, there were no other pregnancies. Mrs B told me that her parents were very 'devoted' people, and she therefore felt extremely unappreciative for saying so, but her parents' home did not feel to her to be a place for children. Her mother kept all the toys in Mrs B's room so that her father, a 'serious academic', would not be disturbed as he read and listened to music in the evenings and on weekend afternoons.

Mrs B's behaviour in the analysis seemed to reflect an immense effort to behave 'like an adult' and not to make an emotional mess of 'my home' (the analysis) by strewing it with irrational or infantile thoughts, feelings, or behaviour. I was reminded of her comments in the opening meeting about the foreignness and sense of unrealness that she felt in my office (feeling that she had stepped out of a Woody Allen film). Mrs B had unconsciously been torn between her need to get help from me and her fear that the very act of claiming a place for herself with me (in me) would deplete or kill me. I was able to understand my fantasy (and associated sensory experiences) of having a brain tumour as a reflection of an unconscious fantasy that the patient's very existence was a kind of growth that greedily, selfishlessly and destructively took up space that it had no business occupying.

Having told me about her feelings about her parents' home, Mrs B reiterated her concern that she would present an inaccurate picture of her parents (particularly her mother), leading me to see her mother in a way that did not accurately reflect the totality of who she was. However, the patient added that saying this felt more reflexive than real this time.

During these exchanges, for the first time in the analysis, I felt that there were two people in the room talking to one another. It seemed to me that not only was Mrs B able to think and talk more fully as a living human being, but that I also felt that I was thinking, feeling, and experiencing sensations in a way that had a quality of realness and spontaneity of which I had not previously been capable in this analysis. In retrospect, my analytic work with Mrs B to this point had sometimes felt to me to involve an excessively dutiful identification with my own analyst (the 'old man'). I had not only used phrases that he had regularly used, but also at times spoke with an intonation that I associated with him. It was only after the shift in the analysis just described that I fully recognised this. My experience in the phase of analytic work being discussed had 'compelled me' to experience the unconscious fantasy that the full realisation of myself as an analyst could occur only at the cost of the death of another part of myself (the death of an internal object analyst/father). The feelings of comfort, resentment and anxiety associated with my fantasy of being an old man reflected both the safety that I felt in being like (with) my analyst/father and the wish to be free of him (in fantasy, to kill him). The latter wish carried with it the fear that I would die in the process. The experience with Mrs B, including the act of putting my thoughts, feelings and sensations into words, constituted a particular form of separation and mourning of which I had not been capable up to that point.

Concluding comments on the concept of the analytic third

In closing, I will attempt to bring together a number of ideas about the notion of the analytic third that have been developed either explicitly or implicitly in the course of the two foregoing clinical discussions.

The analytic process reflects the interplay of three subjectivities: that of the analyst, of the analysand, and of the analytic third. The analytic third is a creation of the analyst and analysand, and at the same time the analyst and analysand (qua analyst and analysand) are created by the analytic third (there is no analyst, no analysand, and no analysis in the absence of the third).

As the analytic third is experienced by analyst and analysand in the context of his or her own personality system, personal history, psychosomatic make-up, etc., the experience of the third (although jointly created) is not identical for each participant. Moreover, the analytic third is an asymmetrical construction because it is generated in the context of the analytic setting, which is powerfully defined by the relationship of roles of analyst and analysand. As a result, the unconscious experience of the analysand is privileged in a specific way, i.e., it is the past and present experience of the analysand that is taken by the analytic pair as the principal (although not exclusive) subject of the analytic discourse. The analyst's experience in and of the analytic third is, primarily, utilised as a vehicle for the understanding of the conscious and unconscious experience of the analysand (the analyst and analysand are not engaged in a democratic process of mutual analysis).

The concept of the analytic third provides a framework of ideas about the interdependence of subject and object, of transference—countertransference, that assists the analyst in his efforts to attend closely to, and think clearly about, the myriad of intersubjective clinical facts he encounters, whether they be the apparently self-absorbed ramblings of his mind, bodily sensations that seemingly have nothing to do with the analysand, or any other 'analytic object' intersubjectively generated by the analytic pair.

Notes

1. It is beyond the scope of this paper to offer a comprehensive review of the literature concerning the development of an intersubjective understanding of the analytic process and the nature of the interplay of transference and countertransference. A partial listing of the major contributions to these aspects of the analytic dialogue includes: Atwood & Stolorow (1984), Balint (1968), Bion (1952), (1959), (1962), Blechner (1992), Bollas (1987), Boyer (1961), (1983), (1992), Coltart (1986), Ferenczi (1920), Gabbard (1991), Giovacchini (1979), Green (1975), Grinberg (1962), Grotstein (1981), Heimann (1950), Hoffman (1992), Jacobs (1991), Joseph (1982), Kernberg (1976), Khan (1974), Klein (1946), (1935), Kohut (1977), Little (1951), McDougall (1978), McLaughlin (1991), Meltzer (1966), Milner (1969), Mitchell (1988), Money-Kyrle (1956), O'Shaughnessy (1983), Racker (1952), (1968), D. Rosenfeld (1992), H. Rosenfeld (1952), (1965), (1971), Sandler (1976), Scharff (1992), Searles (1979), Segal (1981), Tansey & Burke

(1989), Viderman (1979), and Winnicott (1947), (1951). For recent reviews of aspects of this large body of literature on transference—countertransference, see Boyer (1993) and Etchegoyen (1991).

2. Although, for convenience sake, I shall at times refer to the 'intersubjective analytic third' as 'the analytic third', or simply 'the third', this concept should not be confused with the oedipal/symbolic third (the Lacanian [1953] 'name of the father'). The latter concept refers to a 'middle term' that stands between symbol and symbolised, between oneself and one's immediate lived sensory experience, thereby creating a space in which the interpreting, self-reflective, symbolising subject is generated. In early developmental terms, it is the father (or the 'father-in-the-mother', Ogden, 1987) who intercedes between the mother and infant (or, more accurately, the mother-infant), thus creating the psychological space in which the elaboration of the depressive position and oedipal triangulation occurs.
3. What I have said here about the analyst's thoughts and feelings being in every instance contextualised, and therefore altered, by the experience with the patient might seem to lead to the conclusion that everything the analyst thinks and feels should be considered countertransference. However, I believe the use of the term countertransference to refer to everything the analyst thinks and feels and experiences sensorially, obscures the simultaneity of the dialectic of oneness and twoness, of individual subjectivity and intersubjectivity that is the foundation of the psychoanalytic relationship. To say that everything the analyst experiences is countertransference is only to make the self-evident statement that we are each trapped in our own subjectivity. For the concept of countertransference to have more meaning than this, we must continually re-ground the concept in the dialectic of the analyst as a separate entity and the analyst as a creation of the analytic intersubjectivity. Neither of these 'poles' of the dialectic exists in pure form and our task is to make increasingly full statements about the specific nature of the relationship between the experience of subject and object, between countertransference and transference at any given moment.
4. I believe that an aspect of the experience I am describing can be understood in terms of projective identification, but the way in which it was utilised, at the point when it arose, was predominantly in the service of an intellectualising defence.
5. It was in this indirect way (i.e., in allowing myself to draw freely upon my unconscious experience with the patient in constructing my interventions) that 'I told' the patient about my own experience of the analytic third. This indirect communication of the countertransference

contributes in a fundamental way to the feeling of spontaneity, aliveness and authenticity of the analytic experience.

References

Atwood, G. & Stolorow, R. (1984). *Structures of subjectivity: explorations in psychoanalytic phenomenology*. Hillsdale, NJ: Analytic Press.

Balint, M. (1968). The Basic Fault. London: Tavistock.

Bion, W. (1952). Group dynamics: A review In *Experiences in Groups* New York: Basic Books, (1959). pp. 141–192[à].

Bion, W. (1959). Attacks on linking. *Int. J. Psychoanal., 40*: 308–315[à].

Bion, W. (1962). Learning from Experience. New York: Basic Books.[à].

Blechner, M. (1992). Working in the Countertransference. *Psychoanal. Dial., 2*: 161–179[à].

Bollas, C. (1987). The shadow of the object: Psychoanalysis of the unthought known. New York: Columbia Univ. Press.

Boyer, L.B. (1961). Provisional evaluation of psychoanalysis with few parameters in the treatment of schizophrenia. *Int. J. Psychoanal., 42*: 389–403[à].

Boyer, L.B. (1983). The Regressed Patient. New York: Jason Aronson.

Boyer, L.B. (1992). Roles played by music as revealed during countertransference-facilitated transference regression. *Int. J. Psychoanal., 73*: 55–70[à].

Boyer, L.B. (1993). Countertransference: history and clinical issues. In *Master Clinicians on Treating the Regressed Patient*, Volume 2 (ed.), L.B. Boyer & P.L. Giovacchini. Northvale, NJ: Jason Aronson, pp. 1–22.

Coltart, N. (1986). 'Slouching towards Bethlehem' ... or thinking the unthinkable in psychoanalysis. In *The British School of Psychoanalysis: The Independent Tradition* (ed.), G. Kohon. New Haven: Yale Univ. Press, pp. 185–199.

Eliot, T.S. (1919), Tradition and individual talent. In *Selected Essays.* New York: Harcourt, Brace and World, 1960. pp. 3–11.

Etchegoyen, R.H. (1991). The Fundamentals of Psychoanalytic Technique London: Karnac.[à].

Ferenczi, S. (1920). The further development of an active therapy in psychoanalysis. In *Further Contributions to the Theory and Technique of Psychoanalysis.* New York: Brunner Mazel, 1980, pp. 198–217.

Gabbard, G. (1991), Technical approaches to transference hate in the analysis of borderline patients. *Int. J. Psychoanal., 72*: 625–639[à].

Gaddini, E. (1982). Early defensive phantasies and the psychoanalytic process. In *A Psychoanalytic Theory of Infantile Experience: Conceptual and Clinical Reflections*. London and New York: Routledge, 1992, pp. 142–153.

Giovacchini, P. (1979). Treatment of Primitive Mental States. New York: Jason Aronson.

Green, A. (1975). The analyst, symbolization and absence in the analytic setting (On changes in analytic practice and analytic experience.) *Int. J. Psychoanal., 56*: 1–22[à].

Grinberg, L. (1962). On a specific aspect of countertransference due to the patient's projective identification. *Int. J. Psychoanal., 43*: 436–440[à].

Grotstein, J. (1981). Splitting and Projective Identification. New York: Jason Aronson.

Heimann, P. (1950). On counter-transference. *Int. J. Psychoanal., 31*: 81–84[à].

Hoffman, I. (1992). Some practical implications of a social-constructivist view of the psychoanalytic situation. *Psychoanal. Dial.*, 2: 287–304[à].

Jacobs, T. (1991). The Use of the Self: Countertransference and Communication in the Analytic Setting Madison, CT: Int. Univ. Press.

Joseph, B. (1982). Addiction to near death. *Int. J. Psychoanal., 63*: 449–456[à].

Kernberg, O. (1976). Object-Relations Theory and Clinical Psychoanalysis. New York: Jason Aronson.

Kernberg, O. (1985). Internal World and External Reality Northvale, NJ: Jason Aronson.

Khan, M.M.R. 1974. The Privacy of the Self. New York: Int. Univ. Press.

Klein, M. (1946). Notes on some schizoid mechanisms. In *Envy and Gratitude and Other Works*, 1946–1963 New York: Delacorte, 1975, pp. 1–24[à].

Klein, M. (1955). On identification. In *Envy and Gratitude and Other Works*, 1946–1963, New York: Delacorte, 1975, pp. 141–175[à].

Kohut, H. (1977). The Restoration of the Self. New York: Int. Univ. Press.

Lacan, J. (1953). The function and field of speech and language in psychoanalysis. In *Écrits: A Selection trans. A. Sheridan*. London: Tavistock, 1977, pp. 30–113.

Little, M. (1951). Counter-transference and the patient's response to it. *Int. J. Psychoanal., 32*: 32–40[à].

McDougall, J. (1978). Countertransference and primitive communication. In *Plea for a Measure of Abnormality*, New York: Int. Univ. Press, pp. 247–298.

McLaughlin, J. (1991). Clinical and theoretical aspects of enactment. *J. Am. Psychoanal. Assoc.*, *39*: 595–614[à].

Meltzer, D. (1966). The relation of anal masturbation to projective identification. *Int. J. Psychoanal.*, *47*: 335–342[à].

Milner, M. (1969). The Hands of the Living God. London: Hogarth Press.

Mitchell, S. (1988). Relational Concepts in Psychoanalysis: An Integration Cambridge, MA: Harvard Univ. Press.

Money-Kyrle, R. (1956). Normal counter-transference and some of its deviations. *Int. J. Psychoanal.*, *37*: 360–366[à].

Ogden, T. (1979). On projective identification. *Int. J. Psychoanal.*, *60*: 357–373[à].

Ogden, T. (1982). Projective Identification and Psychotherapeutic Technique. New York: Jason Aronson.

Ogden, T. (1985). On potential space. *Int. J. Psychoanal.*, *66*: 129–141[à].

Ogden, T. (1986). The Matrix of the Mind: Object Relations and the Psychoanalytic Dialogue Northvale, NJ: Jason Aronson.

Ogden, T. (1987). The transitional oedipal relationship in female development. *Int. J. Psychoanal.*, *68*: 485–498[à].

Ogden, T. (1988). On the dialectical structure of experience: some clinical and theoretical implications. *Contemp. Psychoanal.*, *24*: 17–45[à].

Ogden, T. (1989). The Primitive Edge of Experience Northvale, NJ: Jason Aronson.

Ogden, T. (1991). Some theoretical comments on personal isolation Psychoanal. *Dial.*, *1*: 377–390[à]

Ogden, T. (1992a). The dialectically constituted/decentred subject of psychoanalysis. I. The Freudian subject. *Int. J. Psychoanal.*, *73*: 517–526[à].

Ogden, T. (1992b). The dialectically constituted/decentred subject of psychoanalysis. II. The contributions of Klein and Winnicott. *Int. J. Psychoanal.*, *73*: 613–626[à].

O'Shaughnessy, E. (1983). Words and working through. *Int. J. Psychoanal.*, *64*: 281–290[à].

Racker, H. (1952). Observaciones sobra la contra-transferencia como instrumento clínico; communicación preliminar. *Rev. Psicoanál.*, *9*: 342–354.

Racker, H. (1968). *Transference and Countertransference*. New York: Int. Univ. Press.[à].

Rosenfeld, D. (1992). The Psychotic: Aspects of the Personality, London: Karnac.

Rosenfeld, H. (1952). Notes on the psycho-analysis of the super-ego conflict of an acute schizophrenic patient. *Int. J. Psychoanal.*, *33*: 111–131[à].

Rosenfeld, H. Psychotic States: A Psycho-Analytical Approach. New York: Int. Univ. Press.

Rosenfeld, H. (1971). Contribution to the psychopathology of psychotic states: the importance of projective identification in the ego structure and the object relations of the psychotic patient. In *Problems of Psychosis* (Ed). P. Doucet & C. Laurin. Amsterdam: Excerpta Medica, pp. 115–128.

Sandler, J. (1976). Countertransference and roleresponsiveness. *Int. J. Psychoanal.*, *3*: 43–47[à].

Scharff, J. (1992). Projective and Introjective Identification and the Use of the Therapist's Self Northvale: NJ: Jason Aronson.

Searles, H. (1979). Countertransference and Related Subjects. New York: Int. Univ. Press.

Segal, H. (1981). The Work of Hanna Segal: A Kleinian Approach to Clinical Practice, New York: Jason Aronson.

Tansey, M. & Burke, W. 1989 Understanding Countertransference: From Projective Identification to Empathy Hillsdale, NJ: Analytic Press.

Viderman, S. (1979). The analytic space: meaning and problems. *Psychoanal. Q.*, *4*: 257–291[à].

Winnicott, D.W. (1947). Hate in the countertransference. In *Through Paediatrics to Psychoanalysis*. New York: Basic Books, 1975, pp. 194–203[à]

Winnicott, D.W. (1951). Transitional objects and transitional phenomena. In *Playing and Reality*. New York: Basic Books, 1971, pp. 1–25[à].

Winnicott, D.W. (1960). The theory of the parent-infant relationship. In: *The Maturational Processes and the Facilitating Environment*. New York: Int. Univ. Press, 1965, pp. 37–55[à].

Winnicott, D.W. (1963). Communicating and not communicating leading to a study of certain opposites. In *The Maturational Processes and the Facilitating Environment*. New York: Int. Univ. Press, 1965, pp. 179–192[à].

CHAPTER NINE

"The play's the thing wherein I'll catch the conscience of the king!" Psychoanalysis as a passion play

James S. Grotstein

Part one

Introduction: Psychoanalysis as a passion play

An erstwhile experience with an analysand caused me—I would like to say inspired me—to rethink what may possibly be the deeper nature of the psychoanalytic process. It was as if a paradigm shift took place within me in regard to our basic conception of the psychoanalytic interaction. I was immediately reminded of a work of mine from long ago and then became aware of similar contributions by Freud (1905), Friedman (1953), Winnicott (1968), Loewald (1975), McDougall (1985, 1989), Modell (1990), Nuetzel (1995, 1999a, 1999b), and others. This new "Aha Erlebnis" then became an Ariadne's thread for me, one that I could see running through many if not all the analyses in my practice that I retrospectively reflected upon and subsequently observed, as well as detected, in supervisions.

Psychoanalysis as a "scripted" and *improvisational play performed in the analytic field*

The epiphany that occurred to me was as follows: The psychoanalytic session, to say nothing of life itself, constitutes an ongoing theatrical play or novel in which we unconsciously beckon and recruit others via our unconscious "casting director" to enter into the sphere of our personal lives so as to play out roles that our unconscious playwright continuously creates in order to *dramatize* incompletely (insufficiently or inadequately) processed moments of emotional significance that still cry for attention in our internal world. Paradoxically, the text (free associations) is "scripted" by a numinous Presence in the unconscious, unbeknown to the analysand and analyst, but plays out in the session as if it were improvisational. The *theater* for this psychoanalytic play is the binary-oppositional structure of the setting, protected by the analytic frame. The binary oppositional structure is the dialectic between the one-person and two-person involvement, i.e., the theater makes room for the actors (the analysand and analyst) to play their roles both as individuals who are separate *and* as an indivisible group or analytic field (Baranger, M. and Baranger, W., 1961–62). *Psychopathology, furthermore, can be considered to be the third actor in a scripted as well as non-scripted play in repertory.*

Psychoanalysis as a dramatic passion play

It is my belief, consequently, that drama constitutes the fundamental function of the psychoanalytic encounter. Was this not implicit when Freud (1912) stated that psychoanalysis could *not* treat a psychoneurosis, *it could only treat an infantile neurosis that had been "transferred" to a transference neurosis?* Further, when he laid down the rules for psychoanalytic technique, was he not unwittingly acknowledging that the success of the psychoanalytic procedure lay in how effectively the analysis was able to expose, so as to *dramatize,* the hidden conflict that was now being transferred to the transference neurosis? The purpose was, in other words to allow the unconscious to come *alive* and thus known (Ogden, 2004).

Drama, an art form which issues from one's internal aesthetic organization, is a latter-day descendant of the "lost c(h)ord"[1] of infancy and of its pre-lexical, "sign-ing" ("sign language?") technique for communication (Peirce, 1931; Silver, A. 1981; Salomonsson, 2007a, 2007b). Action is the quintessence of drama, mental as well as physical action. One must acknowledge that there is a difference between normal mental dramatic action, on one hand, and pathological enactments, on the other. The former presupposes the presence of a reasonably intact alpha-function (Bion, 1962) which in turn presupposes an intact contact-barrier and a binary-oppositional collaboration between the activities issuing from the primary and secondary processes, which, according to Bion (1962), collaboratively constitute alpha-function, and the reality and pleasure principles (Grotstein, 2008b). In so-called pathological enactments, on the other hand, one may find that the previously mentioned functions are compromised.

I believe that these enactments by the analyst which the analysand manipulates the analyst to enact may be due to the analysand's urgent need to arrest any signs of analytic progress because it would herald a catastrophe of the putatively forever regressed portions of the analysand's psychic structure. The analysand, in other words, may be *understandably* seeking to disengage the analyst from his "collusion" with the progressing aspect of the analysand's personality in order to address another cryptic and more urgent portion of the personality that is terrified of progress because of its dread of being left behind and consequently anticipating a catastrophic splitting of the personality that ensues with "progress" (Grotstein, 2009a, 2009b).

But why a passion *play? (Interpretations are not enough)*

The psychoanalytic session is not only a play, not unlike play in child analysis. It is a play of *passion*—in the religious and anthropological (shamanistic) sense—involving transference countertransference as a form of *"exorcism,"* which *pen*ultimately signifies the transfer of demons from the analysand to the analyst and ultimately the obligatory need for the analyst to suffer (the *"passion"*) the *"sacrificial scapegoat"* (Girard, 1972, 1978, 1986, 1987) to complete the transfer of demons. [For references to the shamanistic transfer of demons see: Frazer's (1922) Chapter 40: "The Transference of Evil," pp. 624–633, and Chapter 41: "The Public Expulsion of Evil," pp. 633–650, and Chapter 42: "Public Scapegoats," pp. 651–669; (b) Lévi-Strauss's

(1970). *The Elementary Structures of Kinship*. For references to "exorcism" see the above as well as Whyte's (1974) *A Manual on Exorcism* and Ellenberger's (1970) "The Ancestry of Dynamic Psychotherapy" in: *The Discovery of the Unconscious*, pp. 3–53.]

The "exorcistic rite" of psychoanalysis and the two-person model

The concept of the (shamanistic) "exorcistic rite" in psychoanalysis depends on the employment of the one two-person model in which the analysand and analyst each feels the presence of the same emotional demons. I conceive of the model of the "conjoined twin" as representative of the two-person situation: separate and simultaneously non-separate (divisible and indivisible). This idea expresses Bion's (1992) concept of the binary-oppositional conception in which a "narcissistic" (individual) as well as a "socialistic" (group) personality comprise each person. It also expresses his concept of container contained (♀ ↔ ♂) (Bion, 1962) as well as Winnicott's (1956) idea of "primary maternal preoccupation."

Thus, the one-person and two-person models are operant both simultaneously and alternately. This "combined-operation" model inheres in the following, all of which are cognates of one another and which I wish to place in alignment with one another: (a) the transference ↔ countertransference situation, (b) the "psychoanalytic field" (Baranger, M. and Baranger, W., 1961–62), (c) "transformations in O" (Bion, 1965, 1970), (d) Bion's (1992) personality distinction between "narcissism" (individual qua individual personality) and "socialism" (group personality), and (e) the intersubjective perspective (he "analytic third subject," Ogden, 1994). The conjoined-twin model, which the relationship typologies listed above represent, constitutes the "executive producer" and stage of the analytic passion play.

"The transference ↔ countertransference neurosis" and the narrativization of "the theme of themes"

In light of the above considerations we can consider that psychoanalysis is conducted in part so that the patient's original infantile neurosis (including traumatic neurosis) becomes converted not only into a transference neurosis but also into a "transference ↔

countertransference neurosis." Put another way, the patient's illness constitutes a revelation of an aberration or arrestment imprisoned in a time warp in the ongoing evolution of his unconscious "theme of themes" (unconscious life story) (Grotstein, 1979, 1981, 2000). Psychoanalysis can now be thought of as the conjunction or blending of the patient's unconscious thematics with that of the patient ↔ analyst interaction (co-construction in the analytic field) in the here and now. The co-construction represents a mutual dreaming (Bion, 1992) of the patient's theme. Upon completion, the patient's original theme becomes separated from—but permanently influenced by—co-constructions that had emerged from the analytic field. The "socialist" (analytic field, group) personality now defers to the "narcissistic" (individual) personality to allow himself to become altered by the encounter so that it is truly and truthfully compatible with his nature.

The unconscious dramatic organization

I should like to place the preceding within the enclosure of a supraordinate aesthetic function, drama, one which includes transformations conducted by what Bion (1962, 1965) terms the "alpha-function of dreaming" or the "curtain of illusion." The work of mine to which I alluded are "Who Is the Dreamer Who Dreams the Dream and Who Is the Dreamer Who Understands It?" (Grotstein, 1979, 1981, 2000)" McDougall (1985) states: "Whether we will it or not, our inner characters are constantly seeking a stage on which to play out our tragedies and comedies" (p. 4).[2]

This dramatic organization or faculty seeks to impress the analyst into service as a corresponding actor in a passion play. While each participant overtly *seems* to be directly speaking and relating to one another, they, according to this new vision, are each speaking and relating to each other as serious improvisational actors through an invisible theatrical veil or "curtain of illusion" (Bion, 1965) as if the patient and analyst were each activated by an unconscious, numinous director who has handed each participant a script (*written* by the unconscious playwright but which appears to be *unwritten* to the analytic dyad) which they are to play out.

The connection between psychoanalysis-as—a-play and literature and drama has been described by Sander (2001) and is famously exemplified in Pirandello's (1925) "Six Characters in Search of an Author." Lacan (1966) once stated" "All the while that the ego is speaking, it fails to realize that it is being spoken." The same principle applies to what I am proposing. The free associations and behavior on the part of the analysand and the interventions and enactments by the analyst are initiated by some unknown, unconscious "ventriloquist," the creator of the play. This "ventriloquist" goes by many names, the "Daimon," "dramaturge," the "dreamer who dreams the dream," the ineffable subject of the unconscious" (Grotstein, 1981, 2000), or the "subjugating third subject of analysis" (Ogden, 1994).

The immediate implication of this formulation is that an imperceptible theatrical veil exists between the two participants, conceived both as an indivisible partnership and as two separate individuals, behind which this preternatural Presence, Intelligence, or Gnomon (Daimon) who/which orchestrates, choreographs, and displays the emotions, thoughts, and actions of each—by casting a hypnotic spell on them and then putting words in their mouths which they thinks are their own! This dramatic organization emerges from the "aesthetic domain" or "vertex" (Bion, 1965, p. 38). Psychoanalytic "acting," in other words, constitutes aesthetic action which strives to achieve psychoanalytic "revelation" for "publication" from the unconscious to consciousness (Bion, 1962, p. 50) as well as the "shamanistic exorcism of demons" (the deepest meaning of both transference *and* countertransference). Drama, parenthetically, may be considered to be the "lost c(h)ord" of infantile pre-lexical, sensory-motor language of gesture, one which is as beseeching and persuading as it is revealing. The theater for the play, as mentioned above is the analytic field. The analysand's psychopathology constitutes the third actor.

Psychoanalysis, viewed as demonology and "exorcism," constitute the hidden order of transference and countertransference

I am suggesting that the psychoanalytic encounter is made more comprehensible by the invocation of demonology (as well as angelology) and "exorcism" as metaphoric models to be employed within the context of a religious passion play. Meltzer (1986) advises us, as alluded to above, that the truest meaning of transference is the transfer of mental pain from one person to another. The task of this analytic demonic passion play is to summon he unconscious *demons* to consciousness and portray the painful emotions they signify, following which the symbolic ritual "sacrifice" of the analyst, via "exorcistic" "projective *trans*identifcation" (Grotstein, 2004) transpires. These demons are ineffably selected by a numinous Presence or mysterious Intelligence (Daimon, Gnomon) in the analsyand's unconscious who/which is scheduled to appear as symptoms as well as free associations and "acting in" and/or "acting-out" behavior. A corollary of this hypothesis is that *internal objects are neither kind nor cruel; they are "actors" acting in repertory planted by the numinous playwright to catch our attention so as to be acknowledged by us and processed—but yet are felt as demons.* They are inner beacons or animated distress signals that represent still unquieted mental storms of emotional turbulence in our inner world.

"Exorcism" had once been a recognized form of religious "treatment" for demonically possessed victims as well as being a traditional shamanistic therapeutic practice for primitive cultures (Whyte, 1974). Briefly, it consisted of purging the demonically possessed victim of his demons by a clerical specialist who employed religious imprecations upon the internal Satan and wielded the cross as a purging weapon. In some cases the holy rite consisted of the exorcist's becoming afflicted with the *"transferred"* demons.

The deeper significance of transference, countertransference, container ↔ contained, and the psychoanalytic field

In the vast literature on countertransference a consensus developed that the analyst is vulnerable to his own bidden as well as unbidden emotional responses to his analysand. What was hinted at but never stated was that there was a therapeutic purpose for the countertransference involvement, one beyond empathic resonance, collusion, and unconscious information gathering. Bion (1962) and Winnicott (1969) came the closest to this assumption. Bion (1992) expresses this in his concepts of the analyst's transformations in O but more trenchantly in the following:

> I suggest for a correct interpretation it is necessary for the analyst to go through the phase of 'persecution' even if ... it is in a modified

> form without giving an interpretation. Similarly, he must pass through the depression before he is ready to give an interpretation. Again, he should not give an interpretation while experiencing depression; the change paranoid-schizoid to depressive position must be complete before he gives his interpretation ...
>
> *I do not think ... a patient will ever accept an interpretation, however, correct, unless he feels that the analyst has passed through this emotional crisis as part of the act of giving the interpretation* [italics added] (p. 291).

Winnicott expresses this idea in his concept of "object usage," in which the infant is constrained to destroy the subjective object while the external object (which to the infant are identical) survives the destruction. Put succinctly, the hidden order of container ↔ contained is transference ↔ countertransference, and the hidden order of them both is the need for the analyst to be perceived as the chosen ritualized scapegoat (Girard, 1986), acting within a sacred analytic covenant that is established in order to facilitate the transfer of demons across the intimate "synapse" between the analysand and himself. *Thus, shamanistic exorcism extends and deepens our present conception of (a) transference and countertransference as well as (b) container ↔ contained.*

I take these citations by Bion and Winnicott as tentative evidence that they each were unwittingly linking the process of psychoanalysis to the ancient rite of exorcism—and strongly suggesting that exorcism constitutes the hidden order of psychoanalysis.

The crucifixion as a mythic template for the "therapeutic" "exorcistic" sacrifice of the analyst as "scapegoat"

Perhaps the most famous example of sacred drama as healing narrative is the story of the Crucifixion, a phenomenon which has many parallels in psychoanalytic theory and practice, not the least of which is the need for the passion (agony) to be recognized and mutually experienced by Christians, to say nothing about the importance of the universal phenomenon of human sacrifice and scapegoating that accompanies it (Girard, 1986; Grotstein, J. (2000). I have already put forth the notion that *the religious experience of* ***exorcism*** *may constitute the hidden order of the transference ↔ countertransference phenomena as well as of container ↔ contained.*

As the analysand transfers his painful demons to the analyst, the latter, who upon feeling them "wears" (becomes) them—so as to complete the therapeutic exorcistic act. By extension it would appear that drama, particularly religious as well as psychoanalytic, may be a principal component of *ritual.* Bion (personal communication), as I have already stated above, believed that the analysand would not sanguinely accept an interpretation if the analyst had not likewise experienced it. It may have been that because psychoanalysis had so long been exclusively considered to be a one-person practice rather than a two-person one that the awareness of its dramatic component had been delayed.

The passion play of the crucifixion is the mythic template that embraces this "therapeutic" sacrificial rite. Briefly, in olden times infants were sacrificed presumably in order to propitiate the gods. The biblical patriarch Abraham agreed to sacrifice his son, Isaac, presumably because God demanded it, but when God found Abraham actually poised to commit the act, He relented, and Isaac was spared, but in the covenant that followed, a lamb was chosen for ritual sacrifice instead, and this become a Hebrew tradition thereafter. Human and animal sacrifices were instigated allegedly to pacify the gods, as I alluded to above, but the rationale for the god's desire to be offered sacrifice has never, to my knowledge, been adequately deconstructed.

I believe that the deeper rationale for human or animal sacrifice was for the individual or the group to be able to project their demons onto or into them—because they were innocent, i.e., without guilt (without experience), and therefore convenient containers or repositories for their demons. Insofar as the sacrificial animal or human was felt to be able, in the unconscious phantasy within the myth, to bear and to transcend the demonic projections by virtue of being able to transform the painful act, the sacrificed one became deified, i.e., as the "Pascal Lamb," as Freud (1913) suggested in *Totem and Taboo.* Insofar as the projections succeed in transforming the scapegoat, however, the latter becomes transformed into the devil.[3] Thus, the scapegoat constitutes the deified and the vilified container within the psychoanalytic field. Thus, a vicious circle is created in which the subject first projects his demons into the scapegoat and then fears retaliation by the devil he has created. Exorcism by the psychoanalyst interrupts the vicious circle of projection and retaliation by the analyst's willingness to bear the analysand's demons out of analytic love.

Brief case vignette

I shall now briefly present the case material which inspired my new line of thinking.

R. was a single, early thirtyish physician who consulted me because of intimacy problems with women generally and with his current girlfriend specifically. He had been born in England during World War II and moved with his mother and stepfather to the United States when he was ten years of age. He had no memories of his natural father, who died in action in Egypt during the war. I shall forgo discussing the analytic material relevant to his relationship with his mother, stepfather, and grandparents and to the women he had dated. I shall only epitomize my reverie experience of him—as my experience of how he related a dramatic event to me and my response to it. Prior to this event I had frequently felt there to be a great emotional distance between us—*as if I were dead to him.*

At the beginning of this particular session the analysand spoke of how much he had missed his natural father, yet he was grateful to his caring step-father for having adopted him, offering him a good education, and even sending him through medical school. Then he returned to the theme of his natural father. He stated,

> "There's something I haven't told you that you need to know. Five years ago I returned to England to visit my grandparents. They lived in this village in the West Country. One afternoon after lunch my grandfather and I went to the village pub to get a pint [of beer] [author's brackets]. While there I noticed a man staring at me. I had a weird feeling about him. I asked my grandfather if he knew who he was and why he was staring at me. Rather than answering me, my grandfather took me over to him and introduced the stranger to me. 'R, this is your father!' I nearly fell through the floor! After I returned to may senses, my father told me the following story:
>
> "When I was with the Army in Egypt, your mother met this rich Yank bloke, and they had an affair. When I came home on

> leave from the Army, I learned about the affair and confronted your mother. She and I had a long talk about it. I was a poor bloke with no expectations and wouldn't be able to do for you what this Yank could do, his being rich and all. I was very sad to do this, but your mother and I hit upon a plan to let it be known that I had died in combat so that he could adopt you and take your mother and you to the States where you could have a wonderful education and advantages."

[While listening to this story, I could not help thinking of Charles Dickens' *Great Expectations.*]

When the analysand finished his tale, he looked up toward me from the couch and plaintively asked, "Will you be my father?" Without thinking, yet realizing at the same time that I was enacting a parameter, I immediately said, "Yes!" No sooner had I uttered this than he suddenly changed from his plaintive mood and loudly bellowed, "Why did you do it?! What followed was a lengthy vitriolic attack against a father-me for having abandoned and betrayed him.

Then the lines cited in the title of this contribution came to me unbidden, "The play's the thing/wherein I'll catch the conscience of the king!" In that very moment I began to wonder if I had suddenly been appointed to become an actor who had been pulled against my will into someone else's drama, a drama that could not take place without my participation as a co-actor. Once this vision came to me, I immediately began to wonder if all psychoanalytic sessions were not in fact plays, actually, improvisational passion plays, either verbal or concrete en-*act*-ments. As a result of my musings I then realized that the analysand to whom I just referred had not only in fact felt the feelings he uttered and I had felt the emotions that resulted from his accusatory confrontation of me. I also began to believe that he had been dramatizing his internal world *with* me as well as *to* me in the only communicative way he knew—so that I would get the message; the urgency of his hitherto unresolved pain and my role in its emergence, that it would at last become revealed and then "publicated," so as to complete the incompletely dreamed traumatic event by further analytic dreaming (Bion, 1962, p. 21; Grotstein, 2002, 2004a, 2004b, 2007, 2008a, 2008b).

The mutual hypnotic trance

Earlier, I alluded to my having fallen into a trance state with my analysand. Once I began to think about my experience of being held in this state by the patient, I wondered if this were not a universal phenomenon in all analyses as well as in infant ↔ mother relationships, as has been adumbrated by Winnicott (1956) in his work, "Primary Maternal Preoccupation," and alluded to by Bion (1962) in his concept of container ↔ contained—the need of the infant to *captivate mother's full attention.* I began to wonder why I spontaneously and unthinkingly had agreed with the analysand's unconscious request to accept the role of his father. I then realized that in retrospect I believed that I had fallen into a trance state, a veritable spell. I felt as if I had been mysteriously hypnotized in order to participate in this drama, which would hitherto be thought of as a folie à deux or collusion between the analysand and analyst (Mason, 1994). Of even greater significance, however, was the emergence within me of an emotional compliance with my patient's attacks. I *had* found myself experiencing guilt as a "trial identification" with the patient's accusations and even faintly felt an impulse to offer my heart-felt apology to him. I have elsewhere referred to this phenomenon as the "Pietà transference ↔ countertransference, which, briefly, is the situation that the analysand holds the analyst responsible for his suffering and seeks the latter to say he is sorry (Grotstein, 2000).[4]

The analytic field

The Barangers (1961–62), independently of Bion's work on container ↔ contained and transformations in O but following in the tradition of Racker's work on countertransference, created the concept of an indivisible psychoanalytic field in which the focus of initiative shifted from either participant to the mystique of the field itself. This concept was taken up by a number of authors, amongst whom are Langs, Ferro, and Ogden. Implicit in the concept of the analytic field is the phenomenon of co-construction of the analytic dialogue, but I would hasten to add that, following the results from the co-creation, the analysand must independently assess his own experience of its validity for him. Thus, the analytic field constitutes the "analytic theater." Thus, I once again invoke the model of the conjoined twin: the one-person *and* two-person model constitute a collaborative binary-oppositional structure and function.

Discussion

As I began to generalize this theme as a way of understanding the analytic process, I thought that a new dimension, a new psychoanalytic field, was beginning to emerge, one which might enhance the original concept of an analytic field that had been postulated earlier by Baranger and Baranger (1961–62). I then retrospectively wondered how we traditionally think of our interactions with our analysands, especially about how we believe we relate to them and they to us. I immediately thought of Martin Buber's (1958) "I-Thou" communicative model and noted its directness, openness, and concreteness. Similarly, when we listen to analysands' free associations and observe their behavior, we concretely (without question) believe what we hear from and observe of them while we simultaneously attempt to decipher their messages and manifestations in order to learn the unconscious template from which they emerge.

We speak to one another in analysis, in other words, as if we are in direct contact with each other *without there being an invisible aesthetic, dramatic, mediating veil between us.* I am positing that an invisible veil *does* exist between the analysand and the analyst and that that veil is the "curtain of illusion" (Bion, 1965) or *"dream membrane"* (Grotstein, 2008b). The dream membrane is responsible both for formal dreaming as well as for the role invitations to the analyst (Sandler, 1976, 1993) and analysand to enact the theme of the "mental turbulence," "O" (Bion, 1965, p. 42), and it occupies a reflective mental space between the two.

When all is said and done, we come to the realization that analysts from Freud onward have thought of the process of psychoanalysis as one in which a deciphering of an unconscious cryptogram took place. Its cryptic signifiers consisted of free associations that emerged from the presence of a symptomatic matrix. Along with this assumption were at least four others. The **first** was that the analyst was relating in actuality to another individual, the analysand, much in the same way one would relate in the real world outside analysis—excluding, of course, the fact that the nature of the analytic dialogue consists of free associations and behavior on the part of the analysand and interpretations on the part of the analyst. **Second,** the course of the analysis consisted of progress and resistance on the part of the analysand. **Third,** the course of the analysis was characterized by the emergence of transference and countertransference experiences. **Fourth,** all the analysand's utterances and behavior emerged from his or her unconscious agency, i.e., will (psychic determinism).

The "healthy analysand" as the "actor" who enacts psychopathology

Perhaps I can more clearly explicate my theme in the following way: *It is as if the analysand who consults us is essentially healthy and intact even though suffering from symptoms.* The analysis and its unique setting allow him to present his inner torment for us as drama. He is not, for instance, depressed; he is *showing* us his depression through drama—as if in pantomime or charades. *The unconscious knows but is mute. It needs consciousness or an analyst to read what it knows. The "healthy analysand" is associated with the unconscious "ideal ego"* (Freud, 1913).

Part Two

Psychoanalysis as a passion play

My theme is as follows: one can observe that a sense of concreteness has characterized our conception of the analysand ↔ analyst relationship. Perhaps this point may be illustrated when I employ a different perspective to suggest that psychoanalysis constitutes a *drama, an improvisational passion play,* one in which the analysand is the leading actor who unconsciously invites and recruits, maybe hypnotically ensorcels the analyst, all be it through the unconscious agency of the numinous "third subject of analysis" or the dramaturge, to participate in a *play* in which the dyad is involved in *"playing"* roles that have been unconsciously assigned to them. In citing the quotation from Hamlet in the title of this contribution, I am implying that the play *Hamlet* itself can be likened to an analysis, and that the play within the play that was "produced" by Hamlet reveals that his motive for producing the play was to elicit a confession from Claudius that he had murdered Hamlet's father. In a way it succeeded. Claudius, in *his* prayerful soliloquy, confesses: "My words rise up/My thoughts remain below/Words without thoughts ne'er to heaven go."

The idea that psychoanalysis may constitute a passion play does not dismiss psychic determinism. It affords this concept even more complexity, abstraction, and sophistication. Psychic determinism seen from this perspective would constitute the analysand's unconscious need (drive, will) to *reveal* his or her unconscious agony—and the hidden emotional truth that underlies it—to an analyst for recognition, and acknowledgement by dramatizing it, ideally in words, but inescapably in enactments as well. I am suggesting that the *verbal communication* between the analysand and the analyst (the analysand's free associations and the analyst's interpretations) constitute suspended actions and interactions, as Freud (1911) had anticipated when he stated that *thoughts are trial actions*.

The differentiation between the personality with symptoms and the one who arranges the dramatization of the symptoms

The implications of this hypothesis are many. One is that the analytic relationship constitutes a more aesthetic-symbolic and more evolved interaction than we have realized. Another even more radical implication is that the analysand, from this vertex, can be consider to possess a basically healthy core (ideal ego) underneath his or her alleged psychopathology, as Katan (1954) and Bion (1957) adumbrated when they posited a differentiation existed between the psychotic and non-psychotic personalities in schizophrenia and other psychotic disorders—*and that the pain and turmoil that the patient experiences lie in the discrepancy between his normal self and his symptomatic self*. That discrepancy represents his/her handicap.

The unconscious as "producer" and "drama critic"

All the while one personality is occupied with *enacting* its psychopathology, in other words, another healthier but muted one is both realistically aware of the issues that need to be addressed and is able, through its *dramaturge* (Grotstein, 1979, 1981, 2000) or the "subjugating third subject" (Ogden, 1994), to orchestrate—choreograph a drama to be played out in analysis, one which is improvisational, where the "script" is unknown to the analysand and analyst) but has been carefully crafted by the realistic personality qua dramaturge. Its analytic "production" resembles the game of charades, albeit serious charades, in which the analyst must be able to interpret the signs (Salomonsson, 2007a, 2007b) produced by the analysand and give them symbolic significance as interpretations. This cryptic, numinous inner personality also constitutes a "supervisor" who signals the analyst both when he or she is in error and when he or she has correctly interpreted the salient unconscious issues at hand.

In other contributions I proffered the conception of the "dreamer who dreams (produces) the dream" and the dream audience, the "dreamer who understands the dream" (Grotstein, 1981, 2000). The former corresponds to the first personality I alluded to above, the dramaturge (the instigator and producer of the dream), and the supervisor or dream audience is the latter personality, the dreamer who understands the dream, and thus the emotional meaning of the drama. Both "personalities" are numinous, sentient internal, preternatural Intelligences, Presences, or "Daimons" (in the ancient Greek sense) or "Gnomons. I further hypothesize that if the individual's capacity for alpha-function is sufficient, the internal drama would consist of a closed loop between the two dreamers. When this is not the case, then the dreamer who dreams the dream needs to borrow an analyst's additional alpha-function to address the agony, which has hitherto been incompletely or inadequately dreamed (Grotstein, 2008a, 2008b).

Analytic resistance reconsidered in the light of drama theory

Yet another implication that emerges from this idea is that the concept of analytic resistance must be fundamentally reconsidered. What has been called resistance may be but a *sign* (Salomonsson, 2007a, 2007b) that constitutes the reverse side of unaddressed emotional pain and is clinically dramatized—and thus inversely revealed in the negative. In other words, "resistance" is a genuine member of the play's "dramatis personae." One can now conceive of the analysand as a "*conjoined twin*," one twin being essentially normal (ideal ego) but mute—and aware of his handicap—and reduced to having to dramatize his inner world as his pathological twin for the analyst to understand as well as participate in. In this new way of thinking the analysand is not really resistant. He is *showing (revealing)* his emotional pain by the resistance (Grotstein, 2009a, 2009b).

The importance of the aesthetic vertex: The relationship between drama and narrative

In emphasizing the role of drama in psychoanalysis I am also implicating the importance of what Bion (1965) addresses as the "aesthetic vertex" (p. 38), which in its vast embrace includes the role of the ancient bards, minstrels, storytellers as well as poets, dramatists, and novelists, all of whose creative productions may be considered to fall under the category of *narrative*. Ferro (1992, 1999); Bezoari and Ferro, 1999) have recently addressed the importance of narrative in psychoanalysis, both as a conception of the analytic process and as a desirable component of the analyst's interpretations. Ferro developed his unique theory as an extension of Bion's (1962) conception of the role of dreaming in psychoanalysis (p. 21) (Grotstein, 2007, 2008b). Narrative can be considered to be the linear, diachronic (linear, sequential) transformation of the synchronic (simultaneous and infinite) nature of O. Bion (1962) terms the mental symptoms that emerge in a session the "psycho-analytic object" (p. 68), the painful experience of untransformed O. Psychoanalysis, from this perspective, consequently, can be considered to be the application of narrative (storytelling) which allows for a transformation in linear time of a temporally (infinite, timeless) vertical phenomenon characterized by O.

Brief clinical vignettes

During the course of the analysis of a thirtyish, married woman, who was the heiress of a vast fortune, I gradually became aware of the fact that I had been treating her haughtily and even condescendingly in my interpretations to her and even in my general attitude toward her. In retrospect her free associations seemed to have detected this attitude of mine, but she masochistically (which was her wont) accepted responsibility for it [Racker's complementary transference—countertransference reaction]. I was in psychoanalysis at the time and was able to retrieve childhood memories of my extreme envy of very rich individuals I happened to have met and familiarized with in my elementary and highs schools. My analyst and I interpreted this attitude of mine as an unbidden countertransference whose components were not only my envy in the past of my rich schoolmates but also my earlier-originating envy of my older sister. Later in the analysis of this same patient I found myself mysteriously developing feelings of great anger toward her—mysteriously, because I could not locate the context or cause. A few days later the patient began discussing a frightening event in her childhood. She was about three-years old at the time. She recalled overhearing a loud and highly disturbing quarrel between her parents, following which her father ran downstairs, entered his automobile, and never returned. Her recalling of this event took place just days before I was about to leave for a vacation. My feelings of anger belonged, in this case, to the category of reverie. I felt it as one might feel a countertransference event, but, though I felt it as my own anger, it was in fact a "not-me" phenomenon. I had all along been playing an unconsciously assigned role in a drama that had to be played out so that a traumatic moment from the analysand's past could be recovered and dealt with.

Having stated the above, however, I think, practically speaking, that it is difficult—and maybe even unnecessary—to distinguish between the analyst's countertransference neurosis and reverie, particularly when we think of the analytic field (Baranger and Baranger, 1961–62; Ferro, 1992, 1999) as an enclosure consisting at any given time, of an undifferentiatable transference neurosis ↔ countertransference neurosis, the latter including the countertransference infantile neurosis *and* reverie. This concept gives new meaning to Bion's (1963) idea of P-S D (p. 37). Every individual is simultaneously situated in both.

II

A thirty-four year-old attractive single European female analysand began to develop an intense erotic transference to me. As it intensified, I was struck at my lack of emotional counter-response, i.e., countertransference. As a matter of fact I was repelled by it. Her erotic transference ultimately devolved into a revelation that she had been consistently incested by her brother. Her erotic transference constituted her projective identification with her aggressor brother, and my reverie-feeling of repulsion constituted her having projected her frightened, innocent, repelling self into me. Upon my interpretations, her transference changed abruptly and she felt relieved.

Summary

Psychoanalysis, which consists of the exchange of words and a proclivity to enactments on the part of the analysand as well as the analyst, ultimately constitutes a scripted *and* an improvisational passion play or drama as well as a virtual shamanistic rite, exorcism, the purpose of which is to facilitate the "revelation" and "publication" of hidden traumatic internal objects (demons, unacceptable emotions, traumatic scenes) so as to become known and analytically processed (exorcised) by the combined alpha-functions of the two participants. Since Freud defined "thought" as "trial action" and since I assume that action, trial or otherwise, is inseparable from drama, then psychoanalysis can be thought of as a form of drama which issues from the aesthetic faculty or organization of the analysand and analyst in the form of a theatrical as well as a dream veil. The dramatic organization constitutes an extension of the concept of the psychoanalytic field, or putting it another way, the analytic field is the "executive producer" of the analytic play.

In the course of psychoanalytic treatment the patient's infantile (and traumatic) neurosis becomes transformed into a transference countertransference neurosis within the structure of the psychoanalytic field, during which, under the watchful ear of the analyst's reverie, the original infantile neurosis becomes modified and even healed. The exorcistic rite is the hidden order of psychoanalysis.

Notes

1. "Lost c(h)ord" conveys both the original umbilical cord and the musical relationship that Trevarthen (1980, 1999) holds to be the fundamental communication mode that transpires between the infant and its mother.
2. (I am indebted to Gemma Corradi Fiumara (2008, footnote 26).
3. In olden day portraits of the devil the latter frequently appears with horns, cloven feet, and a tail. The descent from the lamb or the goat is obvious.
4. See Kubie and Israel's (1955) paper, "Say You're Sorry."

References

Baranger, M. & Baranger, W. (1961–62). La situation analitico como campo dinamico. In *Problemas del Campo Analitico*. Buenos Aires, 1969, pp. 124–164.

Benjamin, J. (1995). *Like subjects, love objects: essays on recognition and sexual difference.* New Haven, CT: Yale University Press.

Benjamin, J. (2004). Beyond doer and done to: An intersubjective view of thirdness. *Psychoanalytic Quarterly, 73*: 5–46.

Bezoari, M. & Ferro, A. (1999). The dream within a field theory: Functional aggregates and narrations. *Journal of Melanie Klein and Object Relations, 17*: 333–348.

Bion, W.R. (1948). *Experiences in groups.* London: Tavistock, 1961.

Bion, W.R. (1957). The differentiation of the psychotic from the non-psychotic personalities. In *Second Thoughts.* New York: Jason Aronson, pp. 43–64.

Bion, W.R. (1962). *Learning from experience.* London: Heinemann.

Bion, W.R. (1963). *Elements of psycho-analysis.* London: Heinemann.

Bion, W.R. (1965). *Transformations.* London: Heinemann.

Bion, W.R. (1970). *Attention and Interpretation.* Tavistock Publications, London.

Bion, W.R. (1992). *Cogitations.* London: Karnac Books.

Bion, W.R. (1997). *Taming wild thoughts.* London: Karnac.

Buber, M. (1958). *I and thou.* (Trans.) W. Kaufmann. New York: Schribner's & Sons.

Ellenberger, H.F. (1970). *The discovery of the unconscious: The history and evolution of dynamic psychiatry.* New York: Basic Books.

Fairbairn, (1952). *Psychoanalytic studies of the personality.* London: Tavistock and Routledge & Kegan Paul.

Ferro, A. (1992). Two authors in search of characters: The relationship, the field, the story. *Rivista di Psicoanalisi, 38*: 44–91.

Ferro, A. (1999). *Psychoanalysis as therapy and storytelling.* London & New York: Routledge.

Fiumara, G.C. (2008). *Spontaneity: A Psychoanalytic Inquiry.* London: Routledge & Psychology Press. In press.

Fliess, R. (1942). The metapsychology of the analyst. *Psychoanalytic Quarterly, 11*: 211–227.

Frazer, J. (1922). *The Golden Bough.* Vol. *II*: *Taboo and Perils of the Soul.* Third Edition. London: Macmillan.

Freud, S. (1905). Psychopathic characters on the stage. *Standard Edition, 7*: 305–310. London: Hogarth Press, 1953.

Freud, S. (1911). Formulations on two principles of mental functioning. *Standard Edition, 12*: 213–226. London: Hogarth Press, 1958.

Freud, S. (1912). Recommendations to physicians on the psycho-analytic method of treatment. *Standard Edition*, 2: 305–322. London: Hogarth Press, 1957.

Freud, S. (1913[1912–1913]). Totem and Taboo. *Standard Edition*, *13*: 1–64. London: Hogarth Press, 1957.

Freud, S. (1914). Remembering, repeating and working-through (further recommendations on the technique of psychoanalysis. *Standard Edition*, *12*: 145–156. London: Hogarth Press, 1958.

Freud, S. (1915). Instincts and their vicissitudes. *Standard Edition*, *14*: 109–40. London: Hogarth Press, 1957.

Freud, S. (1941). On beginning the treatment (further recommendations on the technique of psycho-analysis I). *Standard Edition*, *12*: 121–144. London: Hogarth Press and the Institute of Psycho-Analysis, 1958.

Girard, R. (1986). *The Scapegoat*. (Trans.) Y. Freccero. Baltimore: Johns Hopkins University Press.

Grotstein, J. (1979). Who is the dreamer who dreams the dream, and who is the dreamer who understands it? *Contemporary Psychoanalysis*, *15(1)*: 110–169. Also in (Revised):

Grotstein, J. (1981). *Do I Dare Disturb the Universe? A Memorial to Wilfred R. Bion*. (Ed.), Grotstein, J.S. Beverly Hills: Caesura Press, 1981, pp. 357–416.

Grotstein, J. (2000). *Who Is the Dreamer Who Dreams the Dream? A Study of Psychic Presences*. Hillsdale, NJ: Analytic Press.

Grotstein, J. (2002). "We are such stuff as dreams are made on": Annotations on dreams and dreaming in Bion's works. In: Neri, C., Pines, M. & and Friedman, R. (Eds.), *Dreams in Group Psychotherapy: Theory and Technique* (pp. 110–145). London & Philadelphia: Jessica Kingsley.

Grotstein, J. (2004a). "The light militia of the lower sky": The deeper nature of dreaming and phantasying. *Psychoanalytic Dialogues*, *14*: 99–118.

Grotstein, J, (2004b). "The seventh servant": The implications of a truth drive in Bion's theory of O. *International Journal of Psychoanalysis*, *85*: 1081–1101.

Grotstein, J. (2007). *A Beam of Intense Darkness: Wilfred Bion's Legacy to Psychoanalysis*. London: Karnac.

Grotstein J. (2008a). The voice from the crypt: the negative therapeutic reaction and the longing for the childhood that never was. *Contemporary Psychoanalysis*. In press.

Grotstein, J. (2008b). Revisiting the "royal road" with Bion as our guide. Manuscript submitted for publication.

Hargreaves, E. & Varchevker, A. (2004). In *Pursuit of Psychic Change: The Betty Joseph Workshop*. Hove and New York: Brunner-Routledge.

Hegel, G.W.F. (1807). *Phenomenology of Spirit*. Trans. by A.V. Miller. London: Oxford University Press, 1977.

Heimann, P. (1950). On counter-transference. *International Journal of Psycho-Analysis, 31*: 81–84.

Heimann, P. (1960). Counter-transference. *British Journal of Medical Psychology, 33*: 9–15.

Hinshelwood, R. (2008). Melanie Klein and countertransference: a note on some archival material. *Psychoanalysis and History, 10*: 95–113.

Joseph, B. (1989). *Psychic Equilibrium and Psychic Change*. London: Routledge.

Katan, M. (1954). The importance of the non-psychotic part of the personality in schizophrenia. *International Journal of Psycho-Analysis, 35*: 119–128.

Klein, M. (1926). Psychological principles of child analysis. In *Contributions to Psycho-Analysis, 1921–1945*. London: Hogarth Press, 1950, pp. 140–151.

Klein, M. (1935). A contribution to the psychogenesis of manic-depressive states. In *Contributions to Psycho-Analysis, 1921–1945*. London: Hogarth Press, 1950, pp. 282–310.

Klein, M. (1940). Mourning and its relation to manic-depressive states. In *Contributions to Psycho-Analysis, 1921–1945*. London: Hogarth Press, 1950, pp. 311–338.

Klein, M. (1952). The origins of transference. In *Melanie Klein: Envy and Gratitude and Other Works 1946-1-63*. New York: The Free Press, 1975, pp. 48–56.

Klein, M. (1955). On identification. In *New Directions in Psycho-Analysis*, (Eds.), Klein, M., Heimann, P., Isaacs, S. & Riviere, J. London: Hogarth Press, 1952, pp. 309–345.

Klein, M. (1957). *Envy and Gratitude*. New York: Basic Books.

Kubie, L. & Israel, H. (1955). "Say You're Sorry!" *Psychoanalytic Study of the Child, 10*: 289–299.

Lacan, J. (1975). *Le Séminaire XX*. (1972–1973). Paris: Seuil.

Langs, R. (1976). *The Bipersonal Field*. New York: Jason Aronson.

Lévi-Strauss, C. (1970). *The elementary structures of kinship*. London: Tavistock.

Loewald, H.W. (1975). Psychoanalysis as an art form and the fantasy character of the psychoanalytic situation. *Journal of the American Psychoanalytic Association, 23*: 277–299.

Mahler, M.S. (1968). *On human symbiosis and the vicissitudes of individuation*. New York: International Universities Press.

Mason, A. (1994). A psychoanalyst's looks at a hypnotist: A study of folie a deux. *Psychoanalytic Quarterly, 63*(4): 641–679.

McDougall, J. (1985). *Theatres of the mind: illusion and truth on the psychoanalytic stage*. New York: Brunner/Mazel.

McDougall, J. (1989). *Theatres of the body*. London: Free Association Books.

Meltzer, D.W. (1986). *Studies in extended metapsychology: Clinical applications of Bion's ideas*. Strath Tay, Perthshire: Clunie Press.

Merleau-Ponty, M. (1973). *Adventures of the dialectic*. Translated by Joseph, J. Bien. Evanston, IL: Northwestern University Press.

Modell, A. (1990). Play, illusion, and the setting of psychoanalysis. In *Other Times, Other Realities: Toward a Theory of Psychoanalytic Treatment*. Cambridge, MA: Harvard University Press.

Money-Kyrle, R. (1956). Normal countertransference and some of its deviations. *International Journal of Psycho-Analysis, 37*: 360–66.

Nuetzel, E. (1995). Unconscious phenomena in the process of theater. Preliminary hypothesis. *Psychoanalytic Quarterly, 64*: 345–352.

Nuetzel, E. (1999a). Acting and enacting: a case study in the evolution of theatrical performance. *Journal of Applied Psychoanalytic Studies, 1*: 79–102.

Nuetzel, E. (199b). Psychoanalysis as a dramatic art. *The Annual of Psychoanalysis, 26/27*: 295–313. Hillsdale, NJ: The Analytic Press.

Ogden, T. (1989). *The Primitive Edge of Experience*. Northvale, NJ: Jason Aronson.

Ogden, T. (1994a). The analytic third: Working with intersubjective clinical facts. *International Journal of Psycho-Analysis, 75*: 3–20.

Ogden, T. (1994b). *Subjects of Analysis*. Northvale, NJ and London: Jason Aronson.

Ogden, T. (2004). This art of psychoanalysis: Dreaming, undreamt dreams, and interrupted cries. *International Journal of Psychoanalysis, 85*: 857–878.

Peirce, C.S. (1931). Collected papers. (Eds.), Charles Hartshore and Paul Weiss. Cambridge, MA: Harvard University Press, Vols. I-VIII.

Pirandello, L. (1925). Preface to: "Six Characters in search of an author." In *Naked Masks*. New York: E. Dutton, 1952.

Racker, H. (1968). *Transference and countertransference*. London: Hogarth.

Resnik, S. (1987). *The theatre of the dream.* Translated by Alan Sheridan. London & New York: Tavistock Publications.

Salomonsson, B. (2007a). 'Talk to me baby, tell me what's the matter now'. Semiotic and developmental perspectives on communication in psychoanalytic infant treatment. *International Journal of Psychoanalysis, 88*: 127–146.

Salomonsson, B. (2007b). Semiotic transformations in psychoanalysis with infants and adults. *International Journal of Psychoanalysis, 88*: 1201–21.

Sander, F.M. (2001). Psychoanalysis, drama, and the family: the ever-widening scope. *The Annual of Psychoanalysis, 29*: 279–299.

Sandler, J. (1976). Countertransference and role responsiveness. *International Review of Psycho-Analysis, 3*: 43–47.

Sandler, J. (1993). On communication from patient to analyst: Not everything is projective identification. *International Journal of Psycho-Analysis, 74*(6): 1097–1108. *Study of the Child, 17*: 128–130.

Stanislavski, C. (1936). *An Actor Prepares.* New York: Routledge.

Stolorow, R. & Atwood, G. (1996). The intersubjective perspective. *Psychoanalytic Review, 83*: 181–194.

Trevarthen, C. (1980). The foundations of intersubjectivity: development of interpersonal and cooperative understanding in infants. In *The Social Foundations of Language and Thought: Essays in Honor of Bruner, J.S.*, Olson, D. Ed. N.Y.: W.W. Norton, pp. 316–342.

Trevarthen, C. (1999). Musicality and the Intrinsic Motive Pulse: Evidence from human psychobiology and infant communication In *Rhythms, Musical Narrative, and the Origins of Human Communication." Musicae Scientiae, Special Issue, 1999–2000,* (pp. 157–213). Liège: European Society for the Cognitive Sciences of Music.

Von Hann-Kende, F. (1933). On the role of transference and countertransference in psychoanalysis. In *Psychoanalysis and the Occult.* Ed. George Devereux, pp. 158–167. New York: International Universities Press, 1953.

Whyte, H.A.M. (1974). *A Manual on Exorcism.* Springdale, PA: Whitaker House.

Winnicott, D.W. (1951). Transitional objects and transitional phenomena. In *Collected Papers: Through Paediatrics to Psycho-Analysis*. New York: Basic Books, 1958, pp. 229–242.

Winnicott, D.W. (1956a). Primary maternal preoccupation. In *Collected Papers: Through Paediatrics to Psycho-Analysis.* New York: Basic Books, 1958, pp. 300–305.

Winnicott, D.W. (1968). Playing: Its theoretical status in the clinical situation. *International Journal of Psycho-Analysis, 49*: 591–599.

INDEX